Chinese Television and Soft Power Communication in Australia

Chinese Television and Soft Power Communication in Australia

Mei Li

ANTHEM PRESS

Anthem Press
An imprint of Wimbledon Publishing Company
www.anthempress.com

This edition first published in UK and USA 2021
by ANTHEM PRESS
75–76 Blackfriars Road, London SE1 8HA, UK
or PO Box 9779, London SW19 7ZG, UK
and
244 Madison Ave #116, New York, NY 10016, USA

First published in the UK and USA by Anthem Press 2019

British Library Cataloguing-in-Publication Data
A catalogue record for this book is available from the British Library.

Library of Congress Control Number: 2021932490

ISBN-13: 978-1-78527-979-9 (Pbk)
ISBN-10: 1-78527-979-3 (Pbk)

This title is also available as an e-book.

CONTENTS

ILLUSTRATIONS

Figures

Tables

ACKNOWLEDGEMENTS

This book could not have come to fruition without the kindest support and help emotionally and intellectually from many people at various times and in numerous ways. The biggest debt of gratitude goes to Prof. Naren Chitty AM, whose extremely generous guidance, encouragement and support were the most important factors that assured completion of this study. I would also like to thank Associate Prof. Eric Louw from the University of Queensland without whose encouragement my PhD research may not have come out as a book.

I sincerely thank the scholars and media professionals from around the world who offered encouragement and feedback for my research for this book at different stages. They are (in the order of my meetings with them) Prof. Joseph Nye, Prof. Jian Wang, Prof. Jin Jianbin, Prof. Fan Hong, Prof. Shi Anbin, Ms Li Wensha, Prof. Zhong Xin, Prof. Gary Kreps, Prof. Jan Mellisen, Prof. Hugo de Burgh and Prof. Daya Thussu.

Special thanks are due to Prof. Zhang Yuqiang, Dr Ye Hongyu, Associate Prof. Huang Dianlin, Prof. Huang Kuo, Ms Yang Ning, Ms Mei Yan and Ms Guo Chun for their support when I was conducting research in Beijing and Washington DC.

I am also tremendously grateful to the anonymous respondents in Australia and China for their time and valuable insights.

I would also like to thank the team from Anthem: Ms Megan Greiving, Mr Tej P. S. Sood and many others for their support during the publication process.

Last but not the least, my deepest gratitude goes to my family for their constant love and support and for the joy they have brought to me during the years of hard work as a researcher.

ABBREVIATIONS

ABC	Australian Broadcasting Corporation
AIIB	Asian Infrastructure Investment Bank
ASEAN	Association of Southeast Asian Nations
ASIO	Australian Security Intelligence Organisation
BBC	British Broadcasting Corporation
BRFIC	Belt and Road Forum for International Cooperation
BRI	Belt and Road Initiative
CCTV	China Central Television
CCTV NEWS	China Central Television English news channel
CGTN	China Global Television Network
CIA	Central Intelligence Agency
CIPG	China International Publishing Group
CNN	Cable News Network
CNR	China National Radio
CRI	China Radio International
CPC	Communist Party of China
GRC	Global republican confederacy
IPTV	Internet protocol television
NSW	New South Wales
OBOR	One Belt One Road
PBS	Public Broadcasting Service
PD	Public Diplomacy
PPP	Purchasing power parity
PRC	People's Republic of China
R&D	Research and development
RT	Russia Today
SARFT	State Administration of Radio, Film and Television
S&T	Science and Technology
SBS	Special Broadcasting Service
SCMP	South China Morning Post
SMH	Sydney Morning Herald

TPP	Trans-Pacific Partnership
NWICO	New World Information and Communication Order
WICWS	World Internet Conference Wuzhen Summit
WMS	World Media Summit
WSIS	World Summit on the Information Society
USIA	United States Information Agency
USIS	United States Information Service
VOA	Voice of America

Chapter 1

INTRODUCTION

China's Rise, World Reaction and Puzzles for China

China's rise has been one of the most significant issues in world politics in the last few decades. Celeritous economic growth has greatly boosted China's status in world affairs. Since the adoption of its reform and opening-up policy in the late 1970s, China's economy has experienced a four-decade-long period of high-speed growth. In 2010, it surpassed Japan to become the second-largest economy in the world. IMF statistics recognised that in 2015 it became the largest economy in terms of purchasing power parity (PPP). Although China lags far behind some developed countries for certain indicators, it ranks first in the world in many dimensions: It is the largest manufacturing economy, the largest source country of the world tourism market and the greatest engine of world economic growth. In recent years, its heavy investment in the high-tech industry has made its competition with the United States fiercer in the eyes of analysts.

Accompanying the rise of its economic status has been the growth of its significance in world affairs. In many cases, how to react to a rising China has become a concern for many countries, especially the established great powers. Observers have interpreted the influence of China's ascendance on world order in various ways. Under a realist perspective, the economic rise of China coupled with its growing military budget is inevitably interpreted as a potential threat to the existing world order, one that may trigger conflicts (Al-Rodhan 2007; Mearsheimer 2001). In contrast, neo-liberal theories that focus on interdependence, institutions and globalisation, and the assumption that human nature is benevolent emphasise economic cooperation and inter-dependence among states while recognising a role for politics. Neo-liberal scholars predict that the incorporation of China into the international system through complex interdependence with other major economies will increase the cost of serious conflict and in turn lower the risk of war (Bulkeley 2009; Goldstein 1997; Keohane and Nye 1973). However, there are signs that China is increasingly seeking to retain its own political system and way of govern-ance while integrating into global institutions. The constructivist school with its underpinning assumption that world politics is a *world of our making* (Onuf 1989) holds that states can learn and adopt international rules to avoid confrontation. Constructivists believe in the importance of social construction by the exchange of ideas (Bulkeley 2009; Wendt 1992). From this perspective, some believe that whether China's rise is a threat or not is more about the angle of construction than established fact (Liu 2010).

At the policy level, a wariness that the rise of China will upset the balance of power architecture and threaten the security of China's neighbours and the world has become apparent in policy circles in many countries in recent years. The fear lies in China's high economic growth potential precipitating parallel growth in military power, fierce economic competition, the propagation of social values and norms coloured by Chinese socialist ideology, and assertiveness regarding its territorial claims (Campion 2016; Jeffery 2009; Kristof 1993).

From the Chinese perspective, the wariness of external observers is mostly categorised as an image issue. Presenting a good image has been an important task for the Chinese government when dealing with domestic and international affairs; countering negative framing is standard procedure. Chinese political leaders have attached special importance to China's national image since the reform and opening-up period. Each generation of China's leadership has made statements about China's image in published works and speeches. For example, Deng Xiaoping emphasised the reforming and opening-up image to convince the international society of the country's willingness to open its doors with the aim of building trust and confidence in it (Deng 1994). During Jiang Zemin's administration a decade after the opening-up policy and the Tiananmen Square incident generated positive and negative influences, respectively, national image was regarded by Chinese leaders as a task for China diplomatic strategists (Jin and Xu 2010). In this period, an image of self-dependence, modernisation, reforming and opening-up, anti-hegemony, peacefulness and political stability – with the purpose of serving reformation, opening-up and modernisation – was articulated (Jiang 1999). During Hu Jintao's administration, China experienced a long stable period of wealth accumulation and integration into the world community especially in terms of its economy. Chinese scholars described China's image in political, economic and cultural terms. Politically it was a peace-loving democratic country; economically it was a responsible developing country; culturally it was a civilised country respecting cultural pluralism and harmony in the pursuit of equity and justice (Jin and Xu 2010). Shi (2009), after conducting a historical review of the speeches of the Communist Party of China (CPC) leaders from Mao to Hu, identified six facets of China's image discourse among the top leadership during the past 60 years:

1. China independently follows its own path.
2. It has a large economy that is under reform and opening-up.
3. It is a united country with people as the masters of their own lives.
4. It is culturally prolific and is engaged in civilisational rejuvenation.
5. It enjoys social harmony and people live happy lives.
6. It pursues lasting peace and co-prosperity in the world.

In the most recent administration, Xi Jinping elaborates China's image in a more detailed way calling for the following portrayal. China is a civilised country featuring a rich history, ethnic unity and cultural diversity. It is an Oriental power with good governance, a developed economy, cultural prosperity, national unity and beautiful mountains and rivers. It is a responsible country advocating peaceful and common development, safeguarding international justice and contributing to humanity. It is an open, amicable, promising and vibrant socialist country (Xinhuanet 2014).

China constantly claims that Westerners use double standards to interpret Chinese practices; negative or biased news dominates Western mainstream media coverage of China. 'Demonising China' used to be the term used by some Chinese scholars and diplomats to define what is seen as a strategy that is employed by the outside world, especially by Western democratic countries and their media (Li and Liu 1996). Terms such as 'distortion', 'biased' and 'selective' are always employed to characterise the Western stance and tendencies of media practice when talking about China in relation to certain sensitive topics. This is summarised as the image problem in Chinese mainstream discourse. China's obsession with national image has puzzled many. Historical, cultural and soft power lenses may be used to address this puzzle. From the historical perspective, the sharp comparison between its ancient civilisational grandeur and the humiliating belittlement of its more recent quasi-colonisation has laid the grounds for a discourse on de-humiliation and rejuvenation in China. In exploring the cultural dimension, one discovers traditional values wherein reputation is a pivotal factor for judging performance. There is a historical line quoted frequently by China in global affairs: 'A just cause enjoys abundant support while an unjust cause finds little support' (*De dao duo zhu, shi dao gua zhu*). It initially refers to the ruler's practices of governance, but it has been used frequently in talking about conduct in the international arena. A favourable image is a reflection of 'abundant support'. This could lead to the next point, a more pragmatic one in global governance. A good image generates trust and cooperation, helps to build alliances, fuels the economy and thereby contributes to the successful pursuit of national interests. In contrast, a bad image provokes hostile reactions, damages the economy and undermines the state's security. This is crucial at moments when China makes efforts to promote its initiatives such as the Belt and Road Initiative (BRI).[1] In countries where China has a favourable image, it receives less resistance. For decades, Chinese scholars and authorities have held that China's public diplomacy has had to combat a Western hegemonic discourse (Wang 2014), which complicates the task of presenting a positive image of China and hence influence its national interest (Hartig 2016).

Ramo (2007) attributes China's image puzzle to the misalignment between China's self-perception and other's perceptions of China's image. For example, on the 'China's Rise' case, fear of China's rise seems to be the predominant attitude (Harris 2001; Zhao 2012; Zhou 2012), despite the repeated expression of China's expectation of a peaceful developmental environment by its authorities. China's enthusiastic self-image promotion seems acceptable under the constructivist perspective in international relations while it does not fare well under a sociological deconstructivist approach.

Against this background, public diplomacy approaches such as the development of China's international media witnessed rapid development after the 2008 Beijing Olympic Games. Viewed as an unprecedented opportunity for image promotion through a mega event, the games marked a spotlighted moment for China to display its developmental achievements and culture. However, it also turned out to be an opportune moment for negative coverage. Authorities interpreted this as a demonstration of China's weak discursive power. The following year saw the release of *2009–2020 Master Plan for the Construction of China's Major Media as an International Dissemination Force* and *The Cultural Industry Promotion Plan*. This was to promote the development of China's international media and cultural industries. In addition, the national image orientation of government discourse gradually switched to a discursive power orientation. In practice, the top leadership prescribed a 'going-out' policy in cultural industry and media as a remedy under the framework of a soft power strategy. Besides the rhetorical efforts, institutional and policy developments are other complementary efforts for China to gain exposure in a broader overseas public; it draws on public diplomacy resources such as the Confucius Institute, China Cultural Centre and Chinese international media that have witnessed rapid development since then with their mission to narrate Chinese stories. The task is described as to narrate Chinese stories well, to seek

---

1 The name of the initiative has changed slightly over the years. In September 2015, the official English translation of the project was confirmed as 'the Belt and Road' with the abbreviation of 'B&R' by the Development and Reform Commission, Ministry of Foreign Affairs and Ministry of Commerce of the People's Republic of China (PRC). These are used in current documents and media reports. However, before that, One Belt One Road (OBOR) or BRI were widely used in media reports including the ones analysed in this book. The initiative will be named as BRI in this book for consistency.

deeper understanding and to build discourse power to match its growing big power status.

China's Adoption of Soft Power

The framing of China as a threat or a blessing and its impact on policymaking demonstrates the assumption that ideas, values, norms, knowledge and information are becoming increasingly important in contemporary world politics that has been associated with the notion of 'noopolitik' (Arquilla and Ronfeldt 1999) – which views politics to be based on ethics, ideas and information strategy in the age of the noosphere. In the new era, 'the world is moving to a new system in which "power" is understood mainly in terms of knowledge and the information strategy should focus on the "balance of knowledge", distinct from the "balance of power"' (p. 44). Within this world is noopolitik – politics based on ethics and ideas and information strategy, 'an approach to statecraft, to be undertaken as much by non-state as by state actors, that emphasises the role of soft power in expressing ideas, values, norms, and ethics through all manner of media' (p. 29).

Defined as 'the ability to get what you want through attraction rather than coercion or payments', soft power 'arises from the attractiveness of a country's culture, political ideals, and policies' (Nye 2004, x). Since the coinage of the concept by Nye in the 1990s, soft power is increasingly viewed as the other end of the power scale in complementing traditional hard power. Nye posits that soft power is based on attraction: institutions that are legitimate in the eyes of others (and therefore attractive) will meet less resistance to their wishes than institutions seen as illegitimate (Nye 1990, 167). It has opened a new dimension to analyse power relations beyond the military and economic strength among states.

Soft power has gained due attention in China's policymaking circles and academia in that it aligns with China's goal of earning a favourable environment for its peaceful development and offers a theory-based lexicon to describe its national strength domestically and internationally in a noopolitik context. In his speech to the 17th CPC Congress in 2007, the then president Hu Jintao called for China to 'enhance culture as part of the soft power of China' (Hu 2007, 6). This marks, to a certain extent, the adoption of soft power by China into its developmental strategy.

Many scholars attributed the popularity of the concept of soft power among the top leaders in China to Wang Huning, a political theorist and current member (2019) of the Politburo Standing Committee of the CPC. Although his 1993 article 'Culture as national power: Soft power' introduced Nye's term, 'soft power', his focus is on the role of culture as the pillar of national power. Inspired by Toffler's emphasis on knowledge in the 'power triad' of violence, wealth and knowledge (Toffler 1990), Wang argued in his article that culture subsumes knowledge. He saw the following categories as fitting under the cultural umbrella: political system, national morale, ethnic culture, economic system, science and technology, and ideology. Unlike economic and military resources, culture is diffusive and cannot be monopolised by a single group. These characteristics make it a soft pillar of national power (Wang 1993). In his view, acceptance of a cultural form or practice from Country A in Country B and more widely in the international community may be seen as an effect of Country A's soft power and may add to it. Soft power relies on the international acceptance of certain cultural values and systems. He also thinks that to develop a country's national power in the contemporary world order, from a soft power perspective, efforts should be made in developing industrial civilisation and science and technology, modernising the political system, internationalising domestic culture and localising international culture, enhancing national morale and gaining national acceptance in other countries. Wang's article is more an emphasis on culture as a pillar of national power than purely an introduction to Nye's soft power concept. Judging from his long-term position in the CPC's Central Policy Research Office, his understanding of soft power is a key to comprehending China's soft power policy in terms of cultural soft power.

As in other countries, soft power provided China with a new dimension to calculate its national strength. It offers an approach to identify and include intangible components of national strength in comprehensive national power. Since the 1980s, deviating from Mao's emphasis on military and economic power, Deng proposed that national power should be more comprehensively addressed (Pillsbury 2000). Between the 1980s and 1990s Chinese scholars proposed quite a few measurement models for comprehensive national power (Bulkeley 2009). Intangible/qualitative variables such as international reputation and foreign affairs capability were included (Bulkeley 2009; Hu and Men 2002; Pillsbury 2000).

China's adoption of soft power in its top-level political discourse has allowed its soft power practice to thrive through several programmes and initiatives. These include international media development and programmes like the Confucius Institute, state-funded cultural exchanges, the hosting of the Olympic Games in 2008 and the Shanghai Expo in 2010, and the investment in educational programmes aiming to attract overseas students and the people-to-people elements in the newly proposed Belt and Road Initiative. By analysing the discourse of Chinese scholars' research on soft power, Wuthnow (2008) identifies three mechanisms of China's soft power initiatives: (1) projects for projecting Chinese culture to foreign actors; (2) focus on the developing world with economic incentives; and (3) means to show the status of 'responsible great power' to neighbouring states.

Observing from the practice and academic research in the Chinese context, one can discern a different understanding of soft power in China. The resources for making up soft power are an important topic in soft power debates and an important element to distinguish China's understanding of soft power from Nye's conceptualisation. Although Nye's three soft power resource areas are widely recognised, some scholars see limitations in his model based as it is on the US experience after the Cold War (Hayden 2012; Sharp 2005). In China's case, scholars identify the necessity of breaking the constraints of Nye's original conceptualisation of soft power. Some Chinese scholars basing their analysis on China's situation expand the conventional list of resources of soft power and the measurement of these resources. For example, Chinese scholars Yan et al. (2008) redefine soft power through recognising three components: international appeal, international mobilisation and domestic mobilisation. Following this they provide five quantifying indicators: appeal of political system, cultural allure, power to lay down international rules, mobilisation capacity among the domestic elite and mobilisation capability at the domestic grass-roots level. Men (2007) summarises the core elements of Chinese soft power as culture, ideas, developmental model, international institutions and international image. Similarly, Pang (2005) identified 11 elements for inclusion as soft power resources. These are education system, research system, culture, well-educated population and ordered society, media with international influence, political and economic experience model, theory and concept, success in diplomatic policy and diplomacy, healthy interaction between government and society, virtue and the worldwide appeal based on it, and the sharing of global responsibility.

Different conclusions have been drawn about the significance of China's soft power to the world. Many scholars think that China's soft power is still weak. Nye (2005) himself is not positive about China's soft power development. On the one hand, he calls for a US response to China's rise in soft power; on the other, he claims that it is impossible for China to achieve substantial gains in soft power. He offers three reasons for his pessimistic perception on China's soft power based on the constant negative-opinion poll results about China:

1. China is not a Western democracy.
2. Incorporating soft power as a government strategy is difficult because the target has more control.
3. There is inconsistency between projections through soft power initiatives and the problems in the country.

He gives two specific reasons of the limits of China's soft power: nationalist sentiment in the country and limited civil society participation. In his view, the lack of civil society and its cultural products – like Hollywood movies and pop culture, high-ranking universities and their ideas – are the main deficits in China's soft power (Nye 2011; 2015). Others see constant disjunction between what China says and does in cultural diplomacy projection, while pointing out that other countries may also have the same problem (Albro 2015; Rawnsley 2012).

Although a pessimistic outlook on China's soft power is entertained by scholars such as Nye (2011; 2015) and Shambaugh (2015), other scholars hold different opinions. For example, Kivimaki (2014) notes that China is not primarily trying to persuade others about the benefits and superiority of its own system unlike the United States during the Cold War when it sought to prove the superiority of its capitalist ideology over that of communism. One might say, however, that China is seeking to carve out a place for itself as a great power in the emerging multipolar world where there would be multiple power blocs rather than the two blocs of the Cold War period. According to Kivimaki, as an anti-hegemonic big power seeking complementarity and mutual gain, it is not the purpose of China to promote its ideology and governance model; on the contrary, China has been developing cooperative relationships that aim at win-win outcomes, and China's mainstream discourse aims at seeking acceptance rather than winning. Others think that China's adoption of soft power has lowered the potential risk it brings to the world along with its rise. Cho and Jeong (2008) also think that the swift rise of China's influence in the world is the result of the adoption of soft power in its policies and practice. Ding (2006) acknowledged the achievements of China's overall level of soft power with a successful development model that has won global admiration and a 'new diplomacy' characterised by more active and responsible participation in international affairs, through both of which China's agenda-setting abilities and national image have been strengthened. He concludes in other research that China's efforts to develop soft power resources and rely on soft power will reduce the likelihood of China adopting a revisionist policy. Under this circumstance, the transition process from a rising power to a status quo power will be smoother (Ding 2010). Li and Worm (2011) also conclude that a peaceful rise may not be impossible for China judging from the soft power means and ends. In Li's (2008) view, soft power in China is a means to multiple ends. Firstly, it is widely used by Chinese scholars and top leaders as an indicator of China's world status. Secondly, it is a soft shield for self-defence from misunderstanding of others in the short run and for providing a favourable environment for its development.

Regarding the intended effectiveness of China's soft power strategy, conclusions are also diverse. Glaser and Murphy (2009) conclude that there is no comprehensive national strategy of soft power in China; initiatives such as the Confucius Institute and overseas media outlets are under different state regulatory bodies, and there is a lack of 'coordination among ministries or agencies' and 'no central leading group or leader has been assigned to oversee soft power promotion' (p. 25). Ding (2006) reports that China's soft power efforts have yielded different outcomes in different regions. In South-East Asian countries, the perception of China is more positive; in regions such as the Middle East, Africa and Latin America, however, anxiety over China's rise is alleviated by its challenge to US dominance that is becoming attractive, and the effectiveness of Chinese soft power is very low in Western liberal democracies. Huang and Ding (2006) assume that as an authoritarian state China may encounter difficulties in winning over public opinion in democracies. They also express some optimism in this regard because the intention is to make and implement policies in a more consistent manner. They posit that assessment of the effectiveness of soft power wielding should include the country's foreign policy objectives. Based on the resources identified by Nye, they conclude that there still are gaps between China's foreign policy objectives and its limited soft power resources. Many scholars agree that China's soft power has lagged far behind the growth of its hard power. Some scholars think that a lack of consensus on 'what constitutes Chinese culture and values' restrains China's soft power (Li 2009, 2). Li (2008) discerns a lack of clarity in some aspects of China's soft power. The trajectory through which soft power can be used to achieve specific policy goals is unclear. There are uncertainties related to China's transition that hinder the transformation of the Chinese state and society.

Over the past few years, the development of the situation seems to be beyond the comprehension of Chinese policymakers regarding China's endeavours to improve its image and discourse capacity. The mainstream opinion of the West is becoming hung over by the critiques of China's hard push for soft power that is described as sharp power (Walker and Ludwig 2017), in which the educational and cultural initiatives are portrayed as a means to monopolise ideas, suppress alternative narratives and exploit partner institutions. On the other hand, the Chinese side continues to protest that its international programmes have no intention to export its own political system and values but only to seek understanding. In addition, there is no empirical evidence supporting the real effect of China's soft power initiatives on intended target audiences. Western commentary also tends to portray the operations per se as equal to real influence.

Communicating China's Message through Soft Power Means

In the age of the infosphere, information and the values it delivers have an increasing influence on decision making in international affairs (Arquilla and Ronfeldt 1999). Some scholars observe that changes in world order are closely connected with the reconfiguration of the global communication order. Some posit that one of the most important signs of the establishment of Pax Americana was the abolishment of the news agency treaty by Britain, Germany and France in 1934 in order to ensure the free flow of news and thus prepare the ground for US discourse dominance and US dominance in media infrastructure, and content is an indispensable part of its ability to control global agenda setting (Freedman and Thussu 2012; Louw 2010; Shi 2016). This kind of ability is obviously soft power. In the view of Chitty (2017b), communication media (along with mobility and cultural industries) is a key multiplier of soft power. However, the imbalance of information flow has been the reality in the global stage for decades. Since the release of the MacBride Commission Report in 1980, debates around information flow have been a concern of international communication studies. In the 1980s, much research proved repeatedly the existence of an information gap between information-rich and information-poor states, which provided evidence for developing countries to strive for more voices (Mowlana 1985). Although three odd decades have passed, the situation seems to have changed little. Even in the time of new media when information is easier for more communities to access, studies show that information flow is still US-centred (Hills and Segev 2014;Kim and Barnett 1996; Segev and Blondheim 2013). Media and information imbalance contributes to the weakness of those with deficits in setting agendas and framing.

Thus, the study of the international flow of information has become 'another approach to the study of international relations' (Mowlana 1997, 23). One imperative issue and common reason for some countries to develop their own version of international broadcasting is the belief in the imbalance in information flows between developed and developing countries, the net advantage being with the former. It is worth noting that it is not only developing countries that sense the imbalanced flow of information. For instance, France needed France 24 to spread its own stance and voice in world affairs (Anderson 2006). Other state-supported or state-run broadcasters form the force of what Thussu calls contra-flow of information. To him, the significance of counter-flow resides in reducing inequalities in media access, contributing to a more cosmopolitan culture that may affect national, regional and even international political dynamics in the long run, shaping cultural identities, energising disempowered groups and helping to create political coalitions and new transnational private and public spheres (Thussu 2006, 3). On a similar note, China attributes the negative frames of its rise as a sign of insufficient communication capacity. Such debates indicate the long existence of the condition of post-truth, which also demonstrate the rationality of the constructivist perspective in interpreting world affairs.

CCTV NEWS, with its variant logo, is one of the key institutions being activated internationally by China.[2] As part of the country's soft power machinery, since the 1990s, China Central Television (CCTV), the parent organisation, has been making efforts to become a global media network, with the intent of narrating Chinese stories and getting China's story heard. The expansion of CCTV overseas began in the early 1990s, and the broadcaster has graduated from a modest to a grand-scale operation. In 1990, an international channel was launched targeting overseas Chinese in the East Asian region. In 1992, CCTV-4, known as the Chinese International Channel, was established targeting the Chinese diaspora worldwide. Two years later, an English news team was set up. A year later, an experimental English channel was launched. The English channel, formerly widely known as CCTV-9, was formally launched on 25 September 2000 to broadcast English programmes to major English-speaking countries as a 24-hour international channel. Then under the instruction of the publicity department of CCP, in May 2004, the English channel was relaunched as CCTV International. Since then, further expansion and transformation has happened regularly. In 2004, Spanish and French channels were introduced, and in 2009, Arabic and Russian channels were added. In April 2010, the name CCTV International was changed to CCTV NEWS as a 24-hour news channel, and several other foreign-language channels were set up in the following years. By December 2016, the CCTV International family had five channels broadcasting in English, Spanish, French, Russian and Arabic, respectively. Two offshore branches of CCTV NEWS – CCTV Africa, based in Kenya, and CCTV America, based in Washington, DC – were launched in January and February 2012, respectively (Li 2012; Zhu 2012). On 31 December 2016, a rebranding happened again when the foreign-language channels of CCTV appeared under a new name – CGTN – with multiple social media platforms. This was followed by an even bigger shift with the creation of Voice of China by merging three state-run national networks: CCTV, China National Radio (CNR) and China

---

2 This main research was conducted before CCTV NEWS changed its name to China Global Television Network (CGTN) on 31 December 2016. CCTV NEWS, CCTV-9 and CCTV International are all names that preceded CGTN. Because the main research for this book was conducted during the CCTV NEWS era, it will be used in this book. CCTV itself started off as Beijing Television.

Radio International (CRI), under which CGTN's resources have been further optimised.

In addition to its expansion, CCTV NEWS made substantial improvements in news practice. For example, its American branch, CCTV NEWS America, hired many veteran producers, correspondents and anchors from *60 Minutes*, Bloomberg News, CNN, CNN International, BBC World News, ABC News and so on in the hopes of producing global news with an Asian focus. The launch of the Africa branch is the first initiative in the world to realise the idea of establishing a pan-African television channel, prompting traditional international media outlets such as BBC World and Al Jazeera to follow suit.

Research Objectives and Questions

Under the framework of soft power, China's international broadcasting strategy has more aspects waiting to be addressed. First, there is a necessity to further clarify the soft power conception within the communication process. Nye's version of soft power is through the attractiveness of resources that critics see as unverifiable. Recent research details the dynamics through the introduction of influence. For example, Chitty (2017a) classifies soft power into active and passive categories and equates the former with intended influence and the latter with unintended influence. The influence of attractiveness is imperceptible without the transmission of information and meaning, that is, a communication process that ultimately leads to the creation of consensus about a country's information, behaviour and values among other countries. In this sense, a communicative approach of analysing soft power is necessary to identify the strength generated through the transmission of information in speaking of the generation of information edge from soft power resources to real influence, that is, the mechanism of soft power generation during the communication process.

In addition, there is a need for clear empirical research on what China's soft power has achieved, especially in the context of perceivable fear over it. As in any communication case, the receivers do more than receive information passively – as noted by Nye even if he uses the term 'target' rather than 'receiver' (Nye 2011). They may negotiate readings, constructing their own readings (Fisher and Lucas 2011; Hall 1980). As a country expecting maximum recognition from others, it is not a surprise for China to seek recognition through construction, by the majority in a targeted country, of a meaning congruent with the one it holds; it needs to widely share its experience or to seek wide recognition of its deeds, actions or way of life as legitimate and attractive. The domination of international media flows by the West ensures that Western framing of China prevails in the West. This, the Chinese authorities believe, places the discourse capacity of China in international affairs in a disadvantageous situation.

Previous studies have focused on how the foreign news media frame China (Li 2011) or the media practice in single cases in the framework of soft power push (Wang 2011b), but few have addressed Chinese media's performance holistically within the dynamics of the country's discourse intentions in policy, media contexts and the congruence between the audiences and intended receiver frames. In addition, most of the English literature is based on frameworks conceptualised under Western perspectives. As Zhang (2015) notes, an assessment of China's soft power without exact knowledge of the Chinese definition of it, whom China is targeting and how the messages are received leaves room for questions considering China's large investment with the intent of spreading its perspective and voice in the world against the background of shrinking traditional media market. The two points listed above are the main points this volume tries to address. It seeks answers to them through examining how the frames of China are constructed in the international arena and how its media approach functions with a soft power purpose. As China is trying to make its own voice heard, what kind of frames does it wish to transmit? How are the frames framed by its own mouthpieces and received by their target audiences, and how congruent are these frames at the two ends of communication? And how is this thought to contribute to its soft power strength?

The framing of China varies from region to region as the bilateral relationships between China and other countries vary. Previous research in the area of media and international relations often focuses on great powers such as the United States and the European Union (Rawnsley 1996; Zhang 2011) or African countries (Zhang et al. 2016). However, in the context of globalisation, to earn the goodwill of middle-power countries is of the same importance. This research will choose Australia, a typical middle power belonging to the West, as a destination for Chinese television news. The bilateral relations between China and Australia have been changing as cooperation has deepened in areas such as economy, education, environment, science and research, and tourism. Since late 2007, China has been Australia's largest two-way trading partner in goods and services. The scale of two-way trade has increased more than 1,000-fold to over $100 billion in 40 years valued at $155.2 billion in 2016. China is Australia's second-largest source of visitor arrivals, with 1.39 million arrivals by the end of February 2018. Australia is one of the most popular destinations for Chinese students wishing to study overseas. China is Australia's largest source of overseas students, with over 157,000 students in 2016, and the fifth-largest direct investor, with a value of $41.9 billion in 2016 (Department of Foreign Affairs and Trade 2018).

Strategically, relations between China, the burgeoning power in the world, and Australia, the leading middle power in the Asia-Pacific region, may be characterised as close interdependence (Yu and Xiong 2012). For China, to win the heart of the world means not only winning the fondness of big countries but also the affection of the middle powers. For Australia, with a burgeoning economy and high status, China's policy has a substantial impact on its interests in the Asia-Pacific area. Australia's foreign policy is no longer dependent solely on the United States, which has always been regarded as an ally but is now viewed through the lens of a Sino-Australian-American triangle (Li 2011). For Australians, China, with totally different cultural and political backgrounds, is not as compatible as Western allies. This can be found in many foreign policy decisions and media discourses. As in the case of the Belt and Road Initiative, Australia took much longer to join the Asian Infrastructural Investment Bank than many countries, even those allied with Australia (Rimmer 2015). China's invitation to Australia to join the BRI initiative was met with apprehension in political circles. This stirred waves that placed Sino-Auatralian relations in choppy waters in 2018. To understand China is therefore as much a matter of urgency for Australian policymakers as understanding Australia is a matter of urgency for Chinese policymakers.

Situated within the tradition of international communication, with an international relations lens, this book starts with the following four propositions:

1. Public diplomacy policy elites in China have a clear consensus of a preferred self-projected frame for China.
2. The Chinese government strategically regards CCTV NEWS as an important agency of soft power.
3. CCTV NEWS frames a clear image of China to the target audiences abroad.
4. CCTV NEWS frames of China have an influence on the target audiences' frames of China.

With much of the earlier research focusing on segments of the communication process, a complete picture is not available. To rectify this and to form a picture of CCTV NEWS's capacity to deliver Chinese discourse and perspective, a focus on the whole process, including the sender, media and audience, and the soft power mechanism during the process, will help draw a picture of how China's soft power will be generated through the delivery of its resources. Whether or not the media approach is effective depends on the degree of the frames' compatibility, that is, the framing of China's soft power resources projected by CCTV NEWS and the frames of China in the minds of audi-ence members, in the two stages among the three stakeholders.

In the case of CCTV NEWS, its practice is not confined to being a Chinese broadcaster in the traditional sense; other social media platforms are also used. With the employment of foreign staff, CCTV NEWS's perform-ance has improved dramatically and it is on the way to becoming a global player. From the point of view of soft power expansion, whether or not media can fulfil their role effectively depends on how well they can spread Chinese perspectives among their audiences, ideally through the professional perform-ance of the channel. Considering that various degrees of self-censorship com-monly extant in almost every news outlet, as noted in the political economic perspective of the 'propaganda model' (Herman and Chomsky 2002), the mere fact of state ownership is not a sufficient factor for denying the legit-imacy of the products of CCTV NEWS and the channel's ability to spread a Chinese perspective. Especially, its frequent expansion drives and relaunches have attracted many Western media workers to join the team (Li and Chitty 2017). How the professional dynamic works is a crucial question to answer in order to better understand CCTV NEWS's general role in communicating Chinese perspectives and discourses.

Specifically, the book will seek to discuss the following questions: What kind of images does China intend to deliver to the world? How are China's stories framed in CCTV NEWS and received by the target audiences? How congruent are CCTV NEWS frames of China with those of Australian stakeholders of China–Australia relations in the CCTV NEWS audience in Australia? What role does CCTV NEWS play in China's soft power projection?

This covers the three levels of materials, that is, frames of China through CCTV NEWS in three steps associated with three contexts of framing: the intended frames of communicators, the projected frames in CCTV NEWS and the frames of CCTV NEWS's intended audience in Australia. It also compares the frames of the three contexts and examines the relationship among them in order to evaluate the function of CCTV NEWS as a media tool of public diplomacy and soft power. It chooses for analysis the case of China's BRI, which is regarded as China's most salient strategy of this century, one with huge foreign policy implications. It has been described as a public diplomacy plexus (Chitty et al. 2018). It has drawn great attention worldwide and thus is a good example wherein to investigate the nature of China's dis-course dissemination.

Following this introduction, Chapter 2 reviews the historical cases of infor-mation flow in international affairs and China's soft power strategy through its media approach. It provides a detailed analysis of the strategic implication of international media in image and discourse promotion for China and the influence of Chinese media culture in soft power strategy. It will also review the recent development of Australia's reaction to China's soft power wielding. Chapter 3 goes deeper into theoretical aspects of the communicative approach of soft power. It addresses the construction of international relations, which will be a natural habitat for soft power and associated information strategy. The role of communication and international media is also discussed within soft power and influence dynamics. As a reflection of media culture, professionalism, which not only influences media framing but also is a reflection of power dynamics within the organisation and even the state, is discussed. Chapter 4 presents the findings of the interview research with Chinese and Australian public diplomacy elites. It shows the expectations of the Chinese side on their international media role in the country's soft power projection and Australians' media use in acquiring information related to China in the following five aspects: general impressions of China and detailed impressions on China's economy, culture, political system and science and technology. Chapter 5 presents a framing analysis of how China's BRI discourse is framed by communicators (the Chinese government), the media (CCTV NEWS) and the target audiences in Australia at these three contexts in the information flow. Chapter 6 is a conclusion that compares frames of China in the communication process and implications of China's gains and losses in the international media approach to soft power projection. It argues that international media is still irreplaceable in world politics in setting agendas and framing discourses. However, the effects would be more determined by the framing dynamics of receivers. Although China has built its soft power resources (information infrastructures in this book), the soft power edge that it is exerting is not as sharp as many assumed. Through the discussion, it summarises in detail the mechanism of broadcasting in soft power projection and provides a detailed elaboration of the communicative approach of soft power analysis.

References

Al-Rodhan, Khalid R. 2007. "A critique of the China threat theory: A systematic analysis." *Asian perspective*: 41–66.

Albro, Robert. 2015. "The disjunction of image and word in US and Chinese soft power projection." *International Journal of Cultural Policy* 21 (4):382–399.

Anderson, John Ward. 2006. "All News All the Time, and Now in French." *Washington Post* 7: C7.

Arquilla, John, and David Ronfeldt. 1999. *The emergence of Noopolitik: Toward an American information strategy*. CA: Rand Corporation.

Bulkeley, Jennifer Caroline. 2009. "Perspectives on power: Chinese strategies to measure and manage China's rise." PhD, Harvard University.

Campion, Andrew Stephen. 2016. *The Geopolitics of Red Oil: Constructing the China threat through energy security*. London: Routledge.

Chitty, Naren. 2017a. "Conclusion." In *The Routlege Handbook of Soft Power*, edited by Naren Chitty, Li Ji, Gary Rawnsley and Craig Hayden, 453–463. New York: Routlege.

Chitty, Naren. 2017b. "Soft power, civic virtue and world politics." In *The Routledge Handbook of Soft Power*, edited by Naren Chitty, Li Ji, Gary Rawnsley and Craig Hayden, 29–56. New York: Routledge.

Cho, Young Nam, and Jong Ho Jeong. 2008. "China's soft power: Discussions, resources, and prospects." *Asian Survey* 48 (3):453–472.

Deng, Xiaoping. 1994. *Selected Works Of Deng Xiaoping*. Vol. 2. Beijing: Renmin Chubanshe.

Ding, Sheng. 2006. "Soft Power and The Rise Of China: An Assessment of China's Soft Power in Its Modernization Process." Rutgers, The State University of New Jersey.

Ding, Sheng. 2010. "Analyzing Rising Power from the Perspective of Soft Power: a new look at China's rise to the status quo power." *Journal of Contemporary China* 19 (64): 255–272.

Fisher, Ali, and Scott Lucas, eds. 2011. *Trials of engagement: the future of US public diplomacy*. Edited by Jan Melissen, *Diplomatic Studies*. London: Martinus Nijhoff Publishers.

Freedman, Des, and Daya Kishan Thussu. 2012. *Media and terrorism: global perspectives*: Sage.

Glaser, Bonnie S., and Melissa E Murphy. 2009. "Soft power with Chinese characteristics: the ongoing debate." *Chinese Soft Power and Its Implications for the United States: Competition and Cooperation in the Developing World*: 10–26.

Goldstein, Avery. 2012. "Great expectations: interpreting China's arrival." *International Secutity* 22 (3).

Hall, Stuart. 1980. "Encoding/decoding." *Culture, media, language*:128–138.

Harris, Stuart. 2001. "China and the Pursuit of State Interests in a Globalising World." *Pacifica review* 13 (1):15–29. doi: 10.1080/13239100120036018.

Hartig, Falk. 2016. "How China understands public diplomacy: The importance of national image for national interests." *International Studies Review* 18 (4):655–680.

Hayden, Craig. 2012. *The rhetoric of soft power: Public diplomacy in global contexts*: Lexington Books.

Herman, Edward S., and N Chormsky. 1988. *Manufacturing consent: the political economy of the mass media*.

Hills, Thomas, and Elad Segev. 2014. "The news is American but our memories are… Chinese?" *Journal of the Association for Information Science and Technology* 65 (9):1810–1819.

Hu, Angang;, and Honghua Men. 2002. "The rising of modern China: Comprehensive national power and grand strategy." *Strategy and Management* 3.

Hu, Jintao. 2007. Hold High the Great Banner of Socialism with Chinese Characteristics and Strive for New Victories in Building a Moderately Prosperous Society in all. In *Hu Jintao's report at 17th Party Congress*.

Huang, Yanzhong, and Sheng Ding. 2006. "Dragon's underbelly: An analysis of China's soft power." *East Asia* 23 (4):22–44.

Jeffery, Renée. 2009. "Evaluating the 'China threat': power transition theory, the successor-state image and the dangers of historical analogies." *Australian journal of international affairs* 63 (2):309–324.

Jiang, Zemin. 1999. "Speech at National Foreign Publicity Conference." accessed 1 June. http://news.xinhuanet.com/ziliao/2000–12/31/content_485368.htm.

Jin, Zheng-kun, and Qing-chao Xu. 2010. "National Image Building: The New Task for China's Diplomacy." *JOURNAL OF RENMIN UNIVERSITY OF CHINA* (2).

Kalathil, Shanthi. 2011. "China's Soft Power in the Information Age: Think Again." *Institute fot the Study of Diplomacy*.

Keohane, Robert O, and Joseph S Nye. 1973. "Power and interdependence." *Survival* 15 (4):158–165.

Kim, Kyungmo, and George A Barnett. 1996. "The determinants of international news flow a network analysis." *Communication Research* 23 (3):323–352.

Kivimäki, Timo. 2014. "Soft power and global governance with Chinese characteristics." *The Chinese Journal of International Politics* 7 (4):421–447.

Kristof, Nicholas D. 1993. "The rise of China." *Foreign Affairs* 72 (5):59–74.

Li, Mei, and Naren Chitty. 2017. "Paradox of professionalism: The professional identity of journalists who work across media cultures." *Journalism* (November 2017):1–19. doi: 10.1177/1464884917743175.

Li, Mingjiang. 2008. "Soft power in Chinese discourse: popularity and prospect."

Li, Mingjiang. 2009. "Soft power: Nurture not nature." In *Soft power: China's emerging strategy in international politics*, edited by Mingjiang Li, 1–18. Maryland: Lexington Books.

Li, Shi. 2012. "Mass communication research on China from 2000 to 2010: a meta-analysis." *Asian journal of communication* 22 (4):405–427. doi: 10.1080/01292986.2012.681668.

Li, Xiguang, and Kang Liu. 1996. *Behind the scene of demonizing China (Yaomohua Zhongguo de Beihou(.* Beijing: Chinese Academy of Social Science Press. Original edition, Chinese Academy of Social Sciences Press.

Li, Xin, and Verner Worm. 2011. "Building China's soft power for a peaceful rise." *Journal of Chinese Political Science* 16 (1):69–89.

Li, Xiufang. 2011. *Reading the Contemporary Giant: China's Images in the ABC's Foreign Correspondent Current Affairs Program in the Early Twenty-first Century*: Macquarie University.

Liu, Qianqian. 2010. "China's rise and regional strategy: Power, interdependence and identity." *Journal of Cambridge Studies* 5 (4).

Louw, P Eric. 2010. *Roots of the Pax Americana: Decolonization, development, democratization and trade*: Manchester University Press.

Mearsheimer, John J. 2001. *The tragedy of great power politics*. New York: Norton & Company.

Men, Honghua. 2007. "Assessment and Report of China's Soft Power (Zhongguo Ruanshili Pinggu Baogao)." *International Observations (Guoji Guancha)* 2.

Mowlana, Hamid. 1985. International flow of information: A global report and analysis. N.Y.: UNESCO.

Mowlana, Hamid. 1997. *Global information and world communication: New frontiers in international relations*. Thousand Oaks: Sage.

Nye, Joseph S. 1990. "Soft power." *Foreign policy* (80):153–171.

Nye, Joseph S. 2004. *Soft power: The means to success in world politics*. New York: Public Affairs.

Nye, Joseph S. 2005. "The rise of China's soft power." *Wall Street Journal Asia* 29:6–8.

Nye, Joseph S. 2011. *The future of power*. New York: PublicAffairs.

Nye, Joseph S. 2015. The Limits of Chinese Soft Power. Accessed 23 August, 2016.

Onuf, Nicholas. 1989. World of our making. Columbia: University of South Carolina Press.

Pang, Zhongying. 2005. "Connotation of China's soft Power (Zhongguo Ruanliliangde Neihan)." *Liaowang (Outlook Weekly)*.

Pillsbury, Michael. 2000. China Debates the Future International Environment. Washington, DC: National Defense University Press.

Ramo, Joshua Cooper. 2007. Branding China. UK: The Foreign Policy Centre.

Rawnsley, Gary. 2012. "Approaches to soft power and public diplomacy in China and Taiwan." *Journal of International Communication* 18 (2):121–135.

Rawnsley, Gary D. 1996. *Radio diplomacy and propaganda: the BBC and VOA in international politics, 1956–64*. London: Macmillan Press.

Rimmer, Susan Harris. 2015. "Why Australia Took So Long to Join the AIIB." *Lowy Interpreter*.

Segev, Elad, and Menahem Blondheim. 2013. "America's global standing according to popular news sites from around the world." *Political Communication* 30 (1):139–161.

Shambaugh, David. 2015. "China's Soft-Power Push." *Foreign Aff.* 94:99.

Sharp, Paul. 2005. "Revolutionary States, Outlaw Regimes and the Techniques of Public Diplomacy." In *The New Public Diplomacy: Soft Power in International Relation*, edited by Jan Melissen. Hampshire: Palgrave.

Shi, Anbin. 2016. "China national stratigic communication and the change of world order." 25 December. http://blog.sina.com.cn/s/blog_81651ac20102w7c2.html.

Shi, Zhihong. 2009. "What kind of new China meant to be built." *Current Affairs Report* (08).

Thussu, Daya Kishan. 2006. *Media on the move: global flow and contra-flow*. London: Routledge.

Toffler, Alvin. 1990. *Power shift: Knowledge, wealth, and violence at the edge of the 21st century*. London: Bantam.

Walker, Christopher, and Jessica Ludwig. 2017. "The Meaning of Sharp Power: How Authoritarian States Project Influence." *Foreign Affairs* 16.

Wang, Huning. 1993. "Culture as national power: soft power." *The Journal of Fudan University (Social Science Version)* (3).

Wang, Jay. 2014. "CHINA'S FIRST LADY." *The CPD Blog*, 20 July. https://uscpublicdiplomacy.org/blog/china%E2%80%99s-first-lady.

Wang, Jian. 2011. *Soft power in China: Public diplomacy through communication*. Hampshire: Palgrave Macmillan.

Wendt, Alexander. 1992. "Anarchy is what states make of it: the social construction of power politics." *International organization* 46 (02):391–425.

Wuthnow, Joel. 2008. "The concept of soft power in China's strategic discourse." *Issues & Studies* 44 (2):1–28.

Xinhuanet. 2014. *Xi: China to Promote Cultural Soft Power*.

Yan, Xuetong, Jin Xu, and Zongshi Ma. 2008. "Sino-US Comparisons of Soft Power"." *Contemporary International Relations* 18 (2).

Yu, Chang Sen, and Jory Xiong. 2012. "The dilemma of interdependence: current features and trends in Sino-Australian relations." *Australian journal of international affairs* 66 (5):579–591. doi: 10.1080/10357718.2011.570246.

Zhang, Jian. 2015. "China's new foreign policy under Xi Jinping: towards 'Peaceful Rise 2.0'?" *Global Change, Peace & Security* 27 (1):5–19.

Zhang, Li. 2011. *News media and EU-China relations*. New York: Palgrave Macmillan.

Zhang, Xiaoling, Herman Wasserman, and Winston Mano. 2016. *China's media and soft power in Africa: promotion and perceptions*. Edited by May Tan-Mullins and Adam Knee, *Palgrave Series in Asia and Pacific Studies*. US: Palgrave Macmillan.

Zhao, Qizheng. 2012. *How China Communicates: Public Diplomacy in a Global Age*. Beijing: Foreign Language Press.

Zhou, Hailin. 2012. "An Interpretation of the Influential Power of China Development." *Chinese Journal of Population Resources and Environment* 10 (2):12–23. doi: 10.1080/10042857.2012.10685072.

Zhu, Ying. 2012. *Two billion eyes: the story of China Central Television*. New York: New Press.

Chapter 2

CHINA'S SOFT POWER STRATEGY THROUGH MEDIA

International Broadcasting in International Relations

International broadcasting has always had a role to play in world politics since the beginning of the industry when technology made long-distance transmission of signals possible.

The development of international broadcasting experienced peak moments following the outburst of events in history with the realisation by states of the increasing significance of information. The use of information in dealing with international affairs started during the world wars when states realised that ideological narrative would influence the legitimacy of each side in the war internally and externally. As early as 1917, the US government created the Committee on Public Information targeting both Americans and foreigners, and dissolved it in 1919 following the end of World War I. But the tactics were adopted by countries like Germany during the post-war period (Pratkanis and Aronson 1991), which witnessed the first beginnings of national and international broadcasting around the world, especially in the West: the United Kingdom founded BBC in 1922 and started its Empire Service in 1932, accompanied by Russia (1926), Holland (1927), China (1928, international service in 1941), Germany (1929), France (1931), Japan (1934) and the United States (1942). Then came the period of the Cold War, when ideological war between the socialist bloc and the West entered another peak moment with the dominance of BBC Overseas Service, Voice of America (VOA), Radio Moscow, Deutsche Welle and other proxy stations like Radio Free Europe, Liberty and Asia (Rawnsley 2016). An obvious feature in this period of international broadcasting was its close connection with states. States used broadcasting to mobilise for war or counter the frames of rival parties. In the United States, for example, there were organisations in history like the Office of War Information, which later evolved into part of the Bureau of Public Affairs, and the Central Intelligence Agency, then the Office of the Coordinator of Information with a unit called Foreign Information Service under which VOA was started, in charge of overseeing propaganda related to the US stance at war, providing rhetorical support to allies. The United States Information Agency (USIA) (1953–99) played a significant role after World War II 'to persuade people in other nations that the US national interests and national security policies should be supported' (Hacker and Mendez 2016, 75). This, together with the development of the media and entertainment industry, is recognised as an indispensable element that helped the United States achieve the cultural dominance that accompanies its super power status.

Radio was the main force in international broadcasting during the two world wars and towards the Cold War. The 1991 Gulf War saw the rise of CNN, when the use of satellite and cable television made it possible for round-the-clock live coverage of world affairs; the speed of live coverage had a significant impact on governments in dealing with world affairs. This announced the coming of a new era of international broadcasting. Because of the demise of the Socialist bloc, the ideological confrontation petered out in this period. In addition, worldwide news gathering is an expensive business. Enthusiasm for international news broadcasting gave way to the entertainment industry. The state lost its grip on the industry.

The 9/11 terrorist attacks followed by the growth of terrorism marked the return of the battle of heart and mind in the context of national security. The state actors began to re-emphasise the importance of the information war. For example, in 2011, the then US secretary of state Hillary Clinton stated at the Senate Foreign Relations Committee that the United States was in an information war and was losing to global media networks (Snow 2011). The call for more solutions to win the hearts and minds of those who are vulnerable to anti-American messages and to seek more support for its 'war on terror' frame (Schneider 2015) became a focus in the national security debate of the United States.

The development of international broadcasting has seen its functioning in international affairs attracting state involvement. From the world wars to the Cold War period, the main purpose was war and ideological propaganda. For instance, the early radio capacity of VOA was developed with the help of the US intelligence community. During this period, although the amount of entertainment had increased, 'much of the entertainment had its own ideological flavour, the news predominated and the entertainment served as "bait" for it' (Browne 1983, 205–6). In modern times, most states significantly loosen their reins over broadcasting and many non-commercial broadcasters have turned into public organisations like BBC after the struggle of broadcasters for operational independence; a few remain under state control under different systems. The function of targeting the international audience has transitioned from information services operated under state control to information services for the international market, which aims to present themselves as objective information providers (Hacker and Mendez 2016). But promoting the voices and values is not completely excluded from state agenda although there are different patterns in commercial and public networks. But both types are viewed as important tools for foreign policy.

There are several conceptualisations about the role of broadcasting in world politics. One is mediapolitik (Edwards 2001). We are living now in a media-constructed virtual reality (Said 2008) and using media-generated images to construct meaning about political and social issues (Castells 2004; Gamson et al. 1992). After examining the role media played in events like Pinochet's defeat in Chile, Edwards (2001) posits that media has become the real mass and a national power. He has proposed the theory of mediapolitik addressing the interrelationship between the mass media and politics. He believes that media has the obligation to enrich human interest by covering news events in an ethical and professional way.

Another is the CNN effect. The CNN effect theory proposes that 'news coverage – especially gripping visual storytelling – was influencing foreign policy throughout the world' (Livingston 1997, 3). Round-the-clock cable television has had so profound an impact to policymakers in foreign policy that former US President George Bush famously acknowledged that he had learnt more from CNN than the intelligence body CIA. Livingston (1997) identifies three ways the media may influence foreign policy: as a policy agenda-setting agent, an impediment to certain policy goals and an accelerant to policy decision making. The effects of media on policymaking are not as significant as is claimed in the CNN effect. However, the price a state or a politician may pay could be high if they were not to take the media seriously.

Then comes the Al Jazeera effect. The Al Jazeera effect 'encompasses the use of new media as tools in every aspect of global affairs, ranging from democratisation to terrorism and including the concept of "virtual states"' (Seib 2008, 5). Seib views Al Jazeera as a symbol of the new context which helps cohesion among the Muslim community globally (p. x).[1] Media can be 'tools of conflict and instruments of peace; they can make traditional borders irrelevant and unify peoples scattered across the globe' – to put it succinctly, reshape the world (p. xii).

Information flow is a key concept to discuss the debate. Since the 1980s, new information order has become a wave of focus in international communication. More and more newly independent countries realised the

---

1 This claim needs to be seen in the light of the breaking of diplomatic relations by Saudi Arabia, Egypt, the United Arab Emirates and several other Muslim countries, one of the reasons being Qatar and Al Jazeera's support for the Muslim Brotherhood.

Anglo-American dominance in the media landscape and beyond. They started to call for a more balanced information market. The study of the international flow of information thus became another approach to the study of international relations (Mowlana 1997, 23). Since the 1980s, much research proved repeatedly the existence of an information gap between information-rich and information-poor states, which provided evidence for developing countries to strive for more voices (Mowlana 1985). Behind it was the demand to counter the domination of Western discourse which has not changed much even in the time of social media. This has become an imperative issue and a common reason for some countries to develop their own version of international broadcasting. Countries like Germany (Deutsche Welle, 1992), France (France 24, 2006), Russia (Russia Today, 2005), China (CCTV-9, 2000–2010; CCTV NEWS, 2010–16; CGTN since the end of 2016) and Iran (Press TV, 2009), with the aim to 'diversify the perspectives expressed in international issues debates' in the world broadcasting dominated by the United States and the United Kingdom, to improve national image, have founded their own English broadcasting (Seib 2010, 736). This has formed a force labelled by scholars as contra-flow (Thussu 2010).

In recent decades, public diplomacy and soft power have become another new trend in analysing international communication. Actually, the first use of the term 'public diplomacy' by Gullion gave the operation of international broadcasting during war time a very important status. Recent development of public diplomacy sees the decrease in hyped information operations and the increase in civic engagement to foster mutual understanding and trust for further international engagement. Although scholars like Powers and Gilboa (2007) take the view that the role of transnational news organisations does not fall under any type of non-traditional actors categorised by scholars in international relations, Seib (2010) posits that media organisations are non-state actors that function more than as information delivery systems but in a crucial public diplomatic manner to 'further national interests and wield soft power' (p. 743). Various terms have been absorbed by scholars addressing the relationship between media and public diplomacy, such as 'newspaper diplomacy', 'radio diplomacy' (Rawnsley 1996), 'television diplomacy' and 'headline diplomacy' (Seib 1997), which fall under the rubric of media diplomacy, a concept developed by Cohen (1986) and Gilboa (1998; 2002), which refers to the use of media by country leaders and policymakers to propagate a preferred national image in the international community. Two other concepts addressing media and public diplomacy are media broker diplomacy and mediated public diplomacy. The former refers to international mediation implemented and occasionally initiated by media professionals, especially at times when the two parties are in adversarial stances and no third party is available to help them resolve their differences (Gilboa 1998). Additionally, mediated public diplomacy refers to governmental attempts at influencing the framing of its foreign policies in the global media (Entman 2008; Golan 2013; Wang 2011c). These concepts reveal the instrumental function of media in international relations and sometimes as an independent actor in diplomatic activities.

There is a gloomy outlook on the role of media in the social media age. But as Edwards (2001) has claimed, the cyber age will not replace mass media but rather will build on the media development of former ages (p. 3). It is true that new technology has diffused power to a larger public, but little seems to have changed in the dynamics. It is obvious that social media play important roles in events like the Arab Spring revolution and Occupy Wall Street, but the ability of social media to lead to a better solution has not been proved significantly through these cases. In the case of Trump's use of Twitter to connect to the public, while the traditional role of media in Western democracies as watchdog seems to be challenged, media outlets still offer fact-check services for purposes of verification. In addition, the way the president communicates directly with the public is in some ways an unusual practice – anywhere in the world. Although the battleground has shifted to social media dramatically, arguably it is serving more as a channel for trivia rather than originating essential content, especially in politics/world politics. People cannot usually get coherent narratives from friends' social media posts about what is going on nationally and globally without their friends having accessed media stories, with their frames. In addition, as demonstrated in the 2016 US presidential election, social media, although invested with the advantages of quantity and speed, is vulnerable to misinformation because of the lack of journalistic normativisation among social media users and adequate industry self-regulation of websites. So, the stance is taken here that social media is an advanced channel for media. Although it can bring some changes in certain areas, looking at the whole picture, we see that media continue to function but in the form of omni-media.

China's International Broadcasting as An Important Public Diplomacy Approach

China has been experiencing a dramatic socio-economic and geopolitical transition over the last three or so decades, rising all the way from being a poor, backward country to a world power. It has paid increasing attention to improving its national image through public diplomacy initiatives. Although the term 'public diplomacy' was not widely used in China's public and political discourse until very recently, the practice can be traced back to even before the founding of the PRC. d'Hooghe (2008) cites from Edgar Snow's *Red Star over China* to illustrate the skills of the Communist Party in using media to win hearts and minds. Scholars place China's public diplomacy efforts in three categories: information and cultural programmes (Han 2011) and economic programmes (Jiang and Yan 2015). Developing an international communication strategy was an important undertaking of the PRC in conducting its public diplomacy. The Communist Party began foreign broadcasting in 1941. From the establishment of the PRC in 1949 to the late 1970s, China's international broadcasting (also known as external publicity) was focused on the 'socialist camp' and Third World countries, carrying strong political and ideological content with the aim of developing friendship and sharing socialist ideology with other socialist countries. The media branches used were Xinhua News Agency for print stories and CRI for radio stories (Han 2011). Since the 'reform and opening up' policy was adopted, international broadcasting activities have become more proactive. Wang summarised the several stages of China's external propaganda according to content: provide publicity about New China and support world revolution; enhance reform and the process of opening to outside world; safeguard world peace; denounce the China threat discourse (Wang 2008).

In the early 1990s, the Chinese government began to actively promote international broadcasting activities to shift negative images and win international goodwill for its economic development efforts. Zhao Qizheng, the former director of State Council Information Office, argues that it is urgent for China to 'improve the understanding and recognition of foreign publics on its basic national conditions, values, development path as well as its domestic and foreign policies' as its relations 'with the international environment have become closer after 30-plus years of reform and opening up' (Zhao 2012, 2). Image considerations have long been the core task underpinning the publicity strategy: for a long time, there have been research and top leaders' speeches indicating that Western media's coverage of China has been twisted, biased (Hu 2008) and even demonising (Li and Liu 1996; Xiang 2013; Zhao 2012), all in the extreme sense. In the milder sense, some scholars see a divergence between China's self-perception and perceptions of China by others (Wang 2011a). In China, the reason behind the image issues is widely considered as being stereotyped by others, especially by Western countries with their discourse dominance when pitted against the weakness of China's discourse power (Meng 2012).

Investment in international media saw a huge increase after the Beijing Olympics (Sun 2015). Because the Chinese leadership and scholars realised from the drama during the Olympics, such as the torch relay incidents, the criticism received from Western media regarding Tibet issues and human rights issues, that despite China's organisational ability and economic capacity that enabled it to successfully host a mega media event, China was seriously deficient in international media and discourse power. International public opinion is still in the control of those countries with more competitive media outlets. Arguments have been made that under these circumstances it is impossible to set an effective agenda and turn international opinion because of the strong framing capacity of Western media on issues such as Tibet and human rights (Sun 2009, 2015). After 2008, the transformation in geopolitics and economic order, with China playing an enhanced role, some Chinese scholars formed the view that there is a need for a new information order beyond New World Information and Communication Order (NWICO) and World Summit on the Information Society (WSIS) (Shi and Zhang 2016). Since then, media as a channel of external broadcasting has been included in China's grand strategic plans such as the *2009–2020 Master Plan for the Construction of China's Major Media as an International Dissemination Force*. Six media outlets including the *People's Daily*, China Radio International, CCTV, Xinhua News Agency, *China Daily* and China News Service have been listed as major organisations with special financial support under the plan.

Generally speaking, there are two motivations behind Chinese media expansion strategies. First, China seeks to counteract the imbalance of information flow suffered by the Third World, an imbalance identified by NWICO in UNESCO; NWICO indicated, on the one hand, a quantitative deficit to the disadvantage of Third World countries and, on the other, a negative representation of these countries in the West (MacBride 1980). Second, China seeks to match its rising political and economic power with its discourse power. With its economic success driving its status up in the world steadily, China's rhetoric of international communication has begun to reflect big power status on the world stage (d'Hooghe 2014; Hartig 2012; Wang 2010, 2011a, 2011b;). But China's negative image in the West prevents it from integrating into the global economy as a respected world power (Wang 2011a). It recognises from the lessons from history that 'whoever occupies the public opinion high ground will have the possibility – although it might be only temporary and short-lived – to seize the pre-emptive opportunity, gain the upper hand and in "understanding" and "support" from the international community and the public' (Zhao 2012, 47–48). In recent years, more aggressiveness in the discourse regarding external publicity may be noted, with the rhetoric of China offering solutions to world problems. Xi has urged external publicity media workers, on many occasions, to forge new concepts, categories and formulations that may be circulated in China and abroad (Xi 2013) under the concept of community of common destiny for all mankind – as a Chinese approach to global governance (Xi 2014).

With this mission in mind, efforts have been made in various media sectors. At the institutional level, relevant governmental organisations have been established. In 1980, the Foreign Propaganda Group was formed under the CPC Central Committee. In 1991, the State Council Information Office was established and following this a press conference system was institutionalised. A spokesman system was established in 2003 (Ding 2006). Under the new post-2009 strategy, more significant progress has been witnessed. In 2009, the first World Media Summit was convened by Xinhua News Agency together with major international media organisations (WMSDOHA 2016). In 2010, Xinhua News Agency launched its television service. By 2017, CCTV had expanded its reach by establishing five foreign-language channels, overseas branches in Washington, DC, and Nairobi, and fielding more than 70 reporting teams around the world (CGTN 2017; Zhu 2012). In addition, at the operational level, the major outlets employed local staff as well as adopt technological innovations and greater audience orientation through use of social media; these initiatives have enhanced their practice. The new initiatives have at least made the channel look more like its Western counterparts stylistically.

China's international communication effort is not without challenges. The credibility issue is the main hindrance to effectiveness vis-a-vis the audience, according to many scholars (d'Hooghe 2008, 2011, 2014; Nye 2011). Wang (2011a) analysed the situations and reasons why the perceptions are sometimes different: Some negative images are objective facts that China needs to improve, while others are subjective. Also, she employs psychological theories and concludes that people tend to accept information that is consistent with their existing perceptions to explain the phenomenon; for instance, even if China acts benevolently in some cases, Americans do not necessarily perceive its actions as benevolent. Shi also observed the plight facing China in the projection of its ideals and discourse: China's political discourse, though rooted in attractive traditional political concepts such as rule of law and societal aspirations (such as the Chinese Dream following the American Dream meme), do not easily translate into positive narratives in Western media. What is worse, as Hu and Ji have observed, is that the Chinese side is not quite clear on the question of whether the voice China tries to spread is consistent with its internal context – within the complicated reality in the country – and whether the voice can be decoded by targeted Western audiences as China intends (Hu and Ji 2012).

Because of the visible push by state, China's media expansion was labelled as a 'charm offensive' by some scholars (Kurlantzick 2007). But Chinese scholar Shi (2013) views it more as a 'charm defensive', which is to win hearts and minds in a second country, than an offensive, because it is part of broader

engagements including various levels of interactions between the two countries rather than a one-dimensional form of wielding 'soft power'.

CCTV NEWS: A tool of China's soft power?

Earlier research on CCTV NEWS and its processor channels have focused on
a variety of aspects including its editorial operations (Jirik 2004, 2008, 2015;
Ning 2013), content (Jirik 2008; Ning 2013;Zhang 2013), professional aspects
(Zhang and Simon 2016), audience (Gorfinkel et al. 2014; Zhang 2011) and
its soft power significance (Jirik 2016; Rawnsley 2012; Sun 2015, 2009; Wang
2011b; Wasserman 2016; Zhang 2011).

Jirik, with his unique experience of working for CCTV-9 and then CCTV
NEWS and witnessing the relaunch of the former from a comprehensive
channel to a news channel, offers a comprehensive picture of the operation
of the English channel, especially the dynamics of the power mechanism in
the channel which is seldom seen by scholars who have no experience of the
broadcasting or media practice. A widely known major Chinese journalism
characteristic is that the news systems are part and parcel of the governance
system and there is a guideline that there should be positive reporting regarding
the governing system (Jirik 2008; Li 1991). Anything that may cause social
instability or challenge party principles would not be allowed on air, though
increasingly one finds that there is greater expression of critical opinion in academia. The foundation of the English channel and the successive relaunches
over the years were undertaken under the party's strategic guidance – under
the supervision of Central Publicity Department or the regulatory body, the
State Administration of Radio, Film and Television (SARFT). According to
Jirik, although the launch and relaunch were impelled by strong political vol-
ition, the process reflected a certain degree of negotiation between the authorities and management staff; most of the editorial decisions were made within
the channel. The directives were usually given as suggestions about the party
representative's opinions of good angles for a story, and the significance of
certain events. The editors would respond with their notions of audience's
interest and the way they could narrate the story appropriately. Also, there
were political editors, usually experienced retired journalists, who ensure that
no political errors were made. In the management hierarchy, the top management, being more managers and fewer journalists, always rises within
the CCTV system, working with great caution, facing pressure to leverage
news content. However, editorial control has been shifting more in favour of
newsmakers. The measurement for adoption of topics is their sensitivity (Jirik
2008, 2016). Outsiders would doubt whether the new workers have qualified professional skills as they work in state-run media, which is regarded as

the propaganda machine. But according to Jirik's observation, the domestic journalists are 'extremely good at their job'; they are clearly 'not puppets or marionettes dancing to the tune' of the authorities (Jirik 2008, 1).

China's official preference for positive reporting is viewed as being questionable from the point of view of liberal news values. However, some prefer to see it as a challenge to the Western conception of media watchdog role (Gagliardone 2013; Gagliardone et al. 2010; Gagliardone et al. 2012). Other scholars have tried to analyse the CCTV Africa reports from a new paradigm of constructive journalism characterised by positive reporting with a constructive purpose of representing Africa and building China–Africa relations (Zhang and Simon 2016).

Western media could be influenced so greatly by ratings and circulation-driven news values that they could inordinately feature conflict, crime, deviance, disaster and sex. As indicated earlier, neither does focusing on this mix to the exclusion of achievements, cooperation, development and social harmony represent the best professionalism nor does it on the latter at the expense of problems in a society. Striking a balance between the positive and the negative, and between social and individual interest, remains a constant challenge to the media professional.

Research on the content of CCTV NEWS under logos such as CCTV NEWS and CCTV-9 follows various trends that are sometimes contrary to each other. In many occasions, the Chinese authorities and news workers from the channel expressed their aspiration of building the brand to be a channel that provides alternative perspectives of China and the world to Western media (Jirik 2008; Marsh 2016; Zhang 2011, 2013). This is the point many scholars have tried to confirm. Jirik (2008, 2016) examines the problem of CCTV NEWS being reliant on external materials from international news agencies such as Associate Press and Reuters which supply much of the on-air material and on-the-ground correspondents. He regards this reliance as a contradiction of its mission to be a channel that represents Chinese voices and perspectives. Using content analysis and discourse analysis, Marsh (2016) finds that some similarities exist, including the visual presentation of the programmes and the region covered in CCTV NEWS's African programme *Africa Live* and BBC's *Focus on Africa*. As to whether CCTV Africa presents an alternative to Western media coverage of Africa, she concludes that the frames are 'frequently but not always' similar to BBC's *Focus on Africa* (Marsh 2016, 64). There are more post-production traces in *Africa Live* than those in *Focus on Africa*, which always presents a film completely from on-site (Marsh 2016). She interprets this as a sign of following the official perspectives and warns of the danger of cultural dependence through the use of agency materials that usually reflect the values of US and British organisations. Zhang (2013) found that CCTV Africa devoted much to criticising the West. But three years later, Marsh (2016) observed in her research that it was no longer the case. This may indicate the constant improvement of CCTV Africa's practice. But the contradiction leaves space for further investigation into the channel.

CCTV NEWS, as a relatively young channel, has been exploring a model for greater influence in the global news market. This can be seen from its relaunches over the years. In a study conducted by the staff of CCTV NEWS, the ratio of in-house production to news agency and other external material, in the programme *News Hour*, was found to be 1:2 – similar to the ratios in CNN's *News Stream* and BBC's *Global News*, which are programmes aired in the same time slot. The study further reveals that CCTV NEWS led in the width of news coverage but lagged behind in terms of depth. In addition, a large proportion of coverage of CCTV NEWS is on China-related topics while the other two are on international issues (Wu and Huang 2015). In an evaluation report by CCTV Overseas Centre, the channel's general in-house production capacity increased 21-fold from 2009 to 2012, reaching 38.5 per cent in 2012 (CCTV Overseas Centre 2013). With expanding investment in in-house production, this figure is expected to keep growing. In addition, the employment of experienced media workers from mainstream Western media outlets has strengthened the channel's production capacity, which can be seen from the 17 awards from 2016 to 2018 listed on its official site, including two each from Asian Television Awards and the US International Film & Video Festival, and three from the White House News Photographers' Association.

There is also research assessing the channel's effectiveness to fulfil its aims. Examining CCTV Africa's programme *Africa Live*, Zhang (2013) concludes that CCTV NEWS 'not only aims to guide global views of contemporary Sino-Africa relations, but also to create a discourse on international affairs, as an alternative to a "Western discourse" and [has] the ambition to change the global order' (p. 97). However, one cannot see an alternative discourse in CCTV NEWS, only condemnation of the West and West-led international system and calls for a 'system that allows the co-existence of different systems' (p. 99).

Audience may have been the biggest conundrum to both scholars and the channel. From interviews with the international managers in CCTV, the purpose of CCTV International was to influence foreign public opinion, not to make a profit (Jirik 2008; Zhang 2011). But that does not mean that the audience is not important for the channel. Despite the continuing improvement in news-making, the channel's penetration rate is low. Some research has revealed that much of the audience was intent on learning Mandarin or watching programmes about history and culture rather than news (Zhang 2011). The pilot survey by Gorfinkel et al. (2014) in Kenya and South Africa reveals that there is a 'slightly greater interest and awareness by white audiences in Kenya, and a problem of lack of awareness or sustained interest by black Kenyans and educated pay TV subscribers in South Africa' (p. 86). However, according to a later survey by Guan and Wang (2015), this seems to have been improving although not by much. In the survey, 15.6 per cent of respondents in the US report having watched CCTV NEWS in 2011 more than once. CCTV is ranked third among China-run English media in the US market. In a broader sense, US media is the first source from which Americans learn about China; this is followed by Chinese people, Chinese restaurants, Chinese commodities and the media of mainland China – all in America. This shows that Chinese media has a role even if it may be in the fifth place.

Jirik (2016) analyses the audience challenge from two different aspects: cultural proximity (Straubhaar 1991) and soft power. With regard to cultural proximity, he claims that the use of local staff and local stories are strengths for CCTV NEWS. Regarding the soft power perspective, varying from Nye's understanding that media effectiveness in spreading a country's values depends on its reach, Jirik (2016) argues that to sway a polity, targeting elites is possible. This concurs with Rogers's two-step Diffusion of Innovation model in which messages are sent to the wider society through opinion leaders who are essentially influential elites (Rogers 1962). The target audience of CCTV NEWS are elites, as defined by a member of its management team as 'middle-and upper-class North Americans, as well as people who are interested in issues related to China' (Liu 2014, cited in Jirik 2016). However, perhaps, under a Rogers's model, more could be done to target identified opinion leaders in key areas such as Hollywood or who have a large social media following, so as to influence larger numbers of people.

In the cultural proximity perspective, the audience is mostly passive, without any motivation of information acquisition. This may be true about entertainment media. In reality, for news broadcasting, there is always an audience that seeks information in order to make sense or decisions. Among these would be members of policy and business communities. But, as there are alternative sources, a news organisation needs to be competitive in providing information.

Nye's prognostications for China's international media push are not hopeful. He sees China's ability to successfully generate soft power through media to be hampered by credibility issues associated with state-run media (Nye 2013). But could he not be seeing the wood for the trees here? First, US soft power dominance in terms of its political ideology was ramped by the US government during the Cold War through state-run agencies such as USIA (Thussu 2013). There were also state broadcasters such as VOA, Radio Free Europe and Radio Marti. Second, so-called media credibility is more an ideal than a reality, as articulated by many academic researchers (Boyd-Barrett

1980; Herman and Chomsky 2002; Jirik 2013; Li and Chitty 2017; Paterson 2011) and media specialists like Jirik who used to work for mainstream Western media organisations and was 'cynical about the claims to balance and objectivity made by Western and international news organisations [...] over and against the clear biases evident in the objectivist news tradition that political economic analyses of institutional histories and behaviours and longitudinal analyses of so-called objective news content have consistently shown' (Jirik 2016, 35–38).

But it is hard to deny that credibility is a huge hindrance for CCTV NEWS especially in Western countries. The media system in China is not just a social issue but also one that is deeply intertwined with politics and government. In China, media are state-owned and are part of the power system (Jirik 2008, 28). The ideological narrative followed in the media sector has always adhered to Marxist, Leninist and Mao's thought, as well as Deng's theories and those of later administrations. The function of media is widely recognised to be a Leninist 'transmission belt' for indoctrination and social mobilisation (Shambaugh 2007). The position of the media in the Chinese system is defined as the mouthpiece of the government and the party with the function of positively publicising and explaining the policy of the party and the government, motivating people to work hard towards social and economic goals, providing comprehensive and unbiased views of society and the world, and helping the party and the government in the smooth governance of the country and maintaining established order and stability. As a key part of the Chinese system, it is meant to ensure system stability. Another dimension defining China's media system is the emphasis on safeguarding China's national interest and traditional culture in foreign policy. At the same time, television should be the major information source providing an accurate coverage of society and the world. Furthermore, it is expected to encourage people to be more confident in the country and the values as articulated by the administration (Li 1991). In this sense, positive reporting is regarded higher than negative news, unless negative news can discourage offenders and prevent crime or help find an early solution for social problems without generating social disquiet. From this sense, it is not hard to understand Jirik's thesis; state organs like the Foreign Ministry can advise media about what they cannot report. There is dual track supervision: party supervision by the publicity department focuses on ideology and state supervision by administrative organisations focuses on operations, but without excluding ideological aspects (Liu 2007). Zhao (1998) describes the television system in China to be closer to a public media system.

Professional practice is another dimension through which to understand the dynamics of the credibility problem. Onuf (2004) has posited hierarchy, hegemony and heteronomy as three rules for functional grounds for world politics. He has used the term 'hegemony' 'abstractly to describe a form of rule that manifests itself in a great variety of social arrangements [...] [and] that professionalisation fosters hegemonial rule' (Onuf 1997, 91–92). Professionalism is, after all, a set of norms that engenders a normative hegemony. This may also apply with respect to the norms of journalistic professionalism.

One fact that has to be mentioned here is that since the 'opening up' policy, reform in the media sector witnessed enormous transformation not only in media practice but also in the professional perception of the media workers. Lu and Pan (2002) note that journalism practice and journalism education in China incorporate Western liberal professionalism as part of Chinese professional perception, causing some discordance with traditional Chinese intellectual values and contemporary Chinese socialist values among Chinese media workers. Zhao (1998) points out that the market has joined the party as a mover and shaker. In this context, Jirik, comparing his experience at CCTV NEWS and Reuters, concludes that the lengthy and complicated history of modern Chinese journalism has not resulted in a blunt propaganda (Jirik 2016). He also notes that, ironically, the toughest critics of the propaganda model are Communist Party members while expatriate Western professionals (who previously worked in Western mainstream media outlets) are relatively comfortable with the role as the mouthpiece for the party and state because of the belief that Western journalist values were illusionary. Research by Lee et al. (2006) found that journalists, in big cities like Shenzhen and Shanghai, where media marketisation is mature, articulated having little difficulty in working within the party line while serving the market. In the case of CCTV NEWS, Jirik (2008) found that newsmakers in the channel 'balanced social responsibility and professionalism understood as serving the people with their mouthpiece function and professionalism understood as serving the Party and government' (p. 449) by negotiating tactfully with the authorities. More detail about the professionalism debate will be presented in the discussion in the next section.

Being aware of the warning by scholars against the dichotomous framing of China's media under the party/state and market structure, Jirik (2008) provides another insight: framing China's journalism as 'speaking on behalf of the power structure' (p. 449) or as being against the power structure are equally incorrect because it is part of the power structure – an agency that is at the same time both an instrument and a critic of power.

The management of the CCTV NEWS era summarises the channel's goals as being twofold: to project China's voice worldwide and to become a player in the international news retail market (Jirik 2016). These can be examined within the framework of soft power. This perspective has been adopted by several scholars (Gagliardon 2013; Gorfinkel 2014; Jirik 2016; Marsh 2016; Sun 2009; Wang 2011a; Wasserman 2016; Zhang 2011). But different researchers have drawn different conclusions. Sun (2009) takes it as a 'mission impossible' because in her view, '[g]lobally, the Chinese state media needs to convincingly present itself as a player whose values, ethics, and sensibilities are compatible with, if not superior to, its international counterparts', but in reality, in speaking of influencing public opinion, media content and format and the system they work in are different from those of the West. Marsh (2016) posits that it is questionable to assume that China's state media can be 'harnessed' and 'imposed' by state media when the media are restrained by self-censorship that may be associated with a propagandist media (p. 68).

However, according to Shi (2013), the role imposed on media is to be defensive, not offensive. Gagliardone (2013) holds a more positive view of CCTV and sees the launch of CCTV Africa as a 'mix of strategic decisions and a series of fortuitous events' (p. 29). He thinks the role is meant to enhance perceptions of China not through projecting directly a positive image of China but rather by providing a new way of looking at Africa. It is trying to create an 'Africa rising' narrative. He sees the potential for a mutually enriching encounter between the Chinese and African peoples, and notes that any success in acting as a persuader will depend on CCTV NEWS's ability to offer news about the continent to people where there is a demand for such news. He has described what many researchers have ignored when they place China's values and strategic expansion in the prism of threatening Western values and market share: through the process of development, a mixed and hybridised model, one that draws also on models that developed in different contexts, may emerge. CCTV Africa is a 'transactional venue' where Chinese, African and Western ways meet, while in an internationalising media, 'a major transaction in a venue is the production of hybridity' (Chitty 2009, 64).

Others have taken different approaches such as seeking to prognosticate the direction CCTV NEWS will take or identify the problems it faces. Zhang (2011) points out that it should be made clear how China's cultural and political appeal is projected, whether a China's state-centric, one-actor model is the answer to public diplomacy challenges and to what extent the effort will help to advance China's soft power. Jirik (2016) suggests a way forward for CCTV NEWS, meant to overcome its audience deficit. His recommendation is that it should follow the practice of its rivals and thereby attract audiences that are used to certain practices. He also expressed concern about whether state funding will continue, although CCTV NEWS's management was sanguine about financial support from the government being continued.

Chinese media culture

The professional culture in China is quite different to that in the West, being embedded in the socialist political system where the written rule is for media to be the 'throat and tongue' of the party and the government, and support governance (Sparks 2012). With a *sui generis* political system and an immensely popular social media, China's media landscape is more complex than many scholars expect it to be. Professionalism is usually claimed to be limited because of state ownership of media and the 'throat and tongue' character (Simons et al. 2016; Tong 2011). The commercialisation of the media industry that started in the 1990s has led to a transition to market orientation, but the party line continues to dominate (Qian and Bandurski 2011). Journalism in China suffers from contradictions: culturally, Confucian role expectations for public intellectuals versus liberal expectations of press as watchdog; institutionally, party principle versus people principle (Lee 2005; Tong 2011); and as a product in the market-based conception versus the tool of governance (Hassid 2011; Pan and Lu 2003). But the idea of professionalism is widely accepted by journalists and educators alike and to a certain extent is changing the ideology of Chinese journalism with the purpose of reconstruction and amelioration (Shao and Dong 2016). Another survey indicates that Chinese journalists are taking a realistic attitude towards the idea of journalism and can navigate between party and professional lines (Simons et al. 2016).

It is true for China as it is for the rest of the world that journalistic professional values are ideal and counterfactual (Örnebring 2010). The existing criteria seem simplistic when applied to the analysis of China's dynamically changing and historically steeped reality. Despite the state ownership and the party imperative in the Chinese party-state, scholars discover that in practice, journalists have tried to establish a comfort zone for professional practice (Simons et al. 2016). Even so, the research shows that there is consensus among journalists that adhering to the rules is important when playing the game (Simons et al. 2016, 8). Jirik, comparing his experience at CCTV NEWS and other Western media outlets, concludes that the layered history of modern Chinese journalism, from the Qing Dynasty, is not one that can be reduced to the churning out of 'blunt propaganda' – one early influence having been Western journalism (Jirik 2016, 35–38). He also mentions that the toughest critics of the propaganda model were the Communist Party members, while foreign professionals who used to work in Western mainstream media outlets are relatively comfortable in their roles as mouthpieces for the party and state because of their disillusionment with Western journalistic values which they see as illusionary (Jirik 2016).

As noted by Sparks (2012), the existing research on China's journalism is over-concerned with political influence. Sparks specifies two problems in Chinese journalistic professionalism research:

1. There is much political focus on the cultural-revolution-type totalitarian style which is far from today's true situation.
2. Ideological attachment leads to the illusion that marketisation will precipitate conflict with the party.

Research by Lee et al. (2006) found that journalists in big cities like Shenzhen and Shanghai, where media marketisation is mature, articulated little difficulty in working both within the party line and serving the market. It is important to understand the dynamics of Chinese society, because in the complicated political structure even different administrative levels have different realities. An investigation of the characteristics of a specific organisation will be helpful in understanding the practice and the content. CCTV NEWS's staff structure displays the international mobility of media workers with a mix of local and foreign staff. In this context, the culture must be unique as well as complicated. There must be an internal negotiation to achieve its special identity which guides the practice of the channel.

Two aspects are crucial to understanding the formation of its organisational identity. First, there are multiple forces of influence: apart from the 'dominant structure' of communist ideology, there is a 'residual structure' of Confucian intellectual ethics and an imported media professionalism, as well as a globalisation-spawned market logic (Lee 2005; Williams 1977) that acts on Chinese media workers' identity construction. Wang Han, a successful entertainment programme host from Hunan TV, quoted in a speech an expression by Song Dynasty Philosopher Zhang Zai to express his understanding of the media workers' mission: to ordain conscience for Heaven and Earth; to secure life and fortune for the people; to continue lost teachings for past sages and to establish peace for all future generations. This is a characteristic feature for Chinese intellectuals for hundreds of years under the philosophical idea of *Tianxia* (Under the Heaven). Similar ideas are echoed by many mainstream media workers when they talk about social responsibility. These echoes serve the ideological discourse of the state. This may be an important factor for Chinese media workers to find comfort in the face of external suspicion of their playing a propaganda role and supporting party principles. Second, the formation of an organisational culture in a mixed-culture organisation must be the result of interactions between the channel and the Western staff, which, in a Foucauldian disciplinary manner, demonstrates a certain level of hegemonic rule (Onuf 2014) of the management, on the one hand. On the other hand, the Western staff use their professional expertise to make news reflecting Western values, although there are parameters for a small number of topics where chief editors have the final say. Ultimately, however, media workers may respond to conditions with internal constructions of homonomy that will contribute to a unique identity of the organisation.

The Australian Reaction to China's Soft Power Initiatives

As statistics show in the previous chapter, China and Australia have developed a highly interdependent economic relationship. From 1989 to 2014, this bilateral relationship had been getting stronger although there were ups and downs along the journey on specific issues. This trend reached its peak in 2014 with the finalisation of the free-trade agreement; official relations were upgraded to comprehensive strategic relations, and a high-level dialogue among top leaders of the two states was established.

Until then, the mainstream discourse in Australia towards China was keeping close economic ties while maintaining an alliance with the United States in the midst of occasional ups and downs. But in the years that followed, warnings of the rising influence of China in the region kept growing in the mainstream in scholarly debates, political rhetoric and public and media coverage responding to China's more aggressive stance in regional affairs like the South China Sea and the rapid growth of the new BRI. Australia declined China's offer to co-develop the North Territory under the name of BRI while many other countries embraced it. Some believe that a rising China casts a shadow on the prospect of Australia's economic stability because of heavy dependency on the Chinese market with respect to Australia's mineral exports – its largest economic engine – and the emerging economic sector of international education. As an analysis by Chitty et al. (2018) shows, economic development and security concerns are the main themes addressing China's BRI in Australia. The different stances on the above-referenced issues of the two countries had led to what Australian media called a very low and possibly breaking point of the relationship between the two countries as reflected in some occasions when Australian media reflected on as 'not an ideal celebration' of the 45th anniversary of diplomatic ties in 2017. Australian media called 2018 a 'rollercoaster year' for the relationship.

Beyond the economic and political aspects of relations with China, there are more challenging issues vis-à-vis aspirations for a soft power relationship between Australia and China, which goes beyond soft power playing a part in Sino-Australian relations.[2] If record-high statistics in economic relations

---

2 A soft power relationship in its purest form is not the same as a friendship. One of the characteristics of a pure soft power relationship is that there will be no coercion

demonstrate the continuing stability of trade relations, stumbling blocks have emerged in the path towards a soft power relationship.

As reviewed in one article by Li and Chitty (2018), China has established an all-round public diplomatic network in Australia in person-to-person, institutional- and policy-level exchanges, head-of-state visits/dialogue, programmes such as the Confucius Institute, sister cities, business cooperation and large-scale scientific and educational exchange as well as policy agreements like the free-trade agreement. Another important factor for public diplomacy relations is the large Chinese diaspora in Australia. The 2016 Australian census shows that 3.9 per cent of its population, that is, more than 1.2 million of the Australian population, were of Chinese origin, while 2.2 percent of its population, over five hundred thousand Australian citizens and residents, were born on the Chinese mainland (Australian Bureau of Statistics 2016). This large diasporic population in to some a fortune and foreign policy competitive edge (Munro 2017).

International media outlets from China have also been striving to increase their presence in Australia. In 2016, China Daily made a deal with Australian media company Fairfax to include its supplements in Fairfax newspapers, which has triggered debates about China's influence. This agreement is believed to come to an end in November 2018. In September 2018, mainstream media in Australia covered the news of CCTV NEWS's billboard advertisements in capital cities across Australia about its availability in Foxtel and Fetch TV, which are major players of paid television and internet protocol television (IPTV), respectively. Commenting on this, Australian public broadcaster Australian Broadcasting Corporation (ABC) labelled China's media campaign a 'major threat for democracies'.

But these seemingly soft aspects in the bilateral relations have caused more disturbance in Australian society than that of hard power in recent years. Although anxiety existed for a long time in some cases, for example, as early as 2011, an MP for the political party Greens in New South Wales (NSW) organised a petition to remove Confucius Classrooms in NSW schools and called for a review of the operation of the Confucius Institute. Concerns over Chinese engagement reached a historically high level in recent years with

---

at all exerted between those in the relationship – no use of force or economic inducement. It is possible for friends to use force or economic inducement on each other. The special relationship between the United Kingdom and the United States, the values of European integration, the ideals of peaceful coexistence promulgated by the Non-Aligned Movement in the 1950s and the Rancho Mirage identification of a 'cooperative partnership based on respect and mutual benefit' are all cases that need examination in a detailed construction of an ideal typical soft power relationship (Chitty 2015b).

respect to intensity and scale. The starting point was in mid-2017 when an investigative report covered stories of the ties of Chinese overseas students and business figures to the Chinese government and warned of unwarranted Chinese influence in Australia, especially in the political process. This was followed by a hike in investigations by media, scholars and politicians on the issue. For example, the national public broadcaster ABC launched a feature series with the title *China Influence*. Apart from the aforementioned TV programme, the book *Silent Invasion: China's Influence in Australia* by Australian public intellectual Clive Hamilton demonstrates another extreme case of Australian reaction to China- related issues. In the book, the author labels actors from international students to business figures, from political donor to scientific researchers, as the arms of the Chinese government and tools in a conspiracy to undermine Australia's sovereignty. The exceptions are those Australian Chinese who constantly bitterly criticise China. Although some supporters of the book appreciated the author's courage in raising questions about China, others have pointed out some weak points in the book. The weak points include the following: (1) unfairly categorising some groups specialised in foreign policy as China's proxies; (2) 'much exceptional research and detail sits alongside sometimes hasty conclusions' (Medcalf 2018); (3) some racist overtones are based not on deeds reported but rather because the actor was China; and (4) voice is given only to those who are hostile to the PRC (Brophy 2015).

Although little specific evidence is provided in the above-mentioned cases among the claims of Chinese influence, the concerns have been reflected at the policy level and in political narratives: in 2017, the Australian federal government passed a law against foreign donations in the middle of debates about several Chinese Australian businessmen making big donations to political parties. These donors were believed to have connections with the Chinese government, according to the Australian Security Intelligence Organisation (ASIO). In the same year, a Foreign Influence Transparency Scheme was passed, which requires foreign organisations to register. Confucius Institutes in Australia were informed specifically by email to register under this scheme. In 2017, ASIO tried to provide briefings to 18 universities on potential risks to academic freedom, sensitive research and intellectual property. In August 2018, the federal government banned Chinese telecommunication companies Huawei and ZTE from providing 5G technologies to Australia over the concern that it would 'likely [be] subject to extrajudicial directions from a foreign government that conflicts with Australian law' (Fifield and Morrison 2018). In 2017, the then prime minister Turnbull used the sentence 'The Australian people stand up' (Gribbin 2017) in reference to China's long-term revolution against foreign invasion after announcing the new espionage legislation, which sparked fierce protests from the Chinese government and Chinese diaspora in Australia as well as criticism from some of his fellow Australians like former prime minister Kevin Rudd, who claimed his speech to be irresponsible and an insult to Chinese people, Chinese Australians and Australians.

Some other resolutions have been made in less visible ways. For example, to prevent an increasing number of immigrants from countries with different cultural backgrounds, with Chinese as a major group, the immigration department introduced a permanent residency scheme for New Zealanders, which is widely believed to be an unnecessary move for New Zealanders but a strategy to minimise the number of immigrants from countries like China. According to some Chinese-language social media and feedback from student visa applicants from China, the waiting period for student visa approval, especially for research students, has extended from an average of one month to half a year, even nearly a year in specific cases.

Of course, not all Australians view China's engagement in Australia as interference. Former foreign minister Bob Carr does not. He is the director of the Australia-China Relations Institute, which was initially launched with a donation from a controversial Chinese businessman who lost his permanent residence status, a key figure under attack in the China interference accusation. Carr constantly expresses the idea that every country promotes its interests and there is no evidence of China seeking to interfere in Australian politics. He warns that Australia's future prosperity would need closer ties with China and recommends diplomatic solutions to issues in doubt like human rights issues instead of stirring the anti-China panic.

The angst about China's influence has invited pushback from some quarters of the Chinese community – recent migrants and students and some quarters of the larger Australian community and political establishment. The Chinese authorities have protested that claims of undue influence are groundless, irresponsibly biased, prejudiced against China and an attempt to whip up a 'China panic'. Turnbull's 'The Australian people stand up' comment prompted the Chinese Foreign Ministry to lodge an official complaint with the Australian government. Although statistics have not shown significant decreases in trade with China so far, which is the primary concern in Australia over the relationship with China, most agree that the diplomatic relations of the two countries have reached a new low since 1989. In 2018, groups of over one hundred Australian scholars of China and Chinese issued an open letter, which posits that 'the debate surrounding "Chinese influence" has created an atmosphere ill-suited to the judicious balancing of national security interests with the protection of civil liberties'. And they call for 'an accurate picture of the shifting global situation and Australia's position within it, and [to] engage as wide a range of viewpoints as possible, Chinese and non-Chinese alike' from journalists, scholars and politicians. It also strongly rejects 'any claim that the community of Australian experts on China has been intimidated or bought off by pro-PRC interests'. They have also assayed that no evidence has been seen that 'China is intent on exporting its political system to Australia, or that its actions aim at compromising our sovereignty' (Concerned Scholars of China 2018).

Soft or sharp power?

Although most analysis of China's engagement in Australia is mainly viewed through a soft power prism, there are some who deny the applicability of this prism for aspects of Chinese engagement. For example, Medcalf (2018) writes that what China is doing is not ordinary soft power but sharp power through money, censorship and coercion. He makes references to China's efforts to distort Australia's sovereignty, shutting up critics and the strategic grant allocation. Sharp power was introduced by US scholars Christopher Walker and Jessica Ludwig in late 2017 to refer to the influence from China and Russia through initiatives in media, culture, think tanks and academia which they believe focus on distraction and manipulation (Walker and Ludwig 2017). It posits that with heavy investments in many countries, through state-run/ sponsored media and other programmes like the Confucius Institute, what China is exercising is not soft power anymore but sharp power. The concept has been embraced quickly by some scholars including the father of the soft power concept, Nye.

But a closer look will find the necessity for further clarification of soft and sharp power. Nye (2011) adopts the definition of power as the ability to get preferred outcomes. His analysis of power and soft power is based on the emphasis on resources which he thinks is the basis for power behaviour. The outcome depends on behaviour in context. When defined as resources, power is preferred outcomes conversed from resources through conversion strategies and skills. When defined as behavioural outcomes, power goes through some subjects in certain areas, becoming preferred results by different means. Discussing power in this sense connects both the actor and subject in a relationship. He also identifies three aspects of this relational power: commanding change, controlling agendas and shaping preferences. Resources can be tangible, such as military capacity and economic quantity, and intangible, such as culture, policy and values. The outcomes can be achieved through both hard and soft behaviours. With the former, the methods can be a threat through forces or inducement through payment; for the latter, the methods can be an attraction through persuasion, agenda setting and framing as well as priming. The distinction between hard and soft power is in the approaches used through the behaviours and resources. The process from soft power resources (culture, political values and foreign policy) to behaviour outcomes goes through policy tools, conversion skills and target responses and finally leads to outcomes. Because of the variety of audiences and instruments, the indirectness of the path and the long period for actions to be effective, it is difficult for the government to wield soft power. Alternatively, he sees public diplomacy as a good channel to diffuse soft power (Nye 2011).

Public diplomacy is the process of engaging the public of country B by country A, in order to promote country A's frames, images, values and, ultimately, interests. Public diplomacy involves states, civil society, international organisations in which international broadcasting and diaspora populations are popular forces. Chitty (2017b) has further categorised the following as soft power multipliers: cultural industries, media and mobility. With the evolution of society, the main actor in public diplomacy has changed from government to civil society, which is defined as new public diplomacy (Melissen 2005).

Soft power can be active and passive. For the former, it involves intended influence, reflecting the strategic aspect of soft power. In this context, Nye (2011) emphasises three stages of public diplomacy: daily communication, strategic communication and long-term cultivation of lasting relationships through people-to-people programmes, such as scholarships, exchanges and training programmes, with crucial individuals. Nye, however, does not deny the role of government in the process but views it as a mix of direct government information and long-term cultural relationships by stating that 'each of these three stages of public diplomacy plays an important role in helping governments to create an attractive image of a country that can improve its prospects for obtaining its desired outcomes' (p. 106). He immediately follows with the advice that means will not work without the strength of the content conveyed. So, the quality of the soft power resources and the credibility in promoting them are important.

When we talk about softness of power, we refer to the benign characteristics of its approach. But when we use 'sharp' as an adjective to modify power, it may first lead people naturally to think about the literal meaning: 'Having an edge', or producing a sudden, piercing effect, that is, the efficiency of power. Both malign and benign power can be sharp or blunt. Analysing it from the cases used when referring to sharp power shows that there are also points that are negotiable. Walker and Ludwig (2017) deny the charm offensive thesis and attraction and persuasion thesis of China's and Russia's initiatives. But the cases mentioned can be covered by hard and soft power. It is clear that when one uses coercion or inducement, it is hard, not soft, power. When one uses attraction or projects attraction to persuade others, it is soft power. When the two are combined well, it is smart power. Most research on soft power and public diplomacy can reach the following consensus: soft power is a political concept with national interest as its ultimate purpose; public diplomacy is the dynamic of governmental and non-governmental engagement, and it is the subtle influence of Country A on B through long-term cultivation (Melissen 2005; Nye 2011). Although Nye identified three resources, in reality there are multiple carriers of these resources during the process. Hard power and soft power are convertible in some cases. For example, when the military, a typical hard power resource, is used for rescue missions at disasters or for peacekeeping, soft power is generated; a country engaging with the diaspora community, a typical public diplomacy effort, attracts financial investments, generating economic dividends, which is a typical hard power resource. In addition, strategic grant is a common practice. If one categorises other countries' programmes like Australia's New Colombo Plan and the US Fulbright programme into a benign group, it is questionable to single out certain countries' similar operations into a malignant group because they have invested more or have taken their own national interests into consideration. As reviewed previously, international broadcasting for information, discourse and ideology have long been investigated as a public diplomacy approach although the intended manipulation of propaganda is widely criticised and excluded from the field of public diplomacy. China is a follower in this regard, and there are more countries considering to step in. Angst over China's initiatives like international media and the Confucius Institute is out of the overwhelming negative effect they have. However, at current stage, it seems to be too early to arrive at this conclusion because there is little evidence showing their real reach. A country's continuing investment and from the authorities might be able to be understood as unsuccessful in achieving the expected effect. Soft power is used to achieve one's goals through attraction. If all these have not achieved the expected results and, on the contrary, have generated protests, it might be more appropriate, as Nye has criticised, to recognise that they are counterproductive (Nye 2013). Or blunt power might be a more apposite term, if a new one must be given, which refers to the use of harsh rhetoric that is meant to appeal to the speakers' political base – intentionally abrupt, direct and insensitive in character (Chitty 2019).

Some Chinese scholars and authorities regard the introduction of the term 'sharp power' as a deliberate rhetorical trick to prevent them from promoting their own discourse. They see the sharp power critique as being predicated by anxiety about the decline of Western domination (Shi 2018). Of course, this does not mean that operations by China and other accused countries are beyond criticism. As Shi has pointed out, the transparency problem and questions about the global competency of the people conducting the initiatives exist and need to be dealt with.

A power index released by the Australian foreign policy think tank Lowy Institute shows that the cultural influence of China is far behind the United States. The score covering cultural projection, information flows and people exchange is 49.5 out of 100 for China and 93.9 for the United States (Lowy Institute 2018). The evidence also includes the fact that the image of China in the eyes of the two communication ends are different and even contradictory in many instances. All these indicate that China's soft power projection strategy has a rationale despite all the cards not necessarily being rightly played.

So, in current context, the problem with China's soft power initiatives is not whether they are soft or sharp because there must be some soft power element in it. It is to figure out the characteristics of a Chinese way of soft power operations: What goals does China intend to achieve through initiatives like international broadcasting? How has China been conducting initiatives? What does it mean for the rest to engage with China? And how do different interest groups react to Chinese messages? What role do the initiatives play in China's soft power strategy? These are ideas that this book is trying to unveil through the case of international broadcasting.

References

AustralianBureauofStatistics. 2016. 2016 Census QuickStats. Canberra Australia.

Boyd-Barrett, Oliver. 1980. *The international news agencies*. CA: Sage.

Brophy, David. 2015. "David Brophy reviews 'Silent Invasion: China's Influence in Australia' by Clive Hamilton." March 24. https://www.australianbookreview.com.au/abr-online/archive/2018/218-april-2018-no-400/4663-david-brophy-reviews-silent-invasion-china-s-influence-in-australia-by-clive-hamilton.

Browne, Donald R. 1983. "The international newsroom: A study of practices at the Voice of America, BBC and Deutsche Welle." *Journal of Broadcasting & Electronic Media* 27 (3):205–231.

Castells, Manuel. 2004. "Informationalism, networks, and the network society: a theoretical blueprint." *The network society: A cross-cultural perspective*:3–45.

CCTV Overseas Centre. 2013. Evaluation of international communication. Beijing: CCTV Overseas Centre.

CGTN. 2017. "About CGTN." http://www.cgtn.com/home/info/about_us.do.

Chitty, Naren. 2009. "Frames for internationalizing media research." In *Internationalizing media studies*, edited by D Thussu, 61–74. London: Routledge.

Chitty, Naren. 2019. "The Rise of Blunt Power in the Strongman Era." *Georgetown Journal of International Affairs*.

Chitty, Naren, Dalbir Ahlawat, Mei Li, and D. Gopal. 2018. "The Chinese Belt and Road Initiative and the Indian Ocean Region: Sentiment towards Economic Prosperity and Security implications." *The Indian Journal of Politics* 52 (1–2):1–20.

Cohen, Yoel. 1986. *Media diplomacy: The foreign office in the mass communications age*. Oxon: Psychology Press.

d'Hooghe, Ingrid. 2008. "Into High Gear: China's Public Diplomacy." *The Hague Journal of Diplomacy* 3 (1):37–61.

d'Hooghe, Ingrid. 2014. *China's Public Diplomacy*. Leiden: Martinus Nijhoff Publishers.

Edwards, Lee. 2001. *Mediapolitik: How the mass media have transformed world politics*. Washinton DC: CUA Press.

Entman, Robert M. 2008. "Theorizing mediated public diplomacy: The US case." *The International Journal of Press/Politics* 13 (2):87–102.

Gagliardone, Iginio. 2013. "China as a persuader: CCTV Africa's first steps in the African mediasphere." *Ecquid Novi: African Journalism Studies* 34 (3):25–40.

Gagliardone, Iginio, Maria Repnikova, and Nicole Stremlau. 2010. "China in Africa: A new approach to media development." Based on a workshop report of Programme in Comparative Media Law and Policy, Oxford University and the Stanhope Centre for Communication Policy. Supported by the Economic and Social Research Council.) Oxford: Centre for Sociological Studies, University of Oxford.

Gagliardone, Iginio, Nicole Stremlau, and Daniel Nkrumah. 2012. "Partner, prototype or persuader?: China's renewed media engagement with Ghana." *Politics & Culture* 45 (2):174–196.

Gamson, William A, David Croteau, William Hoynes, and Theodore Sasson. 1992. "Media images and the social construction of reality." *Annual review of sociology* 18 (1):373–393.

Gilboa, E. 2002. "Global communication and foreign policy." *Journal of communication* 52 (4):731–748.

Gilboa, Eytan. 1998. "Media Diplomacy Conceptual Divergence and Applications." *The Harvard International Journal of Press/Politics* 3 (3):56–75.

Golan, Guy J. 2013. "The Case For Mediated Public Diplomacy." http://www.diplomaticourier.com/news/opinion/1527-the-case-for-mediated-public-diplomacy.

Gorfinkel, Lauren, Sandy Joffe, Cobus Van Staden, and Yu-Shan Wu. 2014. "CCTV's Global Outreach: Examining the Audiences of China's 'New Voice'on Africa." *Media International Australia* 151 (1):81–88.

Guan, Shijie & Wang, Liya, and Liya Wang. 2015. "China' s Cultural Soft Power in U.S.: An International Communication Perspective." In *China and the World: Theatres of Soft Power*, edited by Naren Chitty and Qing Luo, 9–29. Beijing: Communication University of China Press.

Hacker, Kenneth L, and Vanessa R Mendez. 2016. "Toward a model of strategic influence, international broadcasting, and global engagement." *Media and Communication* 4 (2):69–91.

Han, Z. 2011. "China's public diplomacy in a new era." In *The People's Republic of China today: Internal and external challenges*, edited by Zhiqun Zhu, 291–310. Singapore: World Scientific.

Hartig, Falk. 2012. "Cultural diplomacy with Chinese characteristics: The case of Confucius Institutes in Australia." *Chinese journal of communication* 5 (4):477–480.

Hassid, Jonathan. 2011. "Four models of the fourth estate: A typology of contemporary Chinese journalists." *The China Quarterly* 208:813–832.

Herman, Edward S., and N Chormsky. 1988. *Manufacturing consent: the political economy of the mass media*.

Hu, Jintao. 2008. Speech at the second plenary session of the 17th central committee of CPC.

Hu, Zhengrong, and Deqiang Ji. 2012. "Ambiguities in communicating with the world: the "Going-out" policy of China's media and its multilayered contexts." *Chinese journal of communication* 5 (1):32–37.

Jiang, Fei, and R. Yan. 2015. "China High-speed Rail: A "New Business Card" in the Age of Public Diplomacy." In *Blue Book of Public Diplomacy: Annual Report of China's Public Diplomacy Development 2015*, edited by Qizheng Zhao and Weizhen Lei, 213–236. Beijing: Social Sciences Academic Press.

Jirik, John. 2004. "China's News Media and the Case of CCTV-9'." *International News in the 21st Century*:127–146.

Jirik, John. 2013. "The world according to (Thomson) Reuters." *Sur le journalisme About journalism Sobre jornalismo* 2 (1):pp. 24–41.

Jirik, John. 2015. "The CCTV-Reuters relationship." *Media at work in China and India: Discovering and dissecting*:201–227.

Jirik, John 2016. "CCTV News and Soft Power." *International journal of communication* (10):3536–3553.

Jirik, John Charles. 2008. "Making news in the People's Republic of China: the case of CCTV-9." PhD, The University of Texas at Austin.

Kurlantzick, Joshua. 2007. *Charm offensive: how China's soft power is transforming the world*. New Haven: Yale University Press.

Lee, Chin-Chuan. 2005. "The conception of Chinese journalists." *Making journalists: Diverse models, global issues*:107.

Lee, Chin-Chuan, Zhou He, and Yu Huang. 2006. "'Chinese Party Publicity Inc.' conglomerated: the case of the Shenzhen press group." *Media, Culture & Society* 28 (4):581–602.

Li, Mei, and Naren Chitty. 2017. "Paradox of professionalism: The professional identity of journalists who work across media cultures." *Journalism* (November 2017):1–19. doi: 10.1177/1464884917743175.

Li, Mei, and Naren Chitty. 2018. "An overview on China's public diplomacy in Australia." In *Public diplomacy studies*, edited by Debin Liu. Beijing: Social Science Academic Press (China).

Li, Xiaoping. 1991. "The Chinese television system and television news." *The China Quarterly* 126:340–355.

Li, Xiguang, and Kang Liu. 1996. *Behind the scene of demonizing China (Yaomohua Zhongguo de Beihou(*. Beijing: Chinese Academy of Social Science Press. Liu, Fucheng. 2007. *China media system innovation*. Guang Zhou: Southern Daily Press.

Livingston, Steven. 1997. Clarifying the CNN effect: An examination of media effects according to type of military intervention. Joan Shorenstein Center on the Press, Politics and Public Policy, John F. Kennedy School of Government, Harvard University.

Lowy Institute. 2018. Asia Power Index. Sydney: Lowy Institute.

Lu, Ye, and Zhongdang Pan. 2002. "Imagining Professional Fame: Constructing Journalistic Professionalism in Social Transformation (Chengming de Xiangxiang: Shehui Zhuanxing Guozhengzhong Xinwen Congyezhe de Zhuanyezhuyi Huayu Jiangou)." *Journalism Studies (Xinwenxue Yanjiu)* 4:17–59.

MacBride, Sean. 1980. *Many voices, one world: Towards a new, more just, and more efficient world information and communication order*. Lanham: Rowman & Littlefield.

Marsh, Vivien. 2016. "Mixed messages, partial pictures? Discourses under construction in CCTV's Africa Live compared with the BBC." *Chinese Journal of Communication* 9 (1):56–70.

Medcalf, Rory. 2018. "Silent invasion: the question of race." *The Interpreter*, March 24. https://www.lowyinstitute.org/the-interpreter/silent-invasion-question-race.

Melissen, Jan. 2005. "The new public diplomacy: Soft Power in International relations." In *The new public diplomacy: Soft Power in International relations*, edited by Jan Melissen. New York: Palgrave Macmillan.

Meng, Jian. 2012. "Talk at the Symposium of National Image Construcction and Transcultural Communication." National Planning Office of Philosophy and Social Science. http://www.npopss-cn.gov.cn/GB/219506/219507/17591993.html.

Mowlana, Hamid. 1985. International flow of information: A global report and analysis. N.Y.: UNESCO.

Mowlana, Hamid. 1997. *Global information and world communication: New frontiers in international relations*. Thousand Oaks: Sage.

Munro, Kelsey. 2017. The Dragon and the Kangaroo: 45 years of Austrlia China relations. SBS.

Ning, Jing. 2013. "CCTV-9's coverage of the Iraq War and the evolution of English language television news in China." Rutgers University-Graduate School-New Brunswick.

Nye, Joseph S. 2011. *The future of power*. New York: PublicAffairs.

Nye, Joseph S. 2013. "What China and Russia don't get about soft power." *Foreign Policy* 29 (10).

Onuf, Nicholas. 1997. "Hegemony's Hegemony in IPE." *Constituting International Political Economy, London*:91–110.

Onuf, Nicholas. 2004. "Humanitarian intervention: the early years." *Fla. J. Int'l L.* 16:753.

Onuf, Nicholas. 2014. "Rule and Rules in International Relations." *Lecture at the Cluster of Excellence: The Formation of Normative Orders, Goethe University Frankfurt/Main* 5.

Örnebring, Henrik. 2010. "Reassessing journalism as a profession." In *The Routledge Companion to News and Journalism*, edited by Stuart Allan. London: Routledge.

Pan, Zhongdang, and Ye Lu. 2003. "Localizing professionalism: Discursive practices in China's media reforms." *Chinese media, global contexts*:215–236.

Paterson, Chris. 2011. *The International Television News Agencies*. New York: Peter Lang.

Powers, Shawn, and Eytan Gilboa. 2007. "The public diplomacy of Al Jazeera." In *New media and the new Middle East*, edited by Philip Seib, 53–80. Berlin: Springer.

Pratkanis, Anthony R, and Elliot Aronson. 1991. *Age of propaganda*. New York: W.H Freeman.

Qian, Gang, and David Bandurski. 2011. "China's emerging public sphere: The impact of media commercialization, professionalism, and the Internet in an era of transition." *Changing media, changing China*:38–76.

Rawnsley, Gary. 2012. "Approaches to soft power and public diplomacy in China and Taiwan." *Journal of International Communication* 18 (2):121–135.

Rawnsley, Gary. 2016. "Introduction to "International Broadcasting and Public Diplomacy in the 21st Century"." *Media and Communication* 4 (2):42–45.

Rawnsley, Gary D. 1996. *Radio diplomacy and propaganda: the BBC and VOA in international politics, 1956–64*: Macmillan Press.

Rogers, Everett M. 1962. *Diffusion of innovations*. New York: Free Press of Glencoe.

Said, Edward W. 2008. *Covering Islam: How the media and the experts determine how we see the rest of the world (Fully revised edition)*: Random House.

Schneider, M. 2015. "US public diplomacy since 9/11: The challenges of integration." *International public relations and public diplomacy*:15–36.

Seib, Philip. 2008. *The Al Jazeera effect: How the new global media are reshaping world politics*: Potomac Books, Inc.

Seib, Philip. 2010. "Transnational journalism, public diplomacy, and virtual states." *Journalism Studies* 11 (5):734–744.

Seib, Philip M. 1997. *Headline diplomacy: How news coverage affects foreign policy*: Greenwood Publishing Group.

Shao, Baohui, and Qingwen Dong. 2016. "An Exploratory Study on Journalistic Professionalism and Journalism Education in Contemporary China." *Journalism and Mass Communication* 6 (4):187–200.

Shi, Anbin. 2013. "Strategies and objectives to attract new audiences abroad." Forum Media Entwicklung, Promoting Alternative Views in a Multipolar World: BRICS and their Role in Developing Media Markets, Berlin, 10 October, 2013.

Shi, Anbin. 2018. "Dissect the concept of Sharp Power." *Opipinion*, 28 March. http:// opinion.people.com.cn/n1/2018/0326/c1003-29887627.html.

Shi, Anbin, and Yaozhong Zhang. 2016. "Building new global communication order: interpreting the historical trace and reality consideration of Chinese solution (Gouian quanqiu chuanbo xinzhixu: jiexi 'zhongguofang'an' de lishi suyuan he xianshi kaoliang)." *Journalism Lover* (5).

Simons, Margaret, David Nolan, and Scott Wright. 2016. "'We are not North Korea': propaganda and professionalism in the People's Republic of China." *Media, Culture & Society*:0163443716643154.

Snow, Nancy. 2011. "Information War 2011." *CPD Blog*, 24 November. http:// uscpublicdiplomacy.org/blog/information-war-2011.

Sparks, Colin. 2012. "Beyond political communication: towards a broader perspective on the Chinese press." *Chinese Journal of Communication* 5 (1):61–67.

Straubhaar, Joseph D. 1991. "Beyond media imperialism: Asymmetrical interdependence and cultural proximity." *Critical Studies in media communication* 8 (1):39–59.

Sun, Wanning. 2009. "Mission impossible? Soft power, communication capacity, and the globalization of Chinese media." *International Journal of Communication* 4:19.

Sun, Wanning. 2015. "Slow boat from China: public discourses behind the 'going global'media policy." *International Journal of Cultural Policy* 21 (4):400–418.

Thussu, Daya. 2013. *Communicating India's soft power: Buddha to Bollywood*. New York: Palgrave Macmillan.

Thussu, Daya Kishan. 2010. *International communication: A reader*. London: Routledge

Tong, Jingrong. 2011. *Investigative journalism in China: Journalism, power, and society*. New York: Continuum.

Walker, Christopher, and Jessica Ludwig. 2017. "The Meaning of Sharp Power: How Authoritarian States Project Influence." *Foreign Affairs* 16.

Wang, Chen. 2010. Speech at 2010 National External Publicity Congress. Xinhuanet.

Wang, Hongying. 2011. "China's image projection and its impact." In *Soft power in China: Public diplomacy through communication*, edited by Jian Wang, 37–56. Hampshire: Palgrave Macmillan.

Wang, Jian. 2011b. *Soft power in China: Public diplomacy through communication*. Hampshire: Palgrave Macmillan.

Wang, Longqing. 2011c. "Journalists, media diplomacy and media- broker diplomacy in relations between mainland China and Taiwan from 1987–2009 [electronic resource]." Australia: Macquarie University.

Wang, Y. 2008. "Public Diplomacy and the Rise of Chinese Soft Power." *The Annals of the American Academy of Political and Social Science* 616 (1):257–273. doi: 10.1177/ 0002716207312757.

Wasserman, Herman. 2016. "China's "soft power" and its influence on editorial agendas in South Africa." *Chinese Journal of Communication* 9 (1):8–20.

Williams, Raymond. 1977. *Marxism and literature.* Vol. 1: Oxford Paperbacks.

WMSDOHA. 2016. "About World Media Summit." accessed 2 January. http://www.wmsdoha2016.com/about.

Wu, Weihong, and Zheng Huang. 2015. Brief analysis on the self-producing capacity of CCTV – NEWS: the comparison of News program of CCTV NEWS, BBC and CNN. In *international Communication.*

Xi, Jinping. 2013. Adress at national conference on publicity ieology work. People's Daily.

Xi, Jinping. 2014. Xi Jinping Delivers Important Speech in Germany, Stressing China Will Unswervingly Adhere to the Path of Peaceful Development.

Xiang, Debao. 2013. "China's image on international English language social media." *Journal of international communication* 19 (2):252–271. doi: 10.1080/13216597.2013.833535.

Zhang, Xiaoling. 2011. "China's international broadcasting: A case study of CCTV international." In *Soft Power in China: soft power through communication,* edited by Berlin, 57–71. Hampshire:Palgrave Macmillan.

Zhang, Xiaoling. 2013. "How ready is China for a China-style world order? China's state media discourse under construction." *Ecquid Novi: African Journalism Studies* 34 (3):79–101.

Zhang,Yanqiu, Matingwina Simon. 2016. "Constructive Journalism: A New Journalistic Paradigm of Chinese Media in Africa." In *China's Media and Soft Power in Africa. Palgrave Series in Asia and Pacific Studies.* Edited by Zhang Xiaoling., Herman Wasserman, Winston Mano. New York: Palgrave Macmillan.

Zhao, Qizheng. 2012. How China Communicates: Public Diplomacy in a Global Age. Beijing: Foreign Language Press.

Zhao, Yuezhi. 1998. *Media, market, and democracy in China: Between the party line and the bottom line.* Vol. 114. Illinois University of Illinois Press.

Zhu, Ying. 2012. *Two billion eyes: the story of China Central Television* New York: New Press.

Chapter 3

INTERNATIONAL RELATIONS, INFORMATION FLOW AND SOFT POWER

Constructing a Rising China

Chapter 1 briefed the scenario of understanding China's rise from different perspectives of international relations theories; in those realist perspectives – the economic rise of China coupled with its growing military budget – the assertive stance towards territory disputes is always interpreted as a potential threat to the existing world order which would highly likely lead to a Thucydides trap (Allison 2017). With liberal theories, China's engagement with international organisations was seen as a move towards the integration into the world system and the democratisation of China's political system. However, the centralisation of domestic power in recent years in China has caused growing anxiety about the prospect of this expectation.

Both realist and liberal theories posit an anarchic international system and take material aspects such as economy, military, behaviour and interests as the core factors of analysis. But they cannot adequately interpret the issues around a rising China. The interference frame of China falls into the extreme simplification of international relations. First of all, it focuses too much on the material capacities which assume that rising economic and military status leads to conflict over resources. Human history demonstrates that population explosion does not exhaust resources but stimulates the development of technology which expands world wealth at an unprecedented rate. In addition, the world power structure is more complicated than mere material capacities as realists emphasise; soft power is an obvious example, which is not strictly defined but widely adopted as part of power discussions. Second, the simplification reflects the one-dimensional vision, which has neglected the complication of cultural difference with what is characterised as Eurocentricity by intellectuals. Reality shows that many policymakers in the West are puzzled by the fact that there is an increasing trend of patriotism among Chinese returnees, instead of the push of democratisation in the Western sense. There are more profound social, political and cultural factors that deserve investigation. Wendt (1995) has criticised the liberalists for neglecting the role of individuals and the relationship, social construction of knowledge and different understanding between different cultural groups. Third, the liberalists expect the integration of all states into the liberal institution. But the existing problems perplexing the world reveal that many issues stem from the integration process because of different world views from different cultural perspectives and the incapability of people to deal with such dissonance. And from the detailed view such as that which Harari (2014) presents in his review of the history of humankind, liberal institutions are part of the evolution of human society; even those who thought that liberalism would be the end of history began to reflect on its problems which it cannot solve. It is also powerless to win a universal consensus, let alone the fact that the superpower United States has withdrawn from promoting universal values to stress America first. At this crossroads, academia demands a more open-minded framework to examine what is happening. Constructivism provides a useful complementarity to the above-mentioned perspectives in this regard.

Constructivist international relations and the construct of world politics

Constructivist international relations view the situation in which the state, like the individual, exists in *a world of our making* (Onuf 1989). From a broad social theoretical point of view, Onuf (2013, 2016) assumes that deeds done, acts taken and words spoken are all facts; people and societies construct each other. He emphasises the role of language (both representational and performative) and rules in reality construction and professionalisation in dealing with interactions among states. In his eyes, rather than in an anarchic status, states are regulated by rules with hegemony, hierarchy and heteronomy serving as functional grounds for world politics (Onuf 2014). Wendt (1992), holding a similar conceptualisation of constructivism, in an attempt to go beyond the traditional realist thesis and liberal theories, proposes that the interactions of international actors are shaped and influenced by identities and ever-changing normative institutional structures. According to constructivists, the fundamental structures of world politics are social instead of strictly material; material objects have different meanings in different situations and international relations are not merely impacted by power politics but also by ideas. They emphasise identity, social norms and culture in the social construction of meaning in understanding social facts in international relations (Finnemore 1996). In this sense, in international relations, allies and enemies are shaped by certain ideational and cultural contexts, and changes in the mature of social interaction among states can lead to significant shift towards international relations (Baylis et al. 2013; Jefferson et al. 1996).

Following the constructivist tradition, Chitty (2017b) characterises the contemporary world order as 'a condition of rule' or 'no anarchy' (Onuf 2014), a global civil society (Kaldor 2003; Onuf 2004) together with its moral economy (Calabrese 2005) as a weak global republican confederacy (GRC), 'evolving institutions of world governance, actors and cultures that include both rule-making and ruling elites as well as the ruled and recusants' (Chitty 2017b, 11). The governing institutions such as states, organisations under the United Nations and economic institutions such as those of the Bretton Woods system are diplomatic forums where the legal actors of the GRC interact to shape and reshape of the confederacy. Following the principle of republicanism which promotes the common good of the whole over the good of individuals, the GRC provides a framework for world order. The global polity 'is based on internationally accepted rules and states and non-state actors adhering to the consensual rule-making and rule framework as well as outlaws ad recusants and polities that have not been accredited by the system' (Chitty 2017b, 11). The goals of the GRC align with enhancing human security and consist of both multilateral institutions and bilateral relations within the members of nation states and civil society organisations. Among the GRC, 'there are systemic processes for incorporation, proscription, containment or destruction of out-groups' (p. 12). The proposal provides a framework or umbrella to talk about world politics in a way beyond anarchy and disentropy.

The working dynamics within the GRC

In speaking of the dynamics of control, Onuf (2014) has identified three types of *rules* that consist of the governance of international relations – hegemony, hierarchy and heteronomy – which associate with directive-rules, instruction-rules and commitment-rules. In his understanding, rules are tools for social control, and rule is a system for the distribution of privilege. In Onuf's view, exercise of social power means domination. Hierarchy, hegemony and heteronomy are all connected with dominance and might induce desires for autonomy. Onuf uses these terms to address the whole picture of the rule of politics and world politics. In a broader sense, within the GRC, the states as actors can also be seen as individuals with the desire to gain autonomy, which characterises one aspect of world politics. Examining from the individual perspective, Chitty conceived that the great puzzle for man in a society is to maintain autonomy while accepting a measure of favourable heteronomy – pointing to the psychological response of serenity in the concept of homonomy discussed by Angyal (1969), in relation to belonging to a system

(Chitty and Dias 2018). 'Every concept reveals itself to be a metaphor' (Onuf 2016, 1). An assumption is made here that individual mindset could form a force of group consciousness within similar contexts. Homonomy is used here in a broader sense in a context of global governance.

Power, another core concept in world politics, may offer a tool with which to portray world order. In Onuf's words, power is the mode of social control (Onuf 2014). Power is classically defined as the ability to get others to do what they otherwise would not do (Dahl 1957). Nye (1990, 2004, 2011) further categorises power into hard power and soft power and concludes that soft power is the more favourable strategy in a time where interdependence is the mainstream trend of world politics. He goes further by distinguishing the active and passive approaches of soft power. The former refers to the method with intended efforts to make things attractive while the latter refers to the attraction embedded in an actor's values (Chitty 2017b; Nye 2011). With the strong scale of world power, some scholars prefer influence to power in speaking of relations. Taking Lasswell's view (Lasswell 1950) treats power as a special form of influence; he quarters power/influence in international relations thus: (1) intended influence/active hard power; (2) unintended influence/passive hard power; (3) intended influence/active soft power; and (4) unintended influence/passive soft power. Within these distinctions of influence/power group, Chitty reconfigured influence/power, hegemony, heteronomy, homonomy and autonomy according to influence/power dynamics. Hegemony is the form of power through which dominant groups are integrated in laws, rules, norms, habits and even general consensus (Gramsci 1971). In the long history of world politics, the hegemonic position of certain countries or values always exists despite the ups and downs of specific countries. In Chitty's conception, hegemonic status can generate a condition of heteronomy on others. This can be further received in three ways: with unhappy acceptance of heteronomy, with happy acceptance through homonomy likely because of an acceptable balance of heteronomy and autonomy, or with rejection of heteronomy. The latter will result in autonomy if the rejection can be sustained. If we expand the process further, a personal response of homonomy may further strengthen the status of hegemony as an acceptable hegemony. Ironically, this may be regarded as a soft power effect. Putting the scenario into the dynamics of global governance, hegemonic status can generate the effect of heteronomy to others. There could be in affected countries an unhappy acceptance of the condition of heteronomy, or a happy acceptance in affected countries because of the hegemonic state's soft power – through individual psychological responses to homonomy – or a rejection of hegemony which, if successful, would lead to autonomy for the affected countries or a drive to achieve autonomy. In today's networked society, pure forms of autonomy are almost impossible, as recognised by Onuf (2014). Individuals (in the sense of both the states and non-governmental organisations [NGOs]) operate in networks. From this point of view, it is possible for a national or cumulative, rather than an individual, psychological response of homonomy.

The assumption of the GRC can be understood from two aspects. First, it places world politics under a united lens of global governance. As Harari has pointed out, human society is now living under a globalised ecological economic and scientific system. But the political system is still under the national level. We need a globalised identity (Harari 2018). There is a need for a bird's-eye view to integrate the differences in the chaos of nationalist uprising. Second, it gives the public its due position. These two aspects take the analysis away from the realist anarchy and the constant conflict over the limited resources. From this aspect, there needs to be a consideration of how to facilitate globe homonomy. This highlights the importance of the flow and interpretation of information. Such a global condition of homonomy equates with harmonious coexistence in a community similar to the Confucian ideal of *He* (harmony), which was originally used to portray the situation where various rhythmic sounds responded to one another 'in a mutually promoting, mutually complementing, and mutually stabilizing way' and then was expanded to a more broader sense in ancient Chinese literature. '[Philosophically], harmony presupposes the existence of different things and implies a certain favourable relationship among them' (Li 2006, 584). In *Analects*, Confucius adopts *He* as a criterion for the good person (*Junzi*) in his famous saying 'The *Junzi* harmonises but does not seek sameness, whereas the petty person seeks sameness but does not harmonise' (*Junzi he er butong, xiaoren tong er buhe*) (*Analects 13.23*). He posits *Li* (rites) as the device to achieve harmony. Mencius, another key figure in Confucian philosophy, also emphasises *He* by listing it as one of the most important things in human affairs: '[Good] timing is not as good as being advantageously situated, and being advantageously situated is not as good as having harmonious people' (*Tianshi buru dili, dili buru renhe*) (Mencius 3B.1, cited in Li 2006, p. 585). Harmony in Confucianism can occur within the individual level, at the level of a family with a harmonious relationship among individuals and at the level of the community, the nation, the world and the universe. In the context of world politics, *He* finds its place at the third level. The author will argue here that with the emphasis on the well-being of the governed in the republics proposed by Western philosophers, GRC bears similarity in the sense of the ultimate aim of the whole community of the world.

Noopolitik, information flow and soft power

With the innovation of technology, the proliferation of new organisations and power, noosphere has gained increasing importance in world politics. The term 'noosphere' was coined by French theologian and scientist Pierre Teilhard de Chardin (1965), referring to the realm of the mind. It refers to an information processing and information structuring system beyond the geosphere and bio-sphere (Arquilla and Ronfeldt 1999). It calls for the 'analyst and strategist to think in terms of the roles of ideas, values and norms' (p. 20). Within the noo-sphere, 'the world is moving to a new system in which "power" is understood mainly in terms of knowledge and the information strategy should focus on the "balance of knowledge", distinct from the "balance of power"' (Arquilla and Ronfeldt 1999, 44).

A concept associated with the noosphere is noopolitik – politics based on ethics and ideas and information strategy, 'an approach to statecraft, to be undertaken as much by non-state as by state actors, that emphasises the role of soft power in expressing ideas, values, norms, and ethics through all manner of media' (p. 29). It emphasises the importance of cooperative advantages in addition to traditional comparative advantages and competitive advantages. Under the framework of noopolitik, traditional strategies are fused with new implications: in the economic realm, it means the ability to shape legal structures and norms; military strategy should focus more on the shaping of partners with mutual security arrangements; in the political realm, the partici-pation of non-state actors is valued. To build a cooperative global noosphere, Arquilla and Ronfeldt have identified that both the bottom-up grass-roots effort to foster cooperation and top-down model to establish strategy are important.

As a security strategy for the United States, Arquilla and Ronfeldt put the US values, norms and ideas as models to be shared by the world. But in reality, the concept may have less attraction to the United States than to China because, as the authors have mentioned, the United States already has much capital in areas such as political values and norms, which echoes those in soft power (Nye 1990; 2004; 2011). In a global sphere, the openness required by the noosphere means openness to others' values, ideas and norms, and this, to a certain extent, decreases US dominance. On the contrary, China, with its rising status in the world economy, is eager to seek recognition of its ideas, values and norms; increase its discourse power; and find legitimacy of its values that may be significant to the Western world. If looked at carefully, the concepts proposed by Xi Jinping, such as 'Community of Common des-tiny of Mankind' in 2013, and 'Shared Future in Cyberspace' (Xi 2016), are evidence of the effort to propose ideas and norms to the global noosphere.

Based on these ideas – BRI and the founding of the Asian Infrastructure Investment Bank (AIIB), the World Media Summit (WMS) and World Internet Conference Wuzhen Summit (WICWS), together with the international media expansion – China can be analysed in the prism of information processing and structuring approaches (Shi and Zhang 2016). We can see from the aforementioned initiatives that China is actively trying to diffuse its own stance and values to the information flow which will determine the construct of what is going on.

In noopolitik, information is an important resource. In practice, how information interplays within world politics is another important question. In as early as the 1980s, Mowlana (1985) started to view international information flow as an analytical framework in international relations studies. He argued that our power in 'national and international system involves more than just the reallocation of economic, political, and technological values and bases. It involves multidimensional factors with authority, legitimacy, and will play crucial roles' (p. 5). Mowlana emphasises that 'control of the distribution process is the most important index of the way in which power is distributed in a communication system' (Mowlana 1997, 30). Thus, he has proposed a two-stage international flow of information model which helps understand the dynamic process of international communication. The process consists of the production stage where messages flow from the source or communicator to the production of the message and the distribution stage, which consists of message distribution and the destination or recipient. At each stage, there are intra- and extra-media variables like ownership, economic resources and technology and so on.

Through the information flow, different actors (governmental, transnational and individual) send and receive messages with different effects (change in nature of power, change in nature of resources, change in values and perceptions of individuals and change in national and international systems), which in turn have an impact on individuals, institutions, inter-group, ethnic and minority groups, nation states and the globe. In the end, there will be consequences in issues and policies.

From the perspective of global public opinion, this process can be called, in Chitty's terms (Chitty 1994), 'communicating world order', in which information travels through the dynamics within states and interstates and influences the trajectory of discourse formation. Since the Cold War, information flow has been dominated by Western countries, especially the United States. At the time of the global media boom, Thussu (2010) noticed the contra-flow of information represented in media industries by Bollywood, Al Jazeera and CCTV NEWS towards a new cartography of global communication.

Although Mowlana did not use the terms 'soft power' and 'public diplomacy' in his book *Global Information and World Communication*, which was first published in the 1980s, he differentiated between tangible resources and intangible resources in the power dynamics of international communication. The former consists of factors such as economics, technology, politics, cultural and educational products and military. The latter constists of belief and value systems, ideologies, knowledge and religion. This anticipates some of the distinctions between hard and soft power resources, particularly the second category where all the items listed above could be soft power resources. The first includes some soft power resources (cultural and educational products) too. Also, the international communication he refers to here is more than communication through media but has the broader sense of public diplomacy.

Chitty (2017b), from a cooperative perspective of soft power, proposes a global governance based on an attractiveness generated through civic virtue, aligned with the humanistic republican values of GRC. He posits civic virtue providing '[t]he impulse to influence on behalf of the nation, whether in relation to civil or cultural diplomacy, high politics-related public or traditional diplomacy'. Civic virtue prompts the organisations, citizens and media of one country to engage in soft-power-enhancement activities that demonstrate virtue or virtuosity (Chitty 2017a,b). This offers a new framework for the networked world and the flow of information.

'Information creates power' (Nye 2011, 103). Soft power is the use of attraction in culture, political values and foreign policy instead of military or economic approaches to influence others to do what one state intends to achieve (Nye 1990). International broadcasting, as indicated in the history of its development, is an indispensable channel to diffuse one's information as a carrier of culture, values and policy orientations. As reviewed in the previous chapter, the power transition in history demonstrated that having an information edge is an important factor in shaping knowledge, normalising one's discourse. Nye and Owen (1996) posit that the American information edge accumulated from investments in information-processing technologies – space-based surveillance, direct broadcasting, and high-speed computers during the Cold War – is a multiplier of its diplomacy and soft power. Freedman and Thussu (2012, cited in Thussu 2013) also observe that with the former state-strategic approach, together with the later civil approach where through its private media organisations' expansion around the world, the United States establishes its dominance in infrastructure (such as networks, cyberspace and the spectrum) and content. These, together with its political, economic, technological and military superiority, allowed the United States to successfully acquire the ability to make its vision and version of global events into a global agenda. This kind of ability is Nye's sense of soft power. Other scholars come to similar conclusions that the change of world order is closely connected with the reconfiguration of the global communication order. One of the most important signs of the establishment of Pax Americana is the abolishment of the news agency treaty among Britain, Germany and France in 1934 in order to ensure the free flow of news and thus prepare the ground for US discourse dominance (Louw 2010; Shi 2016). The attractiveness of a country's institutions involves the transmission of information and meaning and, ultimately, the creation of consensus on that country's information, behaviour and values among other countries. So Chitty (2017b) concludes that media (along with mobility and cultural industries) is a key multiplier of soft power. Imbalance of information contributes to the weakness of those with deficits in setting agendas and framing and denies such countries an important soft power multiplier (Chitty 2017a; Nye 2011).

Soft power is often discussed in the context of communication. Nye (2011) elaborates on three facets of power behaviour with both hard and soft approaches: to induce others to do what they otherwise would not do; to change others' framing and agenda; and to shape subject's preference. The hard-power approach to all three dimensions involves the use of force or induce-ment while the soft power approach is through attraction and/or institutions. During the process, Nye emphasises the importance of interpretation and persuasion to ensure the success of policy. In the age when power is diffusing from state actors to non-state actors, Nye sees the importance of public dip-lomacy – the indirect form of diplomacy aims to influence other countries by way of communicating with the publics of the countries – 'as a means of promoting a country's soft power' (p. 94). He segments public diplomacy into three stages in the generation of soft power: everyday communication – the explanation of domestic and foreign policy decisions; strategic communica-tion – public relations campaigns that reinforce certain themes or advance certain policies; development of lasting relations with exchange programmes targeting key individuals. Among the three stages, he emphasises the mass media approach, which plays an important role because of its audience reach and its capacity to draw public attention and set the agenda. Thussu (2013) examines the history of US soft power and its becoming dominant in the wake of World War II, and discloses the importance of story framing by way of state media in telling 'America's story to the world' (Thussu 2014, 7). The usage of mass media can 'correct daily misrepresentations of their policies as well as try to convey a longer-term strategic message' (p. 107). Viewing soft power as a communication-based activity, Zaharna (2004, 2009, 2010) proposed a theory of soft power differentials based on the two aspects of communication appre-hension: linear process and relational process. Under the linear process, states use the strategic communication approach and a mass communication model to exercise the power of persuasion or control. In this model, messages are designed by states and delivered through mass media. Within the relational process, messages are exchanged through networks and through relationship building which Zaharna characterises as public diplomacy.

Public diplomacy is normally regarded as the extension of traditional diplomacy. The modern sense of public diplomacy can be traced back to Edmund Gullion, a former US diplomat who founded the Edward R. Murrow Centre of Public Diplomacy at Tufts University. His concept of public diplomacy was summarised in an early brochure of the centre as

> [D]eals with the influence of public attitudes on the formation and exe-cution of foreign policies. It encompasses dimensions of international relations beyond traditional diplomacy; the cultivation by governments of public opinion in other countries; the interaction of private groups and interests in one country with another; the reporting of foreign affairs and its impact on policy; communication between those whose job is communication, as diplomats and foreign correspondents; and the process of intercultural communications. Central to public diplomacy is the transnational flow of information and ideas. (Cull 2009, 19)

Gullion's definition located the transnational flow of information and ideas at the centre of international affairs. And the Edward R. Murrow Centre of Public Diplomacy[1] itself built upon Murrow's legacy as an outstanding journalist who witnessed the decisive role played by radio in winning people's minds during World War II (Seib 2010).

International broadcasting as an effective way in public diplomacy has been addressed by many scholars. But as widely criticised in the concept itself, vagueness exists in the elaboration of the relationship between soft power and public diplomacy, and further that of soft power and international media. Many scholars take for granted Nye's assumptions to analyse international media practice under the framework of soft power (Sun 2009; Wang 2011; Wasserman 2016). A few scholars like Chitty (2017b) posit that electronic networked media is one of the channels and multipliers of active soft power in the literature on soft power. However, no specific research has addressed how the interaction occurs, and what the mechanism might be is still an unanswered question. Framing theory provides analytic tools in this regard. The following sections will discuss it further.

---

1 Recognising shifts in relative importance of technologies, the centre is now called The Murrow Centre for the Digital World and addresses cyber, media and public diplomacy.

Framing: Organisation of experience

Frames are the 'schemata of interpretation' (Goffman 1974, 21), the way individuals classify, organise, and interpret life experience to make sense of them; the 'persistent patterns of cognition, interpretation, and presentation, of selection, emphasis, and exclusion' (p. 7); the 'central organizing idea or story line that provides meaning to an unfolding strip of events' (p. 143). Frames serve as 'central part of a culture and are institutionalised in various ways' (p. 63). In brief, a frame should be treated as a meta-communicative message (Van Gorp 2005). It offers a perspective for researchers to understand the way people organise and interpret information.

Goffman (1974) observes that in order to process new information effectively, individuals employ a 'schemata of interpretation' or 'primary frameworks' to 'locate, perceive, identify, and label' occurrences (pp. 21–24). In the course of understanding reality, instead of asking what reality is, framing theorists ask the following question: Under what circumstances do we think things are real? In their eyes, the important thing about reality is our sense of its realness. A further question would then be: Under what conditions is such a feeling generated? To answer this question, the focus should be on the devices that make the 'reality' rather than the results of the making. As Goffman puts it, one looks at 'the camera and not what it is the camera takes pictures of' (1974, 2). 'To frame is to select some aspects of perceived reality and make them more salient in a communicating text, in such a way as to promote a particular problem definition, causal interpretation, moral evaluation and/or treatment recommendation for the item described' (Entman 1993, 52). Framing is thus a process of giving meaning and interpretation. Framing involves selection and salience. It could contain substantial connotations because frames highlight and include some elements while excluding others (Borah 2011) and thus is the core of public opinion formation (Chong 1993).

Framing consists of 'collective efforts' (Goffman 1974, 21). The participants in the framing process are the meaning initiator, the message receiver and the interaction between them in the meaning negotiation. In addition, social reality can be viewed and interpreted from diverse perspectives (Chong and Druckman 2007). The frame is moderated by the characteristics of individuals and a social group or the group's interpretive schemas and other attributes in the social environment (Ardèvol-Abreu 2015). Because of their nature as information schema, frames can trigger knowledge and activate 'stocks of cultural morals and values, and create contexts' (Cappella and Jamieson 1997, 47). As Chong and Druckman (2007) have argued, frames are not all equal in strength. It depends on frequency (the number of times the frame is repeated), accessibility (the audience's familiarity with the frame) and relevance (the importance of the frame to the issue or audience). This explains the frame differentiation among different groups on the same issue.

In recent years, scholars in framing studies have turned to a constructive dimension which emphasises the cultural context of frame making, communicating, receiving and interpreting. Frames detail the relationship between various intertwined elements which determine how an issue or a topic would be defined and interpreted (Van Gorp 2007). Frames work differently in different contexts and they are not natural entities but socially constructed ones. They can be constructed by different producers, for example, journalists, politicians and the public (Vliegenthart and van Zoonen 2011). Thus, there is a classification of individual frames and media frames. Because of the leeway for stakeholders in constructing the meaning of issues, frames can be strategic in nature. Various stakeholders, such as social movement organisations, political actors and so on use strategic methods to diffuse meaning to influence framing for specific purposes (Gamson and Modigliani 1989; Tewksbury et al. 2009).

The existence of frames in social construction is invisible (Gamson et al. 1992) and, thus, strategic framing might be used to serve the power mechanism by strategic framing (Van Gorp 2007). 'They can be products of a variety of actors in a variety of matrices – whether international organisations, states, media, corporations or non-government organisations or actors and audiences within these – to name the principal categories' (Chitty 2015a, 9).

Framing usually happens in three steps: the reception of message, the integration of prior knowledge with the newly received information and the construction of a discursive model, and the formation of the new recognition (Ardèvol-Abreu 2015). Because of cultural lenses, there can be multiple frames of the same event from different interpreters at different stages of the communication process (Van Gorp 2007). This indicates that when interpreting a phenomenon or event, investigation from different cultural contexts is essential.

Frames are powerful mechanisms that can help define and solve problems and shape public opinion (Entman 2010). At the same time, they are also potentially useful in identifying the strategic messages created by practitioners in areas such as public relations and public diplomacy. Frame theory also offers the methodological potential to connect the study of perceived and portrayed national images in analysing news discourse (Pan and Kosicki 1993), the process of news construction and the framing effect (D'angelo 2002; Scheufele 1999).

The drama that has unfolded in Australia–China relations demonstrates how significant a role framing can play in bilateral relations. All of a sudden, the interference frames dominated the media and public debate, which lead to the downturn of bilateral relations of the two states, domestic policy changes and political struggles. If we look carefully, concern about China's influence was there for many years among certain groups but was not taken seriously.

China's presence is increasing gradually. For some, it signifies new hope for a dependable partner. But the framing of the *Four Corners* report broke the balance and then the frames changed sharply. The connection the report referenced as evidence was deemed to be not solid in the lawsuit lost by media outlets that released the story. Many challenge the validity of the accusations. However, the frames of Chinese influence have been imprinted on the discussion relegating the economic cooperation frames to the background.

The constructivist view holds that our construction of world affairs matters in international relations; it is rational to emphasise the importance of information and communication. The formation and exercise of soft power, to a certain extent, are matters of communication. Constructivist framing analysis is able to capture frames of messages delivered by states to the audiences through non-coercive public diplomacy.

Framing process

Framing has become a widely used theory in media studies and political communication where media frames and individual frames are distinguished. Efforts have been made by various scholars towards developing an integral framing process. In news-framing studies, many scholars have tried to synthesise the process into different models, and these are often characterised as having an effects orientation. It is understandable that industry and government have an interest in effects to justify expenditure on communication campaigns. As stated earlier, the approach taken in this book recognises the intent of communicators to cause effects; it draws on aspects of framing models that map such intent but takes a different approach. It focuses on the congruency of frames between the information sender, the media and the information receiver, which has drawn nutrition from previous research.

Snow et al. (1986) proposed the concept of 'frame alignment', which refers to the mechanism between the social movement and individuals in the form of frame bridging, frame amplification, frame extension and frame transformation in the whole process.

Scheufele (1999) proposes four framing processes for framing research in the three stages of information inputs, processes and outcomes: frame building, which refers to the dynamics of speakers selecting certain frames; frame setting, which focuses on the 'salience of issue attributes' and the interplay between media frames and audience perceptions (p. 116); individual-level effects of framing, which address the influence of frames in thoughts and attitudes and subsequent behaviours; and journalists as audience, which looks at the how the media frame can be affected by different social sponsors (p. 115). Scheufele's model aims to investigate the framing effect by addressing the links of frame building, frame setting, individual-level framing processes and feedback from individual-level framing to media framing.

With three information flows, D'Angelo's (2002, 880) model of the news-framing process consists of three sub-processes with more comprehensive coverage. The sub-processes are frame construction flow, framing effects flow and frame definition flow. During frame construction flow, signifying elements of meaning are carried by framing devices (Cappella and Jamieson 1997; Pan and Kosicki 1993). What frames have effects is determined by a variety of elements from external discourses to individuals' prior knowledge. This indicates that framing effect is an interactive flow instead of a one-way flow. Frame definition flow indicates the finalisation after the previous stages of flow.

De Vreese (2005, 52) also emphasises the communicative processes of framing. He divides the process into frame building and frame setting. The frame building stage stands between news production and news text, and the determining factors include internal (editorial policies, news values) (Shoemaker and Reese 1996), external (such as interactions between journalists and the elite) (Gans 1979; Snow et al. 1986; Tuchman 1978) and social movements (Snow et al. 1986) that influence the structural qualities of news frames. Frame setting is the stage between the news frames and the specific effects they have. It is the contest between the news frames and the audience's previous knowledge. The result would be attitude or behavioural changes at the individual level or collective actions such as decision making about societal affairs.

The four models presented above are all from the point of view of the travelling of news. Matthes (2012) drew framing into the context of political campaigns and proposed an interdisciplinary research project which reflects the three sets of reciprocal processes among the political actors, media actors and citizens as actors, and, for the first time, brought together the three separate but closely linked framing actors into one analysis (Matthes 2012, 255). His findings suggest that media content is usually governed by political elites with political logic but that citizens' frames are shaped by argument-based frames that were not suggested by political elites or media.

In the context of political communication, frame dominance and contestation matter. With the aim of better explaining how the opinions and moods composing a frame of the 9/11 attack travel from the White House to elites, news organisations, the media texts and then the public and who thus wins the framing contest, Entman (2003, 419) proposed the 'cascading network activation' model. This model explains the way interpretive frames are activated and are transmitted from the top level of a strategic system to the network of social elites and on to news organisations, media texts and the public, and the flow of feedback upward from the lower levels. During the process, Entman emphasises that public opinion is usually a dependent variable, but it sometimes influences elites through feedback; thus, there is an upward flow from the public to the decision makers. He also takes the view that all actors in the process are under conditions of uncertainty and pressure, and process the information with prior knowledge and limited time for comprehensive comprehension. The further the flow travels, the less thorough the information becomes. The advantages of this model lie in its acknowledgement of variations within the levels of the system, its capacity to explain whether elite dissent emerges, the guidance on what information in the news is important to policymaking and the reflection of the flow from audience to policymakers.

Similarly, but in a constructivist vein, Van Gorp (2007) also proposes an encompassing framing model which consists of frame selection and construction, key events and the interaction with frame sponsors, and the interplay between media content and receivers. Constructivist and receptionist perspectives are elaborated on below.

Different from research that focuses on one part of the framing process, for example, media frame or individual frame, the models reviewed above all view framing as an integrated process. In the communication process, especially in transnational/transcultural communication, new frames will need to contest dominant frames through what are called by Entman (2003) counter-frames – that are alternative narratives – to compete with the dominant frames which have a discursive power in international relations. In the international discursive contest scenario, framing would be meaningless without the investigation of frames among the communicator, media and the audience. One fact needs to be emphasised in framing relationships: framing does not happen in a vacuum; it is embedded deeply in the dominant culture (Van Gorp 2007). For individuals, the better the external frame fits its internal schema, the easier it is to accept the new frames. At the societal level, the media frames that resonate with the dominant culture will find more social acceptance (Entman 2004). Frame makers, the media and so on consciously or unconsciously emphasise certain aspects and reflect certain aspects of social reality or certain groups' interests (Entman 1993; Gamson 1988; Gamson and Modigliani 1989). Consequently, framing reflects certain power dynamics. This will explain the emergence of frame sponsors with strategic purposes to intervene in the framing process by not only advocacy but also observable activities such as speech-making, interviews, advertising, articles and so on (Gamson and Modigliani 1989). According to Tromble and Meffert (2016), public officials are frequent sponsors of media frames. The frame that shares a similar background to the information available to receivers would undoubtedly gain easier acceptance (Chong and Druckman 2007). Under this circumstance, there is the possibility for the existence of dominant frames (Entman 2003). 'Television imagery is a site of struggle where the powers that be are often forced to compete and defend what they would prefer to have taken for granted' (Gamson et al.1992, 391). However, the fragmentation effect of media makes media discourse vulnerable for challengers such as social movements to provide alternative constructions of reality (Gamson et al.1992, 391).

For effects-oriented framing theorists, the potency of framing depends on the influence it has on the receivers – attitude change or action. On the other hand, for constructivist theorists, the potency would lie in the ability of determining congruence or the lack thereof of frames between different parties to a frame relationship. The constructivist Van Gorp (2007) posits that cultural resonances contribute to the acceptance of familiar frames. Similarly, Price et al. (2005) conclude from their research that despite exposure to frames, individuals draw their opinion on certain issues from limited patterns of religious, moral, legal and personal discourse. Thus, audience frames are drawn after negotiation with media frames, which is a collective process by individuals with similar backgrounds, rather than mere exposure to media frames.

From a sociological perspective, Vliegenthart and van Zoonen (2011) note that media production and reception will be affected by individual differences, social and cultural contexts, structural divisions and power dynamics: 'Frames are part of a collective struggle over meaning that takes place through a multiplicity of media and interpersonal communication; draws from a range of resources, among which are news media and personal experience' (p. 112); only strong frames can affect opinions.

All the above-mentioned literature leads to the fact that receivers' previous experience influence the way they negotiate reception.

International Broadcasting and Soft Power

Revisiting international broadcasting in the soft power mechanism

The previous chapter briefly reviewed the history of international broadcasting engagement in international relations. This section will discuss pertinent theoretical issues.

Boyd (1997, 446) identified four motivations for broadcasting internationally by both state-run and private organisations: to enhance national or organisational prestige; to promote national or organisational interests; to attempt religious, ideological or political indoctrination; and to foster cultural ties. In the age of satellite-delivered television era, Straubhaar and Boyd (2002) added two more motivations: to see ads for multi-country products and to sell access to pay-TV broadcasts. To Browne (1982), international broadcasting is an instrument of foreign policy and a mirror of society, a symbolic presence, a converter and sustainer, a coercer and intimidator, an educator and an enter-tainer. All these roles of international broadcasting directly and indirectly echo Nye's conception of the three stages of public diplomacy (government to government, government to people and people to people) in wielding soft power as mentioned above. With the development of globalisation and tech-nology, the world has stepped into the junction of the biosphere and infosphere (Chitty 2017b). Technology has shortened the distance between human beings. However, while diffusion of technology does not guarantee mutually recognised symbols and meanings, reorientation of value systems can.

One aspect of the ambiguity of soft power is how the three resources identi-fied by Nye lead to foreign policy advantage (Reich and Lebow 2014). In Nye's view, soft power resides in power resources, but from a constructivist stance, power resides in the particular relations in which 'abilities are actualised' (Guzzini 2009, 7). International broadcasting can be viewed, on the one hand, as the information diffuser through which attraction in the resources are trans-mitted into the receivers' eyes and, on the other, as a multiplier in the field of public diplomacy in which relationships are established (Chitty 2017b).

Following Zaharna's soft power differential model, mass media in public diplomacy may be viewed as a channel to wield soft power; networked com-munication facilitates the generation of soft power (Zaharna, 2010). However, in reality, the two channels are impossible to separate. Networked communi-cation is communication among individuals and organisations. Most of the time, information from mass media can be the primary source of informa-tion for networked communicators. How much they rely on each of the three channels (A, B, C) identified in Figure. 3.1 below depends on the expertise they possess. For example, diplomats and scholars will depend more on their own information-acquisition channels during exchanges with their counterparts in other organisations or countries. In the dynamics of framework, the gener-ation of soft power means the wide acceptance of A's culture, value system and policies. And the wielding of soft power is to have B do willingly what is in A's favour. The success of the former will render what happens in the latter as a natural consequence. From this sense, the generation of soft power means the acquisition of discursive power. During the information flow process, the ideal effect will be the achievement of the recognition of A's belief, values and policies in B or the emergence of *sui generis* conditions of homonomy in rela-tion to the larger system.

Following this logic, it is easier to understand the great enthusiasm in investing in international broadcasting in some countries. From the world wars through the Cold War, state-run broadcasting has demonstrated its use-fulness in spreading host countries' voices, values and discourses, with models such as VOA, BBC, Deutsch Welle and so on (Castells 2007; Seib 2010; Shi

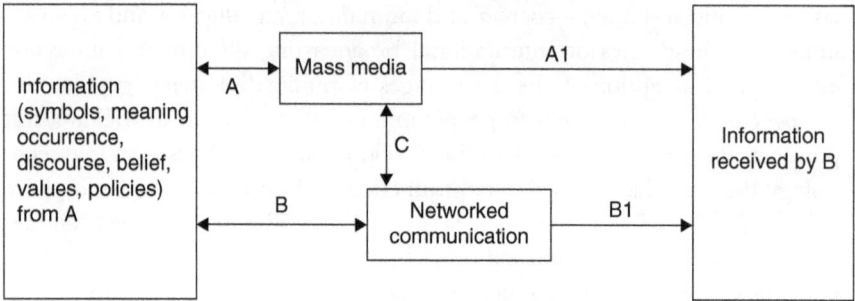

Figure 3.1 Information flow

2015; Thussu 2013). With the development of satellite transmission and globalisation, commercial networks like CNN provided a new model for international broadcasting. The rise of Al Jazeera witnessed the upswing of Islamic discourse in world politics, which has inspired countries like China to promote their own discourse through international broadcasting.[2] After the 9/11 terrorist attack in the United States, a new wave of information war seems to have arisen. In recent years, Russia Today (RT) has drawn a great deal of attention with its strong anti-West discourse; it has been embraced by certain left- and right-wing groups in some Western countries although it has been criticised by those at the centre. It will be useful to consider the non-Western types of ownership and operational models used by organisations such as RT when operating in the West. These could be characterised as being financially hybrid – part-commercial and part-state-sponsored – state-owned broadcasters. Within the same ownership pattern, there are different operational dynamics because of the differences in media systems in different countries. Sponsored by the UK Parliament, BBC's operations are characterised as that of an independent organisation while RT and CCTV NEWS are known to be under strict state control. From a soft power lens, the difference may be used to explain the different soft power approaches. In speaking of soft power resources, the United Kingdom is on top in almost every aspect in comparative polls (Monocle 2015; Portland 2016). What it needs to do is to showcase and strengthen its attractiveness. China and Russia are in a totally different situation due to their own political and value systems. To foster attractiveness, CCTV NEWS and RT need to persuade potential audiences to accept or

---

2 In the history of CCTV NEWS, the official discourses on its status have changed many times. At the beginning, the leaders of the Publicity Department and designers of the channel used the terms 'China's CNN' and 'China's Al Jazeera' to articulate the visibility goals of CCTV NEWS.

at least understand them, if potential audiences are not going to stay away because they view these broadcasters to be on the 'dark side'. In other words, these broadcasters need to gain discursive capacity. In this sense, RT's anti-Western discourse is not hard to understand although it may not be easy to accept, except by the extreme left and right in the West. Would they be better off targeting opinion leaders among mainstream audiences with less anti-Western rhetoric? CCTV NEWS claims to be determined to fill the air-waves with neglected stories while using news considered 'hot' in the West as audience bait.

Cultural considerations: Professionalism as an index of media framing culture

Culture is an important factor in the information flow and framing process (Mowlana 1997). The fact that '[c]ommunication research does not function in a political vacuum' (Mowlana 1997, 207–8) makes the concept of power a very relevant issue. And 'frames are a central part of a culture and are institutionalised in various ways' (Van Gorp 2007). The context in which media workers conduct their routine work can be seen as media culture in a broader sense. Media culture, in turn, is embedded in a broader social polit-ical context and can reflect, to a certain extent, even broader power dynamics. Media culture can be found to have its maximum usage in what is widely called 'professionalism'.

Professionalism is related to profession; it is regarded as an organising prin-ciple of an occupational cohort. The professional's work is based in a theor-etical body of knowledge, shared values and norms, and common purpose (Gade and Lowrey 2011). Journalistic and scholarly evangelism of democracy has been shaped by the good qualities, rules and ideals espoused by this body of knowledge. Journalistic professionalism is evaluated on the basis of adher-ence to these values and norms (Dahlgren 2010; Gade and Lowrey 2011; Li and Chitty 2017; Waisbord 2013; Zelizer 2005).

The existence of different media systems in the GRC determines the diver-gence in professionalism. The divergence of professional values relies first on political culture (Chilton 1988), and where reified by the state, it is the political system that underpins the working environment. The contention here is that in liberal democracies, the terms 'political culture' and 'media culture' may be more applicable, while in polities where media is controlled by the state or/and ruling party, the terms 'political' and 'media system' are appropriate to indicate the comparative centralisation of media control mechanisms. Thomas Jefferson's advice 'in all cases to follow truth as the only safe guide, and to eschew error which bewilder us in one false consequence after another in endless succession' as 'inculcations necessary to render the people a sure basis for the structure of order & good government' (Jefferson 1819) reflects liberal theory that has informed the press. Freedom of expression and press ownership and the notions of public service, insistence on verity, comprehensive treatment of subject matter in objective, non-discriminatory and expeditious ways are among values associate with professionalism in the literature (Deuze 2005; Gade and Lowrey 2011; Hanitzsch 2007; Siebert et al. 1956; Weaver et al. 2009).

But it is fair to say that, empirically, because of variations in political systems and political cultures, there are no universal professional values of journalism. Even in Western countries, values are not always consistent (Kepplinger and Köcher 1990). Within an ideal liberal political culture, journalism as a profession is based upon the value of upholding democracy through providing citizens the information they need to self-govern (Kovach and Rosenstiel 2007). This is the mainstream discourse employed to judge world journalism, although there is more than one model around the world as demonstrated by the four theories of the press (Siebert et al. 1956) and the later three models of media and politics by Hallin and Mancini (2011). Ideal typical values are challenged by multimedia, multiculturalism as well as multinationalism (Deuze 2005). In Australia, for instance, the position that media should support government policies and transmit favourable images of political and business leadership is not without advocates (Hanusch 2008). Scholars with non-Western roots are trying to explore alternative narratives such as journalistic ethics under the framework of Islamic, Buddhist or Taoist philosophy (Gunaratne 2009, 2013; Hamada 2016).

News media has experienced dramatic disruption in the last few decades. The first disruption was through new media, where users choose variously from a smorgasbord of media technologies (Madianou and Miller 2013). The second was the spreading across borders of television news production values that are associated with the libertarian press whose natural habitats are liberal democracies. Countries like Russia and China, within their public diplomacy strategies, have launched foreign-language channels for their state-owned broadcasters and founded overseas branches. They believe that they could generate more soft power abroad through sending messages via these channels. Osipova (2017) has questioned the effectiveness of their use because they have deficits in relation to the professional values identified above; notably, they are not seen as warranted by or believable in the West.

In an age characterised by the pull of globalisation, national and local cultures have pushed back. Some scholars identify the emergence of a transnational global professionalism (Reese 2001); however, a single package of journalistic values has not been identified. These include those who take into consideration institutions (including levels of analysis in some instances) and epistemologies (Deuze 2005; Hanitzsch 2007; Li and Chitty 2017; Reese 2001). There has also been the suggestion that the notion of professionalism should be examined more objectively, after delinking it from its Western ideological construction and relying on a 'journalistic logic' (Waisbord 2013).

Another confusing aspect of journalistic professionalism is the puzzlement about describing it. When placed within certain journalistic cultures and ideologies, in mainly liberal contexts, the specific ideals adopted are different (Deuze 2005; Hanitzsch 2007; Reese 2001). Reese (2001) takes the view that professionalism is a problematic concept that is vulnerable to different interest groups. These may be identified as the power dynamic and operational groups; disseminators and interpreters are the journalistic roles (Hanitzsch 2007; Li and Chitty 2017).

To investigate the cultural influence around international broadcasting, media culture can be a good point to start. It can include the investigation of the political system and traditional culture in the formation of media culture. One way to get to this is through examining the frames of a media organisation's staff about themselves as media workers and the organisation they serve. The frames can reflect the impact of external and internal factors, which include the professional values they cherish in their work, on power relations reflected during media practice. Another way is to analyse the content of media production, which can be treated as a result of the interaction among the factors.

Soft Power as a Communicative Approach of Power Relations

In the construction of world politics, communication skills play a unique role. '[T]he long-term, deep structural forces and the dynamics of the power relations are making communication the central process in global, national, and local social organizations' (Harari 2014, 209). Harari has highlighted three types of communicative skills in human history relating to the ability to describe the environment, social relations and abstract concepts. The ability to conceptualise 'allows frame creation that organizes society over time' and that is 'elaborated as ideology' (Chitty 2017b, 13). Framing is the basis of human interaction. Power relations among the actors are realised through interaction, which can be viewed as the communication of symbols, information and values. 'For soft power to be activated it needs to be cast as a message, be articulated attractively, as assertives, directives or commissives that are intrinsically attractive' (Chitty 2017b, 27). Culture, value system and foreign policy only become meaningful at two ends of a communication process.

Information, the core element in any sort of communication, is an important dimension in power exercising. According to Lasswell (1950), influentials who wield political power depend upon the success with which they manage their environment. This implies skill in handling flows of symbols, violence and goods and services, depending on the type of influential. At the same time, influential must withstand the attacks of other groups of aspirant influentials who strive for ascendancy through the use of every method at their disposal. In practice, this is likely to mean a struggle for power in which the victory goes to the influential who wields most effectively the symbols of the common destiny (Lasswell 1950). Similarly, Haas (1992) views that 'control over information and knowledge is an important dimension of power and that the diffusion of new ideas and information can lead to new patterns of behaviour and prove to be an important determinant of international policy coordination' (p. 3).

Hayden (2003) has noted the interdependencies among the macro level of the nation state and society, the meso level media organisational actors and the micro level of the individual citizen. These interdependencies shaped not only the collective interpretation of the events but also the collective reaction and subsequent consent given to the representative government. Locating media under Nye's three facets of power places it under the soft approaches of power dynamics. It is apparent that attraction and institutions are involved in the transmission of information and meaning, and, ultimately, the creation of consensus or acceptance of the original country's information, behaviour and values among other countries. This will create power as Nye claims (2011). Hayden (2017) views soft power as a congregation of practical reasoning that 'informs linkages between strategic arguments about communication power and the subsequent practice of public diplomacy' (p. 5). Possessing soft power implies the capability of a state to maintain certain types of compliance or action and prescribe normative values for other states. These aspects echo the discursive function of international media. In his definition, power is in terms of 'control over the particular base values as well as in terms of the flow of interchanges between the main sectors of society reflecting the ability to act and to affect something' (pp. 4–5). Belief and value systems are the core in defining the nature and parameters of action. He views these as the context in understanding international relations and information flow.

Chitty (2017b) posits that electronic networked media is one of the channels and multiplier resources of active soft power in the study of soft power. In his civic virtue model (p. 26), he posits virtue-based behaviours such as listening, engaging in dialogue, exchanging values for mutual benefit, developing mutually beneficial relationships and so on as the key practices in civil diplomacy. He reconfigures the passive soft power sources into heritage and contemporary ones which both consist of intangible (knowledge, behaviour and culture) and tangible (historical sites and artefacts under the rubric of heritage, and cultural products under the rubric of contemporary culture) categories; cultural-industrial, media and mobility channels are regarded as soft power multipliers, tools of cultural diplomacy. He further distinguishes public diplomacy (between governments and public between countries or within one country through media, mobility or cultural production to build sustainable and mutually beneficial relationships), civil diplomacy (engagement between the civil society and government within one country or civil groups with/ or government with counterparts in other countries to promote cooperation for mutual interests) and cultural diplomacy (practices through state or non-state actors draw on heritage or contemporary culture using media, mobility or cultural production to build sustainable mutually beneficial relationships) (pp. 18–19). In all the three types of public diplomacy, the key thread is the transformation of ideas, products and so on through communication.

But there is one point missing in many discussions, that is, the existence of infrastructure does not guarantee soft power. If a broadcasting has no audience, it is impossible for it to transit any information. So we can assume that from international broadcasting to soft power, there are two different layers of interplay. The first layer consists of information diffusion and projection: the voices of one nation and the stance and the virtues it carries. Only those received as attractive will contribute to the accumulation of soft power strength. At the second layer, communication has the potential to wield soft power as a multiplier. With the edges accumulated at the first layer, information in this layer can have an effect in achieving policy goals of the original country. This is where soft power can be wielded.

Understanding China's international media push in the communicative dynamics

The theoretical perspectives discussed above offer an applicable analytical framework to understand China's image issues and its discursive power promotion. First of all, according to the constructionist perspective, framing among countries can be viewed within the linked processes of meaning and experience construction. The opinion of a country as a whole (whether a majority view or a patchwork of group views) is a result of meaning negotiation in itself and others. Framing as the 'schemata of interpretation' (Goffman 1974, 21) can be adopted as the analytical tool of the process. Because of inter-subjectivity, every group forms its experience based on its own environment; the divergence of framing is understandable and unavoidable to a certain extent. At the same time, however, it leaves space for improvement through spreading a core message that favours one side (the information war during the Cold War being a good example) or promoting mutual understanding through showcasing the good side of a culture. A country that expects maximum recognition from others, as does China, must gain recognition by construction, by the majority in a targeted country, of a meaning congruent with the one China holds; it needs to widely share its experience or have wide recognition of its deeds, actions or way of life as legitimate and attractive. The strategic communication approaches and public diplomacy initiatives employed by states seem to be explicable from this aspect. From this sense, the importance of noopolitik is self-evident. China's enthusiasm in promoting its image seems to find an acceptable interpretation from this constructivist perspective, to contrast the international relations constructivist making of world politics with the analytical social scientific method of constructivism. Some scholars like Rawnsley (2012, 2015) claim that China's public diplomacy has the aim of being liked. But on examining the Chinese mainstream discourse, the terms usually used to label the country are those such as peace-loving, victim, socialist, revolution, anti-hegemonic, developing, major, cooperator and autonomous (Wang 2003; Wang 2011). From the latter angle, it is more like a process of battling with a biased perception by other states, especially the West that usually frames China as a weak state subject to US rules, sneaky and adept at scheming only for its own interests, an oppressor, an enemy, a negative existence (Liu 2014) and a definite war-maker if not contained by the United States (Kagan 2017). From the international relations constructivist perspective, what China is doing in its communication strategy for the economic zone connecting by the One Belt and Road initiative can be viewed as constructing the narrative of what its president proposed as 'a community of common destiny'.

It is useful to note the role of language, the tool by which social experience is accumulated (Berger and Luckmann 1966) and social rules are delivered (Onuf 1989), in understanding image construction and discourse contest. Image is a kind of knowledge accumulated through social experience. In this sense, it is fair to conclude that image is transmitted in terms of language. Although it is easier to link image with visual signs, in the case of image of certain states, it is more in the form of language. For example, when people say China is a threat, the linguistic feature is more obvious and enduring. When taking power relational dynamics into consideration, discourse, as a regime of truth (Foucault 1979) that influences social relations and knowledge systems through language (Fairclough 1992), sustains image, although it contains not just image. Having particular access to discourse and communication means having one of the social resources that generate power and dominance. Framing has been called, by some scholars, an approach to analysing discourse which is between the behaviourism of content analysis and the structuralism of discourse analysis (Pan and Kosicki 1993). In the international sphere, which is posited by Chitty as a weak GRC (Chitty 2017b), the discourse power model exists. It is possible to assume that in this kind of confederacy, as within a society, discourse by a particular group has the dominant power to define certain relationships or statuses. In this regard, the framing of one country's image and status could be determined not only by itself within world politics but also by forces that have more access to it. Pan and Kosicki (1993, 58) posit that 'framing analysis is not constrained within the content-free structuralist approach of news discourse,' rather, 'it retains the systematic procedures of gathering data of news texts in order to identify the signifying elements that might be used by audience members'. To China, the problem puzzling mainstream perception is the unescapable trap of threat image that prevents it from engaging deeply in world affairs. This can be verified through the framing process model by comparing the degree of congruence or incongruence in different framing contexts.

A Process Model of Information Flow

As mentioned earlier, in the networked society, mass media not only serves as a channel to diffuse messages from the two ends of an information flow process but also partly provides messages for the networked communication. As Zaharna (2010) points out, the 'global communication era is defined by connectivity, interactivity and cultural diversity' (p. 4); at each stage, it is impossible for the flow of information to be one-directional; feedback will always influence the way information is framed at the beginning. In addition, during each stage of the process, framing is at work, which could influence the way the receivers frame the information they get at each stage. Due to the background differentiation of the receivers, information through every medium will be different, more or less, from the original one. Especially when travelling through different cultural filters, the information from Country A or Organisation A to audience at Country B or Organisation B, which is A's intended target, must change due to multiple filters (see Figure 3.2). After the filtration, different outcomes will be emerging, homonomy or heteronomy, which will lead variously to happy acceptance or even rejection of the information from A by B. In this regard, the process of what A is framing, how it is re-framed by different media forms in the middle and then how the targeted audience at B will interpret how it would reflect the dynamics of the multi-framing process.

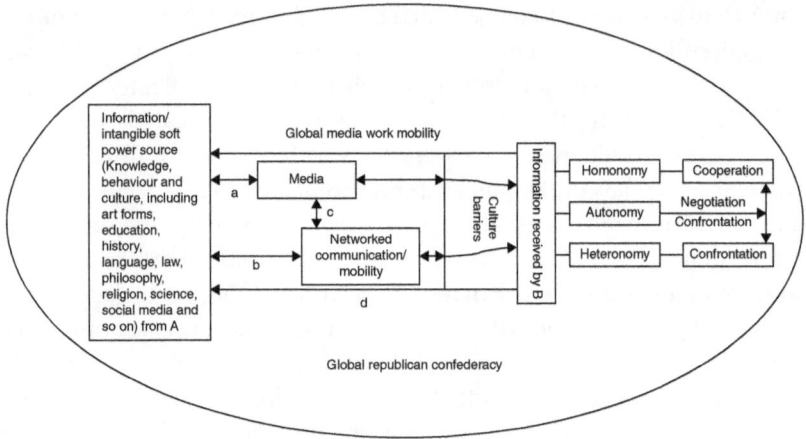

Figure 3.2 Soft power model of information flow

Some details need to be mentioned here: First, the information matters mainly to the stakeholders. As Nye has emphasised, attention is a scarce resource (Nye 2011). The reason why Australian people are interested in information about China must be because it is relevant to them. Second, the framing of information will be influenced by many factors. These include stereotypes, political factors, historical relations and political systems, which can be under a broader culture base (Chitty 2015a). Thus, cultural elements are also an important variable in the information flow process which can be reflected by the different framing results. Culture is a broad concept that can be understood as a 'complex whole which includes knowledge, belief, art, morals, law, custom and any other capacities and habits acquired by man as a member of society' (Tylor 1871, 1). It is very difficult to incorporate all the elements of the culture into a single analytical framework. But as mentioned earlier, professional culture can reflect to a certain extent the broader cultural influence around it. In the case of CCTV NEWS, there is now a hybrid journalistic culture due to the recruitment of foreign staff. The organisational frame of the professional culture – the role of this in society and the way organisations frame issues – can reflect not only the culture of the organisation itself but also the dynamics of the broader relationship between the organisation and the state political system. Its professional identity as an organ of the state leaves with the targeted audience in the West the impression that CCTV NEWS is a propaganda tool. This framing of an organisation will definitely impact the effectiveness of its reach, which in turn will push the media organisation to take into account audience frames.

Reconciling the Chinese public diplomacy model with cross-cultural audience framing

To avoid the potential confusion among scholars from different perspectives of research in communication and cultural studies, this subsection will briefly wrap up the main framework of this research. This project is primarily situated within the tradition of the field of international communication while engaging with international relations with a focus on soft power and communication under the broad cultural context. To avoid long-term but futile debates of framing collision on issues like China being a threat among different social groups, which further result in division of global opinion, this project absorbs the stance of viewing world opinion within the GRC while admitting the differences among the states but emphasising mutual good and benefit (Chitty 2017b). From the constructivist point of view, this project holds the basic understanding that soft power, as an influence sans coercion or inducement, is basically a communication process – one whereby messages of attraction of heritage and contemporary culture of one country are delivered through personnel mobility, media and cultural industry, the virtuosity of the content and style of the message delivery playing a key role (Chitty 2017b). The concept of soft power is meaningful only in the context of relations (domestically and internationally) where a certain degree of influence is expected to be achieved.

The aforementioned literature shows that public diplomacy activities with the purpose of soft power can be grouped into three layers: state-initiated activities, state-funded activities implemented by the civil society and cultural action initiated and run purely by the civil society. The third category, with no specific diplomacy aims, is huge in scale but may not always deliver messages that are deemed effective from the point of view of the state's soft power expectations. But their delivery of information is easier for the recipients to accept. In this sense, public diplomacy is essentially a top-down activity although elements can be implemented through the civil society. This project will focus on the mechanism of message delivery with the soft power purpose, specifically through the channel of media.

Being aware of the deficit in the investigation of the audience end in the soft power debate (Chitty 2017b; Gillespie and McAvoy 2017), the imbalance of world information flow (Thussu 2013) and the differences in the China narrative in Chinese and Western media, this project will look at the process from both ends: the initiator and the recipient. Listening is said to have great importance for global governance, international relations and public diplomacy (Chitty 2017b; Cull 2008; Onuf 2014). From Nye onwards, the discussions of soft power always emphasises the importance of the target, a behaviourist term, though Nye also emphasises the importance of listening and notes varied audience responses (Nye 2011). The inclusion of recipients of a soft power message is to examine the effectiveness of China's international media approach and explore the mechanism of message-framing between the two ends of the process. In this regard, Hall's encoding and decoding theory provides a useful insight in that it emphasises the active role of the audience in the interpretation of messages under the influence of a social context (Hall 1980). Constructive framing analysis used in this project can, on the one hand, take the contextual elements into consideration and, on the other hand, reflect the cognition formation process whether or not they read the message delivered.

Culture is a complicated concept that can be viewed from different lenses (Jacob 2017). Here, Sorrells's definition of culture, as a system of shared meaning (Sorrells 2015) which influence people's framing of things, is used. But it will only hold the position that culture is a background factor which can, in varying degrees, influence people's framing. As elaborated earlier in this chapter, public diplomacy activities with soft power purposes are a matter of communication which can be impacted by culture but is not a problem of culture itself. With the aim to fully communicate, cultural barriers can be overcome – this can be seen in many real-life cases. In this regard, culture should not be an excuse of ineffective communication.

References

Allison, Graham. 2017. *Destined for War: Can America and China Escape Thucydides's Trap?* New York: Houghton Mifflin Harcourt.

Angyal, Andras. 1969. "A logic of systems." *Systems thinking* 1:17–29.

Ardèvol-Abreu, A. 2015. "Framing theory in communication research. Origins, development and current situation in Spain." *Revista Latina de Comunicación Social* (70):423.

Arquilla, John, and David Ronfeldt. 1999. *The emergence of Noopolitik: Toward an American information strategy.* CA: Rand Corporation.

Baylis, John, Steve Smith, and Patricia Owens. 2013. *The globalization of world politics: an introduction to international relations.* Oxford: Oxford University Press.

Berger, Peter L, and Thomas Luckmann. 1966. *The social construction of reality: A treatise in the sociology of knowledge, Garden City, NY: First Anchor.* NY: Random House.

Borah, Porismita. 2011. "Conceptual issues in framing theory: A systematic examination of a decade's literature." *Journal of communication* 61 (2):246–263.

Boyd, Douglas A. 1997. "International Radio Broadcasting in Arabic A Survey of Broadcasters and Audiences." *International Communication Gazette* 59 (6):445–472.

Browne, Donald R. 1982. *International radio broadcasting: The limits of the limitless medium.* Connecticut: Praeger Publishers.

Calabrese, Andrew. 2005. "Communication, global justice and the moral economy." *Global Media and Communication* 1 (3):301–315.

Cappella, Joseph N, and Kathleen Hall Jamieson. 1997. *Spiral of cynicism: The press and the public good.* Oxford: Oxford University Press.

Castells, M. 2007. "Communication, power and counter-power in the network society." *International journal of communication* 1 (1):29.

Chilton, Stephen. 1988. "Defining political culture." *The Western Political Quarterly*:419–445.

Chitty, Naren. 1994. "Communicating world order." *Journal of International Communication* 1 (2):100–119.

Chitty, Naren. 2015 "Analysing Soft Power and Public Diplomacy" *Jilin University Journal Social Sciences Edition* 55 (3).

Chitty, Naren. 2017. "Soft Power, Civic Virtue and World Politics." In *The Routledge Handbook of Soft Power*, edited by Naren Chitty, Li Ji, Gary D Rawnsley and Craig Hayden. New York: Routledge.

Chitty, Naren, and Sabina Dias. 2018. "Artificial intelligence, soft power and social transformation." *Journal of Content, Community and Communication* 7:1–14.

Chong, Dennis. 1993. "How people think, reason, and feel about rights and liberties." *American Journal of Political Science*:867–899.

Chong, Dennis, and James N Druckman. 2007. "A theory of framing and opinion formation in competitive elite environments." *Journal of Communication* 57 (1):99–118.

D'angelo, Paul. 2002. "News framing as a multiparadigmatic research program: A response to Entman." *Journal of communication* 52 (4):870–888.

Dahl, Robert A. 1957. "The concept of power." *Behavioral science* 2 (3):201–215.

Dahlgren, Peter. 2010. "Public spheres, societal shifts and media modulations." *Media, markets & public spheres. European media at the crossroads*:17–36.

De Vreese, Claes H. 2005. "News framing: Theory and typology." *Information design journal+ document design* 13 (1):51–62.

Deuze, Mark. 2005. "What is journalism? Professional identity and ideology of journalists reconsidered." *Journalism* 6 (4):442–464.

Entman, Robert M. 2003. "Cascading activation: Contesting the White House's frame after 9/11." *Political Communication* 20 (4):415–432.

Entman, Robert M. 2004. *Projections of power: Framing news, public opinion, and US foreign policy*: University of Chicago Press.

Entman, Robert M. 2010. "Framing media power." *Doing news framing analysis: Empirical and theoretical perspectives*:331–355.

Entman, Robert M. 1993. "Framing: Toward Clarification of a Fractured Paradigm." *Journal of communication* 43 (4):51–58.

Fairclough, Norman. 1992. *Discourse and social change*. Cambridge: Polity.

Finnemore, Martha. 1996. *National interests in international society*. New York: Cornell University Press.

Foucault, Michel. 1979. *Discipline and punish: The Birth of the Prison*. New York: Vintage Books.

Freedman, Des, and Daya Kishan Thussu. 2012. *Media and terrorism: global perspectives*. Thousand Oaks: Sage.

Gade, Peter J, and Wilson Lowrey. 2011. "Reshaping the journalistic culture." *Changing the news: The forces shaping journalism in uncertain times*:22–42.

Gamson, William A. 1988. "Political discourse and collective action." *International social movement research* 1 (2):219–44.

Gamson, William A, David Croteau, William Hoynes, and Theodore Sasson. 1992. "Media images and the social construction of reality." *Annual review of sociology* 18 (1):373–393.

Gamson, William A, and Andre Modigliani. 1989. "Media discourse and public opinion on nuclear power: A constructionist approach." *American journal of sociology*:1–37.

Gans, Herbert J. 1979. *Deciding what's news: A study of CBS evening news, NBC nightly news, Newsweek, and Time*. Illinois: Northwestern University Press.

Gillespie, Marie, and Eva Nieto McAvoy. 2017. "Digital networks and transformations in the international news ecology." In *The Routledge Handbook of Soft Power*, edited by Naren Chitty, Li Ji, Gary Rawnsley and Craig Hayden, 203–218. London: Routledge.

Goffman, Erving. 1974. *Frame analysis: an essay on the organization of experience*. Cambrdge: Harvard University Press.

Gramsci, Antonio. 1971. *Selections from the Prison Notebooks of Antonio Gramsci: Ed. and Transl. by Quintin Hoare and Geoffrey Nowell Smith*. New York: International Publishers.

Gunaratne, Shelton A. 2009. "Buddhist goals of journalism and the news paradigm." *Javnost-The Public* 16 (2):61–75.

Gunaratne, Shelton A. 2013. "Go East young 'man': Seek wisdom from Laozi and Buddha on how to metatheorize mediatization." *Journal of Multicultural Discourses* 8 (3):165–181.

Guzzini, Stefano. 2009. *On the measure of power and the power of measure in International Relations*: DIIS working paper.

Haas, Peter M. 1992. "Introduction: epistemic communities and international policy coordination." *International organization* 46 (01):1–35.

Hallin, Daniel C, and Paolo Mancini. 2011. *Comparing media systems beyond the Western world*. Cambridge: Cambridge University Press.

Hamada, Basyouni Ibrahim. 2016. "Towards a global journalism ethics model: an Islamic perspective." *The Journal of International Communication* 22 (2):188–208.

Hanitzsch, Thomas. 2007. "Deconstructing journalism culture: Toward a universal theory." *Communication theory* 17 (4):367–385.

Hanusch, Folker. 2008. "Mapping Australian journalism culture: results from a survey of journalists' role perceptions." *Australian Journalism Review* 30 (2):97–109.

Harari, Yuval Noah. 2014. *Sapiens: A brief history of humankind*. New York: Random House.

Harari, Yuval Noah. 2018. *21 Lessons for the 21st Century*. New York Random House.

Hayden, Craig. 2015. "Scope, mechanism, and outcome: arguing soft power in the context of public diplomacy." *Journal of International Relations and Development*.

Hayden, Craig A. 2003. "Power in media frames: Thinking about strategic framing and media system dependency and the events of September 11, 2001." *Global Media Journal* 2 (3):146–159.

Jacob, Udo-Udo Jacob. 2017. "Cultural Approaches to Soft Power." In *The Routledge Handbook of Soft Power*, edited by Naren Chitty, Li Ji, Gary Rawnsley and Craig Hayden. London: Routledge.

Jefferson, Ronald L, Peter J Katzenstein, and Alexander Wendt. 1996. "Norms, Identity, and Culture in National Security Policy." In *The Culture of National Security*, edited by Peter J Katzenstein, 33–75. New York: Columbia University Press.

Kagan, Robert. 2017. 'Backing Into World War III.' Foreign Policy, 6. https://foreignpolicy.com/2017/02/06/backing-into-world-war-iii-russia-china-trump-obama/

Kaldor, Mary. 2003. "The idea of global civil society." *International affairs* 79 (3):583–593.

Kepplinger, Hans Mathias, and Renate Köcher. 1990. "Professionalism in the media world?" *European Journal of Communication* 5 (2):285–311.

Kovach, Bill, and Tom Rosenstiel. 2007. *The elements of journalism: What newspeople should know and the public should expect*. New York: Three Rivers Press

Lasswell, Harold Dwight. 1950. *Politics: Who gets what, when, how*. New York: P. Smith

Li, Chenyang. 2006. "The Confucian ideal of harmony." *Philosophy East and West* 56 (4):583–603.

Li, Mei, and Naren Chitty. 2017. "Paradox of professionalism: The professional identity of journalists who work across media cultures." *Journalism* (November 2017):1–19. doi: 10.1177/1464884917743175.

Liu, Yang. 2014. "Discourse and Framing: A Content Analysis Based on Chinese News Quoted by New York Times." *International Proceedings of Economics Development and Research* 77:19.

Louw, P Eric. 2010. *Roots of the Pax Americana: Decolonization, development, democratization and trade.* Manchester: Manchester University Press.

Madianou, Mirca, and Daniel Miller. 2013. *Migration and new media: Transnational families and polymedia.* London: Routledge.

Matthes, Jörg. 2012. "Framing politics: An integrative approach." *American Behavioral Scientist* 56 (3):247–259. doi: 10.1177/0002764211426324.

Monocle. 2016. Soft Power Survey 2015/16.

Mowlana, Hamid. 1985. International flow of information: A global report and analysis. New York: UNESCO.

Mowlana, Hamid. 1997. *Global information and world communication: New frontiers in international relations.* Thousand Oaks: Sage.

Nye, Joseph S, and William A Owens. 1996. "America's information edge." *Foreign affairs*:20–36.

Onuf, Nicholas. 2004. "Humanitarian intervention: the early years." *Fla. J. Int'l L.* 16:753.

Onuf, Nicholas. 2013. *Making Sense, Making Worlds: Constructivism in social theory and international relations.* New York: Routledge.

Onuf, Nicholas. 2016. "The power of metaphor/the metaphor of power." *The Journal of International Communication*:1–14.

Osipova, Yelena. 2017. "Indigenizing soft power in Russia." In *The Routledge Handbook of Soft Power*, edited by Naren Chitty, Ji Li, Gary Rawnsley and Craig Hayden, 346–357. London: Routledge.

Pan, Zhongdang;, and Gerald M Kosicki. 1993. "Framing analysis: An approach to news discourse." *Political communication* 10 (1):55–75. doi: 10.1080/10584609.1993.9962963.

Portland. 2016. The Soft Power 30.

Price, V. 2005. "Framing public discussion of gay civil unions." *Public opinion quarterly* 69 (2):179–212. doi: 10.1093/poq/nfi014.

Rawnsley, Gary. 2012. "Approaches to soft power and public diplomacy in China and Taiwan." *Journal of International Communication* 18 (2):121–135.

Rawnsley, Gary D. 2015. "To Know Us is to Love Us: Public Diplomacy and International Broadcasting in Contemporary Russia and China." *Politics* 35 (3–4):273–286.

Reich, Simon, and Richard Ned Lebow. 2014. *Good-bye hegemony!: power and influence in the global system.* New Jersey: Princeton University Press.

Scheufele, Dietram A. 1999. "Framing as a theory of media effects." *Journal of communication* 49 (1):103–122.

Seib, Philip. 2010. "Transnational journalism, public diplomacy, and virtual states." *Journalism Studies* 11 (5):734–744.

Shi, Anbin. 2015. "Approaching New Internet Information and Communication Order: The Role of Chinese Media." World Internet Conference, Wuzhen Zhejiang, China.

Shoemaker, Pamela, and Stephen D Reese. 1996. *Mediating the message in the 21st century: A media sociology perspective.* New York: Longman.

Siebert, Fred Seaton, Theodore Peterson, and Wilbur Schramm. 1956. *Four theories of the press: The authoritarian, libertarian, social responsibility, and Soviet communist concepts of what the press should be and do.* Illinois: University of Illinois Press.

Snow, David A, E Burke Rochford Jr, Steven K Worden, and Robert D Benford. 1986. "Frame alignment processes, micromobilization, and movement participation." *American sociological review*:464–481.

Sorrells, Kathryn. 2015. *Intercultural communication: Globalization and social justice*. Thousand Oaks: Sage publications.

Straubhaar, Joseph D, and Douglas A Boyd. 2002. "International broadcasting." In *Global Communications*, edited by Yahya R Kamalipour. Belmont, CA: Thomson Wadsworth.

Teilhard De Chardin, Pierre Teilhard. 1965. *The phenomenon of man*. Translated by Bernard Wall. New York: Harper & Row. Translation.

Tewksbury, David, Dietram A Scheufele, Jennings Bryant, and Mary B Oliver. 2009. "News framing theory and research." *Media effects: Advances in theory and research*.

Thussu, Daya. 2013. *Communicating India's soft power: Buddha to Bollywood*. New York: Palgrave Macmillan.

Thussu, Daya Kishan. 2010. *International communication: A reader*. London: Routledge

Tromble, Rebekah, and Michael Meffert. 2016. "The Life and Death of Frames: Dynamics of Media Frame Duration." *International Journal of Communication* 10:23.

Tuchman, Gaye. 1978. *Making news: A study in the construction of reality*. New York: The Free Press.

Tylor, Edward Burnett. 1871. *Primitive culture: researches into the development of mythology, philosophy, religion, art, and custom*. Vol. 2. London: Bradbury, Evans, and Co., Printers.

Van Gorp, Baldwin. 2005. "Where is the frame? Victims and intruders in the Belgian press coverage of the asylum issue." *European Journal of Communication* 20 (4):484–507.

Van Gorp, Baldwin. 2007. "The constructionist approach to framing: Bringing culture back in." *Journal of communication* 57 (1):60–78.

Vliegenthart, R., and R. Vliegenthart. 2011. "Power to the frame: Bringing sociology back to frame analysis." *European journal of communication (London)* 26 (2):101–115. doi: 10.1177/0267323111404838.

Waisbord, Silvio. 2013. *Reinventing professionalism: Journalism and news in global perspective*. Jew Jersey: Wiley.

Wang, Hongying. 2003. "National Image Building and Chinese Foreign Policy." *China (National University of Singapore. East Asian Institute)* 1 (1):46–72.

Wang, Longqing. 2011. "Journalists, media diplomacy and media- broker diplomacy in relations between mainland China and Taiwan from 1987–2009 [electronic resource]." Australia: Macquarie University.

Weaver, David H, Randal A Beam, Bonnie J Brownlee, Paul S Voakes, and G Cleveland Wilhoit. 2009. *The American journalist in the 21st century: US news people at the dawn of a new millennium* London: Routledge.

Wendt, Alexander. 1992. "Anarchy is what states make of it: the social construction of power politics." *International organization* 46 (02):391–425.

Wendt, Alexander. 1995. "Constructing international politics." *International security* 20 (1):71–81.

Xi, Jinping. 2016. Addresse at the Openning of the Second World Internet Conference in Wuzhen. Wuzhen: Zhejiang Province, China.

Zaharna, Rhonda S. 2009. "Mapping out a spectrum of public diplomacy initiatives: Information and relational communication frameworks." In *Routledge Handbook of Public Diplomacy*, edited by Nancy Snow and Philip M. Taylor, 106–120. New York: Routledge.

Zaharna, Rhonda S. 2010. *Battles to bridges: US strategic communication and public diplomacy after 9/11*. New York: Pilgrave Macmillan.

Zaharna, Rhonda S. 2004. "From propaganda to public diplomacy in the information age." *War, media and propaganda: A global perspective*, edited by Yahya R. Kamalipour and Nancy Snow, 219. Oxford: Rowman and Littlefield.

Zelizer, Barbie. 2005. "Journalism through the camera's eye." *Journalism: Critical Issues*:167–176.

Chapter 4

INTENDED AND RECEIVED FRAMES OF CHINA AND THE EXPECTATION ON MEDIA

A Brief Introduction to the Data Collection and Analysis

According to the reviews and discussions in the previous chapters, there are different frames about China's image and policy issues on the Chinese and Australian sides. The image the Chinese side has been promoting for decades, although it has changed with time, is from a progressing to an accomplished country, one that is a cooperative, peace-loving responsible world citizen growing from a low-profile developing country to a big economic power wishing to take on a greater share of global responsibility and contribute to global governance. Chinese mainstream discourse identifies China's struggle through public diplomacy initiatives to counter its unbalanced information status, the bias in other countries' framing of China and to narrate more accurate Chinese stories with the purpose of creating a better understanding, while in the mainstream framing of the Australians, China's culture and political system is at the two ends of the preference scale with the former in the favourable position. Over the decades, China has grown from a backward country to an aggressive threat to Australia. This incongruence in frames of the two sides often leaves individuals as well as policymakers puzzled. For example, having experienced living in both countries, individuals from China always have the impression that at the policy level, Australian policymakers seem to rely on merely their own stereotyped imagination of the 'authoritarian regime', 'lack of freedom' – far from China's reality. On the other side, having given millions of students and immigrants from China the opportunities to be immersed in the Western system, the West witnessed that a growing Chinese middle class failed to push China into becoming a more democratic country as the West had expected. On the contrary, there are an increasing number of patriots in China both among those who reside and those who return to China for convenience of life and prospective opportunities for individual career development. What has caused the difference in their framing?

International broadcasting has been employed as a crucial tool to address this problem. What role can it play in this communicative process? This chapter is going to explore these questions by presenting findings through in-depth interviews with public diplomacy elites from the two countries.

To understand China's frames in the communicative context, it is necessary to uncover the frames and frame changes that happen in the context on a certain topic. However, to understand this, we must first understand under what circumstances this topic is framed. As mentioned in the previous chapters, framing will not happen in a vacuum and will be influenced by many factors. For example, the frames China intends to promote would usefully be influenced by an understanding of the way it is perceived by intended target audiences. This could be viewed as a parameter of their seeing the specific topics. Thus, this chapter looks at the general frames of China in the eyes of the Chinese and their target audiences in Australia. Chapter 2 has identified framing as a cognitive tool.

Data were collected through in-depths interviews with public diplomacy elites in China and Australia. Public diplomacy elites are intermediate experts from four sectors in public diplomacy, including state, corporate, civil society and media sectors (Li and Chitty 2009). And in fields like international relations, only stakeholders/intermediate experts are really concerned with certain topics, those elites with expertise in specific issue areas and are classed as being intermediate because they are a bridge between the policy elites and the general public and are influential in policymaking processes. In addition, they are more accessible than the statesmen who may be constrained from expressing their true opinions (Chitty 2007; Li and Chitty 2009; Wang 2000).

The operationalisation of framing analysis

Framing analysis consists of the detection of frames and the analysis of the dynamics behind them. To detect frames, it should first be understood what they are and what they are made of. Previous research widely consented that the unit of identifying an issue is an interpretive package/a frame package (Gamson and Modigliani 1989; Goffman 1974). An interpretive package consists of a frame and a position. The elements reflecting the characteristics are signatures. The signature elements are divided into framing devices, which suggest integration and synthesis, and reasoning devices, which provide justifications or reasons for a position. Frame suggests that the core organising idea consists of devices such as metaphors, exemplars, catchphrases, depictions and visual images; reasoning devices consist of roots, consequences and appeals to principle.

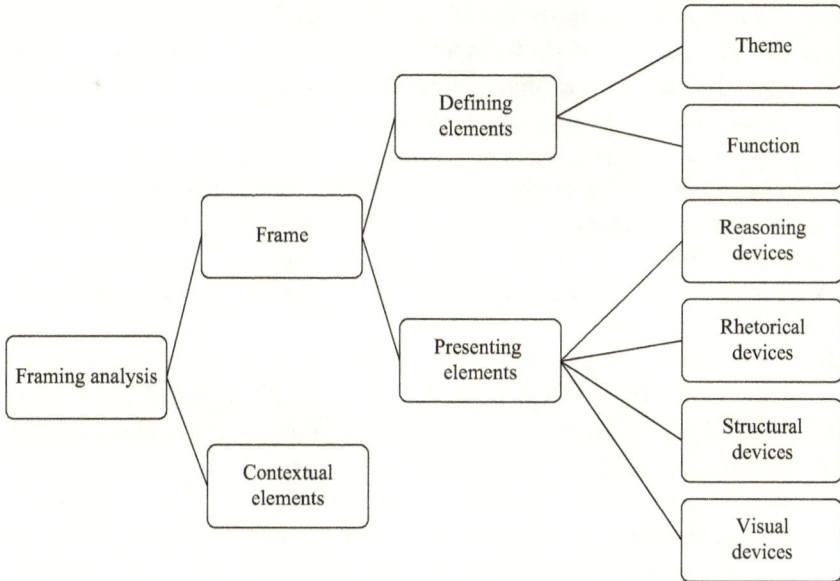

Figure 4.1 Matrix of framing analysis

In this study, framing analysis was conducted by identifying the frames and discussing the contextual issues. A frame is formed through the salience of certain elements. Frames at different stages can be interpreted differently by interpreters from different backgrounds. They are identified through the detection of the components and devices. In this book, a frame is viewed as an interpretive package with defining elements, presenting elements and the contextual elements (Figure 4.1). The defining elements consist of the theme of the frame, the position/stance it holds and the function it has with others. The theme is about the topic or core meaning. The position/stance is the attitude embedded in the frame towards the issue it addresses. In the case of Chinese issues, the stance may be different among different actors. For example, what the Chinese side thinks as positive may be negative to Australian audiences. The function indicates the effect the frame has. It could be informative, persuasive or defensive in the case of China's government documents on OBOR and CCTV NEWS's framing of relevant issues. The presenting elements consist of devices that help highlight certain elements of an issue. It could include the syntactic and script structures and other rhetorical devices like metaphors, exemplars and visual devices. The contextual elements refer to the cultural environment where the frame is formed in certain ways instead of others. It is important to understand that not all the elements exist equally in all stages. For example, in government documents and news texts, the syntactic and rhetorical devices might be more than those in individual frames. Thus, the inductive approach is used to identify as many frames as they emerge. Contextual elements can be identified through the analysis of institutions, the professional practice and so on.

This chapter focuses on the frames of China in the eyes of Chinese and Australian public diplomacy elites, the expectations of the Chinese on their international media role in the country's soft power projection and Australians' media use in acquiring information related to China. Following Nye's discussion of soft power resources, and Chinese scholars' understanding of China's soft power resources, interviews with 35 Chinese and 22 Australian public diplomacy elites between September 2015 and mid-2016 sought the following impressions held by them: (1) general impressions and (2) detailed impressions on economy, culture, political system and science and technology, which could be regarded as manifestations of Chinese virtuosity that generate soft power. In each frame matrix, the theme, position and framing devices were detected with the aim of discovering the way framing occurs.

The participants are coded with a letter and a number. The letter 'c' stands for Chinese participants and 'a' for Australian participants. The numbers were allocated at random at the time of coding.

China in the Frames of the Chinese

To find out how the Chinese people frame the state, during the in-depth interviews, general impressions of China were solicited. Nye's triad of soft power resources and Chinese scholars' understanding of soft power resources, economy, political system, culture and science and technology, which had potential to be considered as examples of Chinese virtuosity, were picked out during the interviews to ask the participants to evaluate China under the above aspects. The main results are presented in the following five sub-sections. To avoid any deviation in interpretation, this book chooses to present the comments from the participants in as detailed a manner as possible. The main opinions from participants are quoted in italics followed by tables hosting the main framing elements. A brief analysis is presented after the each table where there would be an exploration of contextual backgrounds of the framing.

Complex China frame

The individual framing of China by its public diplomacy elites showed complex results. On the question of what the most distinct features to describe China are, most participants used the word 'complicated'. This complexity was reflected in four categories: the ambiguity in national branding, the changing context, the measurement of judgement and the stance held by the observers.

Although a participant mentioned the 24 core socialist values proposed by the ruling party (c14), most felt that there were no clear aspirations that could define the country – like democracy and freedom seen in many Western countries (c14, c21, c34). It seemed that settling on some striking and impressive descriptors for the country was not easy. Bewilderment was detected among the participants.

Another element contributing to the complexity was the rapidly changing context where the defining elements reside. For example, some participants mentioned China's image from the historical perspective by mentioning the peak moments in history; In the Tang dynasty and between the seventeenth and eighteenth centuries AD, the influence of China was far-reaching; there was a decline from the nineteenth to the twentieth century, with an insular policy encountering the rapid and invasive development of the West; the opening-up policy resulted in China's image being restored (a10). It was widely agreed that the situation is in flux, thus making the image hard to capture. As one participant put it:

> It is like a running person, if the mirror is put in a fixed position, what one can see is only a rapid passing figure. (c12)

The complex frame of China also reflected the different judgements arrived at from consideration of different foci of measurements. For example, the closer contact of the leaders with the people, the rapid economic development and dramatic improvement of people's lives (c16, c11, c25 and c35), good governance and stable social life (c17) were seen to add positivity to the judgement of the outside world. But the pollution problems, the ever-increasing gap between the rich and the poor, the relative constraints in the political and cultural environments and ideological control were seen as contributing to negative perceptions. The difference lay in where one chooses or happens to look or to highlight:

> In recent years, the top leaders show close contact with the people, this may be a positive factor in our national image. (c11)
>
> The general impression of China should be becoming better and better because of our achievements in economic development and the improvement of people's life. (c25)

The position to observe is another factor contributing to the complex frame. For example, most participants agreed that the perceptions of China by its people are better than perceptions from people of other countries (c12, c17), and different countries have different views due to varying relationships with China, the differences in ideology and the corresponding interpretation on certain issues (c16).

> *There is difference in our own perception of our country and others. Generally speaking, our own perception is better than others.* (c17)

The framing devices identified under this question included exemplars, quotations of poll results and metaphors (see Table 4.1). For example, the participants mentioned the Tang dynasty and the portrait of Confucius in Voltaire's study to demonstrate the influence of China in earlier times. Contradictory perceptions are cited to illustrate the varied perceptions on China: these are positive Pakistani and negative Japanese perceptions. Different polls were referenced by participants to present different figures. The participants had concluded that the results shown by polls by China's *Global Times* and China International Publishing Group on global public opinion on China were better in general than those from BBC and Pew and that they indicated an image improvement over the years although the degree of preference varied with region.

Economy frame: The main source of attraction

Many participants viewed the economy as the most attractive factor to other countries. First, it was a measurable element; second, it sometimes could be combined with cultural elements like the food and fashion industries and thus generate attraction in other domains.

Also, economic success demonstrated the advantage of other factors, such as the political system, as one participant suggested:

> *The 30 years continuous growth is worthy of attention. It cannot be explained by the economy per se. Some scholars credit it to political system, political model and the approach of governance even the leadership of the Communist Party. So there are theories like Beijing Consensus talking about the Chinese model. This is not done by Chinese, it is by the Westerners. Although the development is slowing down, but the market size is huge, it might to a factor of attraction.* (c12)

c7 echoed this point in relation to the cohesiveness the political system:

> *If the energy is used towards one direction, it (economy) could be an advantage because the governance and policies are stable and continuous.*

Table 4.1 Complex China frame

	Theme	Root	Devices		
			Exemplars	Quotations	Metaphors
Complexity Frame package	The ambiguity in national branding	Traditional vs. modern: No clear position	–	–	–
	The changing context	Seventeenth–eighteenth centuries better than nineteenth–twentieth centuries/In a process of rapid changes	Tang dynasty; Voltaire had a portrait of Confucius	National image poll by CIPG, Pew International Image poll	Lion Running person
	Judging from different dimensions	Good in economy/Bad in air quality, etc.	Leader's engagement with the people; pollution	–	–
	Judging in the position of different beholders	Self-good/Others different	Pakistan: good; Japan: bad	Pew poll, CIPG poll, Global Times	–

But confidence could not hide the problems. Although participants were quite confident in the attractiveness of the economic development, there were problems that were mentioned, such as the irrational economic structure, the modest size of per capita income and so on:

> *Economy can't be ignored; it is big but not strong.* (c18)
>
> *Economy is big in size. Figures show that China has surpassed US in terms of purchase power; it might surpass US quickly with the 7% growth rate versus 2%-3% in US. But China has a large population, four times of that of US. If we count the per capita income, it may need 20 more years to catch up with the US.* (c21)
>
> *China lacks quite a few factors to be a strong economy, for example, Chinese currency is not an international currency, state and individuals are not getting rich simultaneously.* (c14)
>
> *The economic development of China is obvious. But the economic system reform needs to continue.* (c9)

There were also pessimistic views based on the structure of the economy:

> *I am not so optimistic for China to become the strongest economy in 2050. There are complicated elements. The quantity is impressive, but the structure is not good enough. The gap with US is not small at all.* (c5)

The devices presented include exemplars and statistics within a comparative perspective (see Table 4.2). For example, the Beijing Consensus was used by one participant to prove the influence of China's economic development model. When talking about the growth rate, figures were quoted. Also, the comparison with United States was used by more than one participant when talking about the speed and potential of economic development.

Delving into the background of the framing diversity, the responses revealed the relatively sober-minded evaluation on China's economic strength as a source of attraction by the participants. That might be the result of domestic publicity being diffused from a single source, making government policy well known. This may provide a clue as to why terms such as 'political system reform' and 'economic structural reforms' were quoted repeatedly by participants; they are frequently used in the public discourse conducted by the government in the media.

Culture frame: The card of soft power?

Culture has been regarded as an ace card in China's soft power resources. For example, in *The Soft Power 30 2016* statistics, China ranked 28th in general,

Table 4.2 Economy frame

| | Theme | Position | Devices | | | |
			Exemplars	Statistics	Comparisons
	The continuous growth is obvious	Positive	Beijing consensus	–	–
	A factor showcasing the strength of other factors	Positive	–	7% growth rate	2–3% in the United States
	The market is big	Positive	–	1.3 billion	–
	Has the potential to further development	Positive	–	–	–
Economy frame	Large in size but not strong in quality	Sceptical	Currency	–	–
	Large in overall economic size but not in per capita	Sceptical	–	1.3 billion	Four times of that of the United States

and culture ranked 9th, the best index among digital, enterprise, engagement, education, government and polling (Portland 2016). The state has been using cultural soft power in discourse to emphasise the role of culture in its soft power strength. However, the participants' views on culture did not seem to be as confident as expected, although acknowledgements exist.

First of all, there were different understandings of where the attractions in culture resided.

For example, some participants interpreted it as the height of human civilisation and emphasised the richness of its long history:

> *Chinese culture is one form of traditional civilization; it is a representation of eastern civilisation, tested by the long history it is where the value of Chinese culture lies.* (c12)

> *The attraction is huge from the 5000 years accumulation of culture and history. It showcases in the ways of Chinese people's dealing with things, thinking, and architecture etc. This is obvious.* (c3)

Interestingly, within China, the mainstream discourse on its culture is always 'broad and profound', but it seemed that different opinions existed in some participants' minds, which were observable from their responses:

> *I don't think China's culture is very attractive overseas. It may have certain attractiveness to some.* (c11)

> *I think perhaps some of the foreigners are interested in China's culture but they might not be the majority. Some people may have curiosity about it. It is another thing, how much they like it.* (c6)

> *[To say China's culture is] very attractive is inappropriate; cultural exchange may be easier than political exchange with other countries. But not all people like it.* (c8)

> *Those functional elements of culture in which one can seek satisfaction may be attractive to others.* (c7)

> *What element in our culture is attractive? Maybe kung fu, food, acrobatics, Confucius, philosophy etc. the classic things and tourism, nothing else. We think that it is broad and profound, but others might not understand that.* (c5)

The above insight might partly be based on the different understanding of culture itself. Culture is a broad concept which could refer to everything in social life. This makes it hard to form a consistent view. This point was reflected in the responses of the participants.

> *China's cultural influence can be analysed at different levels. The most important part of culture is value system. Our core values are part of common human values, they are*

universal and attractive, such as Benevolence, Righteousness, Courtesy, Wisdom and Trust (Ren, Yi, Li, Zhi, Xin), never do to others what you would not like them to do to you (Ji Suo Bu Yu, Wu Shi Yu Ren). These values provide a philosophical base, this is where the attraction of Chinese culture is. Others are the things that can be exhibited, like Taichi, food, language etc. that people may be interested in. (c12)

When we talk about restoration of traditional values, what are these, feudal monarchy? (c21)

Others held different ideas and expressed concerns on the loss of core cultural values:

But how do we understand culture? Artworks are a good form. But the most important part of culture is values. In the film, all the values are what the Americans advocate: individualistic heroism, freedom and equality. What are the values reflected in our films, it is hard to tell. It may be clear as there are 24 terms socialist core values, but how many people can remember them? For some, we cannot achieve at present, such as socialist justice. I think Xiao *[filial piety] is the core value of Chinese culture.* (c14)

We need to make clear the core values and spirit domestically and cherish the culture inheritance, like its inclusiveness, expansibility and emphasis on peace. But it is very hard; look at the policy-making circles, most of them were trained overseas, what they cherish may not be our traditional culture. (c7)

Cultural attractiveness showed in the process of communication. It seemed that the communication of Chinese culture had not been satisfactory for some participants.

The recognition on arts is high overseas. But we didn't communicate them well. The good side is we have large population which can serve as a medium. (c16)

Culture is abstract, and thus may be misunderstood. The attraction can be created. No culture has instinctive attraction to others. They may be interested in elements that proximate to their own. (c7)

In the field of cultural exchange, it is done relatively well. Like Confucius Institute, the scale is large, but the depth is not enough. The intention is good, but it hasn't been rooted deeply in other countries. It is bluntly described as a channel to promote our culture in the countries that have had concerns on our behaviour, now they will think we are trying to overthrow their values with communism. On the contrary, the US understands our young people well and promotes their culture among our people in an invisible way. We have cultural products that go overseas, like the paintings, but just sold as products. The entrepreneurs are doing the jobs of artists. (c8)

Apart from the traditional elements, we have also those talents who keep pace with the times and their works and designs are on par with the world level, but they are little known. (c3)

The devices detected from the framing of China's culture include exemplars (traditional Chinese traditional values, kung fu, movies, Confucius Institute), depiction (descriptions such as curiosity, not clear, impossible) and comparison (with Hollywood and the United States) (see Table 4.3).

The unexpected lack of confidence in culture might be explained from a historical perspective. In the most recent century, the revolution, the New Cultural activities and the socialist movements almost always denied all traditional values. The adoption of Western culture before and after the opening-up policy further dimmed memories of traditional culture. In the last several decades, reflections on the loss incurred through the denial of traditional culture in recent history has led to a revival of interest in traditional culture. But how well traditional values can be restored may need the test of time.

Political system frame: The best choice?

As to the question on the political system, the answers were even more unanimous than other items. The political system was generally viewed as being suitable to the situation. Most of the participants seemed to be happy with the system:

Every country has its own situation, so independent thinking is important. You can't just follow suit. China should stick to what suits the country and the people best. (c11)

The choice based on unique situations and characteristics that might not be understood by others. This may increase the difficulty for others in understanding... There is an inevitable question on what's behind the continuous growth of China's economy in the last 30 plus years. At first people talked about economics alone. But gradually, it is found out that it also has something to do with the political institutions and model, the governance even the leadership of the Communist Party. Traditional western political economics will draw this conclusion. That's why Beijing Consensus was raised by Remo to discuss the Chinese model. It is not the empty talk on institutional superiority, but a theoretical exploration. (c12)

Basic democratic institutions and the polity of multi-party cooperation, under the leadership of the Communist Party, make sure of the unity of the country. Without this, it may be another situation. Value-building is needed, otherwise, look at USSR. (c8)

Table 4.3 Culture frame

	Theme	Position	Devices			
			Exemplars	**Depictions**	**Comparisons**	
	Representation of Eastern civilisation	Positive	Ren Yi Li Zhi Xin	Representation of Eastern civilisation	–	
	Limited attraction	Sceptical	Kung fu, movie	Curiosity/Certain level of attraction	Hollywood	
Culture frame	Ambiguity in internal recognition	Negative	Ren Yi Li Zhi Xin, Xiao	Not clear	United States	
	Deficiency in communication	Negative	Confucius institute	impossible	Hollywood	

Sometimes we have been too sceptical about our model. There are numerous top research institutions from Western countries that are studying China's healthcare, agriculture. We need to be confident about these and highlight achievements. (c2)

Debates about systemic problems are not rare among intellectuals and even among ordinary people, especially on social media, when incidents happen. 'Many problems in China are caused by the existing system' is a common narrative shared even among people working within the system. The criticism is much stronger from the outside world. Some Chinese participants harshly criticised the current Chinese system, but few were able to propose an alternative; this was especially so because they figured that the cost of system change might be destabilisation of the state.

> *From the normative perspective, it is problematic, but from the practical perspective, the so called best system may not yield best results and vice versa. There are a lot of problems in the Chinese system, but if you merely follow the Western model, it might not work. Reform is necessary, but cannot be done in a hurry. No one can afford the consequence if hasty reform is adopted.* (c5)

> *Of course it faces difficulties, but we have a complicated situation comparing with others.* (c12)

> *Stability is very important, the African journalists I work with think that the very parts of China that are deserving of their study are its stability and [its ability] to develop within a stable environment. It is incredible for China to keep its own stability in such a disturbing world. Pakistani journalists also said Chinese people are amazing to concentrate on development in such a chaotic world.* (c16)

> *It is a relatively effective system at present, it is not perfect. China has many problems, but the situation is special.* (c9)

Despite the suitability with the country's situation, few respondents thought the system to be attractive to others despite the quotation of measures of admiration from some Third World countries in one case. Interestingly, one participant refused to comment because she thought that the question was not reasonable:

> *The American system may not be completely suitable for the US, so it is in China where some parts work well but others may not. From the perspective of national branding, some harsh criticism on China is just because of ideological difference and that people in other countries do not understand China's situation and culture.* (c3)

Table 4.4 Political system frame

	Theme	Position	Devices		
			Exemplars	Depictions	Quotations
Political system frame	The choice of special and complicated	Positive	Economic development/Beijing consensus	Special	African journalists; Pakistani journalists
	Not perfect	Understanding	USSR	Complicated	–

The devices embedded the frames of participants mainly include exemplars, depictions and quotations (see Table 4.4). For example, the Beijing consensus and the collapse of the socialist system of the USSR are mentioned as exemplars. When China was mentioned, adjectives such as 'special' and 'complicated' were used repeatedly by participants.

China is well known for its ideological and speech control. Participants at discussions on the political system may have been influenced by this. But many participants expressed their understanding of the nature of academic research and the anonymous nature of data collection after human ethics protocols were explained to them. A couple of participants did forbid the use of recording devices in advance. Perhaps the answers could be seen as the majority view on the issue. The Pew polls revealed that Chinese perception of their own country is exceptionally positive (PewGlobal 2008–2014), which is congruent with the majority positive responses. In addition, about one-sixth of the participants in the current study have experiences of studying overseas and are aware of the political advantages and disadvantages of both China and the second societies. Their responses demonstrate that although they do not think that China's political system is flawless, their consenting to it is not unlikely.

Science and technology frame

Science and technology (S&T) has become one of China's fastest growing fields in recent years. In the *2014 China National Image Global Survey* jointly conducted by the Centre for International Communication Studies under China Foreign Languages Publishing Administration British multinational market research firm Millward Brown and global online survey company Lightspeed GMI, the average positive evaluations of China's S&T innovation capacity is 64 per cent; in BRICS countries, the average figure was above 80 per cent, the highest being 90 per cent. Similarly, some participants expressed their confidence in S&T development.

> China's investment in S&T is the third in the world now. The number of workers in research and development, and the patent placement are both the 2nd in the world. This is a bonus of economic development. (c10)

> I am confident in China's S&T. They are on the right track. Our scientists got the Nobel Prize last year and President Xi highlighted that at his New Year Speech. The government attaches importance to that and Chinese people never lack the ability of innovation and research. Although the investment cannot always be satisfactory, Chinese people are dedicated. We can see that in the recent Consumer Electronics Show (2016), one third of the products exhibited were made in China. (c7)

Again, large population, state support and market size were viewed as the most important incentive factors for S&T development:

> China has a large population size. Implementation is quick; central control allows people to practice creativity, innovation etc., and [in a] large population [its] very easy for things to come out. There are a lot of Chinese internet entrepreneurs; they are not hampered by systems and processes and bureaucracy. I think that's a positive thing to yield creativity and innovation. (c27)

Scepticism also existed among a small number of participants. For example, c5 thought the gap between China's S&T and that of the United States was huge (although the pace of development was fast), with China's S&T depending mainly on cloning with very few genuine innovations. Core technologies were seen as rarely being developed in China, for example, the engines of passenger planes cannot be made domestically, and in many industries, essential parts need to be imported.

More problems such as industrial transformation capacity, capital-chasing behaviour by entrepreneurs and intelligence protection were also mentioned by participants:

> S&T is stressed by policy making level. But the transformation to industry is weak. And some core technologies are still weak, like automobile engines and software for computers. It is not the problem of policy, but the short-sightedness of entrepreneurs. (c8)

> The speed is good. The problem lies in the innovation and intelligence protection. (c11)

The framing devices included exemplars, statistics and metaphors (see Table 4.5).

Table 4.5 Science and technology frame

	Theme	Position	Devices		
			Exemplars	Statistics	Metaphors
Science and Technology capacity frame	Fast-developing	Positive	Consumer Electronics Show	2nd, 3rd	–
	Lack of innovation	Sceptical	Engines; Software		Clone

China in the Frames of the Australian Public Diplomacy Elites

Australian frames of China, like the Chinese frames, were analysed in both general and specific senses within a matrix of commentary. The general frames of China in the Australian participants' minds demonstrated complexity as among the Chinese participants, in spite of the differences in details. It needs to be mentioned that all Australian participants showed a certain degree of understanding of China through their various experiences. All of them had visited China at least once. Some had become acquainted with China through travel, media and friends or family members; some had, either at the time of the interview or earlier, regular business interactions with Chinese organisations; four had China-related topics as their areas of research expertise. Some of the participants' first visits to China went as far back as the 1970s, before China's opening-up policy was adopted. The main opinions from participants will be quoted in italics followed by tables with main framing elements. A short paragraph of the analysis will be presented after each table where applicable as the exploration of cultural backgrounds of the framing.

Complex China frame

First, there were some aspects that enjoyed a clearly favourable reception, such as a long history replete with colourful cultural treasure (a17, a20); industrious, kind and rational people (a14, a21, a1, a11, a12, a13); abundance of opportunities, impressive cities, unbelievable changes thanks to rapid economic development (a1, a15, a11, a12, a13); delicious food and beautiful scenery (a5) and diversity (a9).

> *If you look at the way in the world, a lot of people seem [to be] going mad, like Trump, lack rationality, so are the protesters. I don't see this in China, in China people seem to be very rational.* (a14)

China is a huge country, with a long history and many people. (a17)

The attractive part of China for me is its tradition and culture, rich culture treasure. (a20)

The positive part of China is that people are very industrious, want to do well, (a21)

In China there are lots of opportunity, very cultural, food, cultural connections and background. (a11)

I love China, its people, culture, beautiful scenery, impressive cities like Shanghai, Beijing. There are huge, unbelievable changes. (a1)

Variations among the people and places are remarkable. (a17)

The most impressive part of China for me is its diversity. (a9)

Also, some negative aspects were clearly identified from the Australian perspective: for example, the environmental issues (a19), the trials around human rights issues and the imprisonment of dissenters (a5), the political system (a20), a more aggressive and bullying stance on issues such as the South China Sea (a8) and the limitation of individual rights (a7).

Environmental damage is a huge problem. (a17)

My worst impression about China is its pollution. (a19)

Political system, from a West[ern] point of view, may be problematic. (a20)

From my perspective, what is uneasy is that people don't always have the opportunities to be individuals. (a7)

One scholar explained that the emphasis on humanity in Chinese culture – the dependency on the benignity and rectitude of the ruler rather than laws and law enforcement – is difficult for Australians, who have a good framework of laws, to accept.

For me one of the difficult things to come to terms with in Chinese culture is its emphasis on humanity rather than discipline or laws. You know in history, Chinese always said if you have a good ruler then the country will be in good order, everything will be good, it all comes from the goodness of the ruler, whereas in the West we tend to think if you have a good government, if you have a good frameworks of laws, if everything is orderly then it is more important than the person. (a2)

A former diplomat-turned-scholar thought the Chinese logic to be problematic and difficult to apply to many situations, as in the dispute of the South China Sea; the Chinese diplomatic discourse has always been that it has been

China's territory since ancient times and that China had maps to support its claim. 'Others may have maps as well; you need to convince people through detailed and logical evidence,' he said (a6).

The general impression reflected some widely recognised problems both among the Chinese and Australian participants. But most aspects fell into the disputed realm not only with the Chinese but also with the Australians. The most salient trend was the people versus government division.

A very common statement about the impression of China among Australian people was that the people are good but the government is not. As already mentioned, people were regarded as one positive factor by some participants.

My observation is that, when I talk with Westerners about Chinese as people, they are usually quite positive. They are more positive than they were because they think the Chinese are fitting into the society well. Some other communities don't fit in the western society; they keep to their own traditions. (a11)

I have an overwhelmingly positive view on Chinese people. So [my criticisms] are nothing against Chinese people, it's against the way in which political and economic direction is headed. (a1)

However, the Chinese people were not always shown in a positive light. For example, those who encountered negative behaviour of certain groups had adopted a negative impression.

[Chinese people] lack public etiquette. (a17)

Chinese people are queue-jumping, loud, and chaotic. (a18)

Having wealth, they don't know how to behave. They don't know how to treat other people in a global community with compassion and respect, but still talk about how much money you've got. There are growing immigrants and a lot of Chinese students coming to Australia to study and I think that's great; the problem is that they live in communities but seldom interact with locals. International relations are starting with grass roots people. If people understand people, it will make things much easier. (a3)

Participant a8 sensed the aggressiveness in the Chinese attitude to others in dealing with issues in international relations.

In 2008, Kevin Rudd gave a speech at Peking University. There was a very articulate Chinese student commenting on Rudd's speech saying that even though he studied China, had been working in China for a long time, knew about a great deal about China and use idioms in his speech, she said that he is not Chinese, he doesn't love

China, there is no reason for us (the Chinese) to listen to his comments or criticism about Chinese circumstances; and as far as she was concerned, that was the end of discussion. Many of her contemporaries share the same horrible nationalistic attitude. Since then, my impression about China changed from positive to concerned.

Another characteristic of Australians' impressions of China was the different levels of concern and scepticism they expressed. In addition to concerns on the nationalistic attitude among the young people as expressed by participant a8, there were other concerns that were embedded in a variety of contexts ranging from the possible threat that China presents to neighbouring countries to the rise of Chinese issues in domestic politics.

I think people in countries like Australia do have human rights concerns in China and also they have concerns for the environment. But I think that the view is on balance positive, when I say on balance, obviously, some Australians do have anti-China views but also balanced views that are positive. (a15)

[We are]) anxious that China can get too powerful and will be pursuing its own satisfaction over others. (a16)

While acknowledging the economic success, concerns were also expressed by some participants on future prospects because of different internal problems they learnt about through various channels.

But you know there are substantial problems, different problems perhaps to the West, but substantial problems, and it has some human rights issues they have to deal with. [The substantial problem] I suppose in the top of my head I would say is how to cope with 'only having had one child' policy for a long time, perhaps there are some social issues we in the west don't hear much about. This is my impression, mainly, maybe wrong, the dismissal perhaps, of having daughters so there are too many men in China, that brings social problems; but also pollution and things like that, very fast growth they are not managing, or they are trying very hard to manage both pollution, and also how to deal with energy in future. Then I guess politically I certainly don't see it as evil empire in any way but it's still a one-party system and they don't have a free vote. (a21)

We have concerns on the strong China, on other strong countries as well. It was unilateral strength; that has problems. It will always be a problem with US relationship and China; it always plays in that context, like South China Sea, whatever. If the US weakens, and China strengthens, you know the world have to adjust to that. (a7)

We've seen 2 million manufacturing jobs lost in 3 years. There are more protests taking place; […] the anti-corruption drive against tigers and flies is important but it be used politically against political enemies. (a1)

Interestingly, the above comments all came with the prospect of China's rise economically and politically in the world stage with the rhetoric of 'yes, it has been very successful/it may become one of the strongest economies, but there are problems'. This may indicate the lack of confidence or the existence of scepticism in China's future development, which has resulted from the information they acquired from different channels. The conclusions varied dramatically when evaluated from different perspectives. This phenomenon reflected in the different perspectives of interpretation of the same issue indicates the participants' information source preferences. In other words, the Chinese found comfort in the state media information, which mainly focuses on positive issues, while the Australian participants favoured Western media, which prefers to believe the pessimistic side. This may be further evidence for selective exposure theory which indicates that individuals tend to believe or access the information that reinforces their pre-existing views, while avoiding contradictory information (Lazarsfeld, Berelson and Gaudet 1968). This in turn will reinforce their sceptical judgement.

Economy frame

The 'economy frames' on China also reflected multi-faceted receptions from the Australian public diplomacy elites. On the one hand, some participants acknowledged that economic success had won for China much admiration. On the other hand, concerns had been expressed over the potential threat and uncertainty in world order as a consequence of China's economic rise. Some participants' knowledge of China's economic development was very direct and focused on the achievements. For example,

> China is going to overtake the US; power is shifting in China's favour; I think there's still a lot of admiration for China's rise economically. (a14)
>
> It [China] is a world leader economically already. (a2)
>
> China is a great power. With 1.3 billion people and the economy which is the second largest in the world, you cannot not be a great power. Whether you want to exercise your power, militarily or some other way, that's a different issue. But at the moment China is no doubt a great power; I mean it is the second largest economy. (a1)

However, not all participants had confidence in the prospect, because of the distrust of the Chinese way of economic operation.

> I thought if China sticks to what they had undertaken in the last 30 plus years, which means keeping the market open and free, this will be something that would place China

in a growth trajectory, which would leave the West's economy behind. But now China is going to take the other direction [the increase of central planning], I think it's very disappointing. We've seen 2 million manufacturing job losses in 3 years. (a1)

It's [China's economy becoming the world largest] going to happen. The issue is whether the growth can be continuing, but I would expect that. (a7)

Concern about the political system was also an element that instilled distrust in economic cooperation with China. As was expressed by participant a21, a renowned economic journalist in Australia:

I do think that people are worried about it, you know if you are a business person […] and you know we had a number of Australians thrown into jail in China and sort of left there without charge, so that makes people nervous I think. Again this is the level of distrust. So if we do this fantastic business with you, will I end up in jail? Of course some of the people have done the wrong thing, and that's probably the source of that, but to be in jail for months without trial as a foreigner, that's very hard for Australians to stomach. If you spoke to Blackmore's CEO, she would say nothing but superbly positive things, she loves China. Some of the businessmen benefit so much from their relationship with China, and Australia has benefited from it, Australia as a country has hugely benefitted from the relationship with China. But there is still a low level of scepticism and I think suspicion is too strong a word, maybe angst. (a21)

China's increasing presence in Australia was another factor that made them feel insecure about many things they used to be very familiar with.

Yes, there could be a lot more cooperation, but also a kind of nervousness around China buying our agricultural land which we were using to produce food, cattle ranches, ports, mines, and all that kind of thing. So China has changed the way it invests in Australia slightly. I do see that in Australia there would be a level of mistrust of China or maybe that's even too strong a word, it's not knowing whether we should be mistrustful, it's not knowing whether we can trust them to be a great trading partner and a friend, or are there other designs. (a21)

I am not sure if China offers to potential partners [an opportunity] to build cooperative relationships in two-way exchange. (a8)

However, participant a14, a scholar who regularly taught in China's top universities, was quite comfortable with Chinese economic operations. He analysed the concern, even hostility, towards China, as a bias and even jealousy.

Economically, the West tends to be very sceptical; they think their way of doing of economics is the best. And I think there's an amount of bias. [There's] another thing that's very difficult to deal with: I think it's a kind of jealousy. You see in the big picture, hundreds of years, what's happening now is that China is rising, the West may still be rising, but it's not rising as quickly as China, but the long-term trend is that the balance of power, the balance of economic forces is changing in China's favour and if that goes on and on and on, China will rise and the West will decline, and China will become No.1 and the West will become No2. So a lot of Westerners don't like that. It's not surprising, is it? If you are No.1, you don't want to be No.2. (a14)

The framing devices detected in 'economy frame' include exemplars, depictions and statistics (see Table 4.6).

Culture frame

Frames of Chinese culture in Australian public diplomacy elites' eyes reflected diversity because of the background differentiation of the participants. First, the profound and historical reputation is well known. For example, the most frequently used adjectives and phrases relating to Chinese culture included appealing, interesting, diverse, cultural treasure, fantastic and rich (a10, a12, a15, a20, a21, a9).

Beyond this impression, there was the multi-layered recognition in terms of both the access to and the nature of culture per se. Culture can be the physical artefacts, the behaviour and the tradition and values of a society. Participants' opinions have reflected some of these elements, respectively, because of their own experiences (see Table 4.7).

For many, culture meant delicious food and hospitable people:

Chinese food is charming; I have a very positive view on that. (a7)

One of the things I always enjoy about, my interest in Chinese things is that I can travel any part of the world and could meet people with shared interests about China. In Europe, US, etc., I can go to the museum see the Chinese architecture; I can go to a town and eat at a Chinese restaurant. These are the great resources of Chinese soft power. (a8)

China's culture has an attractive part, I guess, I travel a lot in the country, Chinese people are very friendly, very hospitable. (a5)

For participants a21, a5 and a2, culture meant the historical and philosophical heritage:

I have to say I don't know enough about Chinese culture but in the past millennium it has been a fantastically rich culture. Perhaps that [became] subdued a bit in the past hundreds of years and now I see it's coming out so I am a supporter of that. (a21)

Table 4.6 Economy frame

	Theme	Position	Devices		
			Exemplars	Depictions	Statistics
Economy frame	Huge achievement/ Bright prospect	Acceptance/ admiration	–	Second largest/Admiration	1.3 billion people/ Second largest
	Uncertain prospect	Suspicion	Job loss/Protest increase	Disappointing	2 million job losses
	Australian's concern about a rising China	Concern	Businessmen thrown in jail	Concern/Suspicion/Distrust/Angst	–

Table 4.7 Culture frame

	Theme	Position	Devices		
			Exemplars	Depiction	Comparisons
Culture frame	Attractive aspects	Positive	Food/ History	Appealing/Very positive view	–
	Multi-layers of cultural elements	Mixed	Behaviour – buying house with cash/ Tradition – family connection	Friendly, hospitable/Benefit a lot/ Strong/Fantastically rich	Hollywood
	Appreciated within multicultural background	Mutual	–	Has its charming aspects like every culture/Similar to many societies	US/Korea/Pacific islands
	Inefficiency in communication	Negative	Confucius Institute	Clearly not working	–

I think the most positive part of China is that China's culture and philosophy have been very strong in history, and Australia has a lot to benefit from bringing two different cultures and philosophies, ways of life together. I believe if you bring together two different ideas or two different cultures, it would be a great source of energy. (a2)

Some traditional values received positive comments, although they were different from the participants' own values and ethics, such as Chinese filial piety, the Chinese collectivist family and the Chinese work ethic.

I used to not like the fact that parents got to work and leave their children to their grandparents. But now I begin to think it is a nice thing because I think it is one way people get respect for the elderly. (a4)

For participant a3, a third-generation immigrant with Chinese origins, culture was seen as the people's public behaviour, which was not necessarily a positive resource for China:

I think the issue with its culture, is behaviour, it's how people behave in business, how they behave with wealth, how they behave towards other people. I think that Chinese people have […], their economy has changed quite quickly for some people and I think that because they used to have been struggling, now they've got money, they don't know how to behave like countries that have had wealth for many years. So I don't think it's a matter of [whether] culture is good or bad; it's about behaviour, behaving ethically in business; behaving in a way that is authentic and in line with people they are cooperating with. Sometimes I don't think that Chinese people would do that, maybe that's the aspect of their culture that impedes it, like saving face and all those sorts of things. (a3)

Participant a7's observation echoed the comment he heard from friends of the bizarre behaviour of Chinese people, such as they buy houses with one million dollars in cash.

One striking feature in the context of the 'culture frame' was that Australia was seen as a multicultural country. In addition, it had intrinsic connections with Western countries. As a result, Chinese culture might not have been viewed as being as unique as many Chinese might have expected.

We are so dominated by American culture; since the 1950s when television came and Australia saw every bit of American popular culture. They have the same sort of Western democratic kind of tradition. (a21)

So I think Australia has an enormous advantage (to integrating different cultures) because where we are in the world, our neighbours are the Pacific islands, New Guinea,

Indonesia, South East Asia, China, Japan, Korea, India, all these different friends have intellectual traditions and we are in the middle of that, very exciting. (a2)

Various parts of Chinese culture are very similar to [those of] other countries, like the importance of family values. I think these values are embedded in other countries as well. But I think the general cultural norms of Chinese society are similar to many societies. (a3)

Like any culture, it has its charming aspects – like every culture. (a9)

China has been promoting its culture through various channels, including organisations like the Confucius Institute. But to some participants, these were not efficient in getting people to know about China's culture, and, thus, there was still a demand for learning more.

[Cultural diplomacy] – It's clearly not working. If the Chinese government brings a song and dance group to perform here, almost all people who go are Chinese. I personally have no problem with organisations like the Confucius Institute. The problems with it in my opinion are not a problem of the Chinese, they are the fault of business bodies who know nothing, very often, or some Chinese who have their own interests. What do they do? They teach Tai Chi, fan dancing, teach people how to make Jiaozi etc., but I am going to say if they make any popular academic cultural lectures, like Chinese Science and Technology History or about the poet Tao Yuanming, and other topics [...] there are hundreds of thousands of subjects, that would be more attractive. (a6)

To tell you the truth, if there is a dance troupe visiting the Opera House from China, I don't rush to see it, because maybe I don't understand that well enough so I don't see if I enjoy it much, but I probably should go and have a look, as my cultural knowledge, I would say, is limited. But the impression is it is also coming along but perhaps China has encouraged from national point of view, business and investment more than they have culture. They really should increase their presence. (a21)

Political system frame: Diversified

Frames on China's political system were also diversified in the Australian public diplomacy elites' eyes. Being used to the democratic system, China's political system was definitely not considered by them to be an attractive one that could be an exemplar. But a certain degree of acceptance existed among some of the elites because of the current dilemma facing Western democracies and discouragement from the countries struggling towards democratisation.

I believe in democracy, but if you look around the world, it's very difficult to say you must have the same political system everywhere. But it's also very difficult to say that democracy works very well everywhere. I'll just make 2 points on this: if you look at Arab Spring that began in 2011, it is run by people loving democracy, but look at the result, and it's terrible. In Tunisia, it is fine; but look at Egypt, Libya, and Yemen. The other point, if you look at the West, which loves democracy for example, in Australia, it, is a good place to live; I don't think our political system is very good. It is terrible the way all the leaders have been thrown out. Moreover, they've done surveys, and the young people don't think democracy is very good. But in China, many people say they like their system very much. It might be because they don't say otherwise because of the supervision, that maybe true, but I do think some people like their system. Our system is a good system, but I don't think it is the best. I think some people, like the Americans, tend to say our system is good, yours are wrong, so you should follow us, they often do that. But it is not necessarily true. (a14)

I am not sure democracy is the best choice. In US democracy, most people don't vote. Look at our democracy; we have had five Prime Ministers in how many [seven] years, so it's a different way [with its own problems]; the proposal of the new airport and the train line, it takes forever. (a4)

Almost everybody says the system is very bad; the worse thing is they've got no alternative. I don't think the system here is quite good. Look at Brexit, Trump, France, every system has its own problems. The good thing here is that Australia is a rich country and children are going to do what they want, you have personally freedom. But now in China your generation has so much personal freedom compared with your parents. What ordinary people are talking is about corruption, no so much about communism. (a6)

Some found legitimacy in the Chinese political system to arise from the demands of the country's immense size and complex situation, although this was not for some to admit.

[Is the political system suitable for the situation?][...] there is probably something true in that, it is such a large country, one that would be very hard to govern in a fragmented way. (a15)

I moderately agree that China's current system is suitable to the situation. It's developing. A lot of people [in China] don't have the knowledge to run [affairs] in a democratic way. Like in stock market, people buy stocks according to the person who are standing next to them. You got government structures to move them along, but you have a large population who don't understand, only small population who do understand. So I think China may need things that are very tightly structured until the economy increases and you've got most people [being] rich. (a27)

It's a big nation, it's gone through some big battles politically and historically, and it's very hard to drive intensive economic progress and intensive social change particularly the growth of all those new big cities without a government that can just be totally focused, so I can understand that most people in China think the current political system is suitable to the country. It's made impressive outcomes. (a7)

China's political system can be a positive resource, we are seeing in the West now the increase in protectionism and insularity, people are looking in and want to exclude the others and the vision in politics makes it very difficult for the political class to do what they believe in the best interest of their country. But in China where political opposition is not a problem, so favourably, the opportunity for the political class to carry out positive reforms is very considerable. The problem is it can also be negative. This is the problem at the moment. So I say that it's in balance. But there are tremendous potentials there for soft power. (a8)

I don't have a strong view that [it] is not suitable. Managing 1.4 billion people is always going to be a difficult job. (a9)

There are so many people. I used to be dogmatic about those sorts of things – freedom of speech is always No.1, but when you look at it from the Chinese point of view, you can understand the speech controls, in order to achieve economically. (a7)

There were doubts about the one-party system in which the concentration of power may lead to its misuse, the potential of decision-making mistakes or the overreaching of power in areas such as the economy, where according to one participant's liberal belief, the market always has the best solution. This doubt extends its shadow on to perceptions of China's ability to play significant roles on the international stage. Significant concerns about the political system were also seen to reside in the individual rights issues often found in specific cases under the communist system.

My view is that to have a communist system, we [need to] know we saw the sins the communism system commits, not necessarily in China. (a21)

I think China has more problems with putting those in prison for what they believe. But things probably have to change because of the internet; technology; people are travelling; people are getting to know what it is like overseas; people are getting wealthier; when people get wealthier, they get more demanding and I guess systems have to change as well. But maybe that's Asian culture that has a different view of freedom. I think China emphasises economy before politics. (a4)

[If] China wants to become a global power, it has to become more responsible – treat its citizens with a little bit more respect, it has to have rule of law that is fair. I think with the middle class becoming richer, they will expect that from the government and the government will change, too. China will change; you can't have a wealthy middle class and not have that middle class expect more say and power. Perhaps it is like Singapore; Singaporeans are prepared to sacrifice some civil rights and democratic

freedoms for a stable and wealthy life. China will probably follow that model [rather]
than [the] Australian model. Probably it won't be a democracy like Australia, but a
democracy like Singapore might be possible. (a5)

From my perspective, what [makes me] uneasy is that people don't always have the
opportunities to be individuals. (a7)

The framing devices detected from the frames include exemplars, depiction and comparison (see Table 4.8).

It is worth mentioning that the starting point of both Chinese and Australian participants seems to be the comfort zone of their own familiar political environment. For the Chinese, radical change may not be a wise choice because democracies have their own problems, and evolutionary reform through continuous progress would be preferable. For the Australian side, the Chinese political system is a problematic one, no matter what improvements have been and will be made under the current system.

Science and technology frame

As for frames on other issues, the Australian frames on China's S&T were also multi-faceted and different in judgement based on participants' own experience or second-hand sources. For example, those who had direct experiences with Chinese mobile phones and high-speed trains were quite impressed with them:

Chinese technology in internet is becoming the best in the world; in many areas, they
surpass anywhere in the world, and are leading the world. (a10)

My impression with China's technology like high-speed trains is [that it is] efficient,
fast, and modern. (a12)

I am amazed at China's ability for rapid and at the same long-time development over
time; also the complexity and depth at telecommunications, like Huawei, Alibaba, and
other massive companies. (a7)

Participant a1 quoted the statistics to confirm China's achievement in S&T: China ranked second in S&T investment and third in innovation and lodgement of patents.

Participant a3 attributed the development of S&T to the large population and China's simplified procedures:

I think China's S&T may have a chance to be stronger due to the large size of
population. Another thing which I thought is fantastic, that is if you have an idea,
you can do it pretty quickly in China, because there isn't the sort of controls, [like]

Table 4.8 Political system frame

	Theme	Position	Devices		Comparisons
			Exemplars	**Depictions**	
Political system frame	Cautious acceptance	Acceptance	Economic development/ People's satisfaction	It is also very difficult to say that democracy works very well everywhere. But in China, many people say they like their system very much.	China's social stability vs. Arab Spring/ China's rapid speed vs. Australian prime minister swaps and public decision inefficiency
	Different level of suspicions	Concern/ Suspicion/ Angst	Centralisation of power/ Arrest of dissents and business person	Concern/Scepticism/Angst	China vs. Australia vs. Singapore on individual rights

say [in] a country like Australia. We have got to go through this authority, that authority. I think being able to do that, it actually allows people to practice creativity, innovation, etc. and I think with the large population, the way things are [easy] and how it is very easy just coming out with something new. I mean if you look at some of the technology entrepreneurs, some of the web entrepreneurs, etc., a lot of them are Chinese. And I think it's just not hampered by systems and processes and bureaucracy. I think actually that's a positive thing to yielding creativity and innovation. (a3)

Again, there were concerns in this area for the possible generation of soft power attractions. For example, participant a8 commented:

I am not sure how much trust [there is] in both directions for technology and information transfer. China certainly developed a space program, all of the other things and technology areas at very rapid rates. But I am not sure how much China offers to potential partners to build cooperative relationships in two way exchange. It seems that China is very keen to operate high-technology hacking facilities and intellectual espionage, these kinds of issues seem to be giving rise to potential conflict, it's not the way to building improved cooperation. (a8)

Framing devices detected in this frame include exemplars, depictions and statistics (see Table 4.9).

The Role of Media

The above framing analysis of public elites' framing of China on different aspects reveals quite different perceptions on each topic. These differences come partly from the difference in experiences and channels of China-related information. It is obvious that for those Australians who had experience with certain topics, the judgement came more from their experiences. For example, with people who have first-hand interactions with Chinese people or Chinese technologies, like high-speed trains or internet products, their narrative of relevant topics tends to be based on feelings. For those abstract topics or those individuals have no direct experience with China, their judgement always come from certain media. For example, high-technology espionage and the imprisonment of dissenters are stories often covered by Western media and at the same time are where the bias lies in Chinese eyes because of the highlights in these stories. Findings on the Chinese expectations of the media push, and the Australian participants' media usage habits, will be discussed in the following two sub-sections.

Table 4.9 Science and technology frame

	Theme	Position	Devices		Statistics
			Exemplars	Depictions	
	Acknowledgement of achievements	Positive	High-speed train/Huawei/Alibaba	Becoming best in the world/Leading the world	China ranks second in S&T investment, third in innovation and lodgement of patents
S&T frame	Different level of suspicions	Concerns/Suspicion	Intellectual espionage	Not sure how much trust in both directions	–

Chinese expectation on media push

This section begins with a discussion of interviews with the Chinese public diplomacy elites, especially journalists' views of Western media coverage of China and their corresponding expectations on China's international media push. As mentioned in the previous chapters, a biased perception by others, especially reflected in press coverage, is one of the most important reasons for China to develop its own international media. The public diplomacy elites' understanding on the issue will offer a channel to further understand the logic behind the state's international communication strategy. The interview results with the Chinese public diplomacy elites reveal a diversified understanding of the issue. For some elites, there were always certain unfavourable discourses from press coverage:

> There are always biased coverage of China in the Western media; it is obvious, especially on issues such as polity, human rights, freedom of speech and South China Sea. Sometimes, as media people, we feel very angry. For example, the 3.14 incident targeting ordinary citizens (the riots happened in Lhasa in 2008), was described by many Western media as heroic protests; CNN even used fake pictures. But we always cover terrorist attacks which happened in their countries, such as the Boston Marathon Bombing as terrorist attacks; never tried to justify the evil attacks on civilians. I am not saying we are perfect in all these issues; China has a lot of problems; with such a large population, so complicated a situation, China cannot solve all the problems at once; I think many Westerners just ignore the efforts we are making – the government is endeavouring, the people are endeavouring; a sound civil society is forming gradually. (c18)

> [Much negative reporting on China] is not just bias, but on purpose – to discredit. They are telling the world China is bad; China's overseas business activities are with no good intention. (c2)

> As a media worker, I think there is much biased coverage on China in Western media. For example, on the issue of RMB devaluation, they are unanimously against China and leave the impression that China will collapse soon. (c13)

> Even our undergraduate students can come to the conclusion through simple content analysis of the so called mainstream Western media coverage that they are discrediting China. (c19)

> The discourse context is unfair to China. There are many state-funded media outlets, BBC is one of them. When others entered the market, no one judged them on that; but when we enter the market, everyone is talking about state-funding, suddenly it became a problem. (c6)

> Sometimes the positive reporting is increasing, but at crucial moments, on the important political and diplomatic issues, the bias is still obvious. (c10)

Some participants viewed the non-objective media coverage as misunderstanding caused by cultural and ideological differences or sometimes the source of their information.

> *The judgement of other countries on China is always based on their own value out-look; it is not appropriate; the main reason may be the limitation of their information resource.* (c3)
>
> *No one is perfect. Sometimes the bias is caused by the difference in cultural background.* (c6)
>
> *Little reportage on China is objective. It is because the ideological intentions of others and the weakness of our communication power.* (c8)
>
> *Their people won't read it if they cover only good things. A US correspondent said, after he had lived in China over 30 years, he found out that the foreigners are not misunderstanding China, they just don't understand China.* (c33)

Some thought that the perception on China is close to what it is and found an explanation for the unfavourable coverage at the dissemination of information:

> *It [foreigners' perception on China] is close to objective, but there is some bias which is inevitable. Most information spreads through media; while one characteristic of media is that bad information travels faster.* (c10)
>
> *China in other countries' eyes may not be so amiable. Too many reports on the economic achievements may make others feel you are a threat.* (c4)
>
> *In general, I think the judgement is objective, but there are some communities who do not agree or appreciate the Chinese way of dealing with things.* (c10)
>
> *We couldn't tell our modern story well, the story of talents with international views. They are the main force pushing China's continuous development.* (c3)
>
> *In results of Western polls, China's image is falling. But the Chinese poll results see the rise of positive perceptions. It should be becoming better because the economy keeps growing and the country is more open politically.* (c10)

On the question of the role of media in soft power strategy, the following views were expressed:

> *Firstly, media could play certain roles in soft power. It could be a component of soft power strength as a tool of bridging over the understanding chasm through creating a more informed public and proliferation of stories responsibly told.* (c29 and a12)
>
> *We cannot calculate the proportion of the role media can play in promoting soft power of one state, but it does play certain roles when necessary. For example, when the US and UK were involved in wars and during the Cold War period, they had their*

international media playing roles. When they try to promote their values of democracy and freedom, they need international communication. (c7)

In the context of an unbalanced international public opinion, the role of international media for China was seen as more specific: to check the balance of information flow on China-related topics.

The bias on China's image is partly because negative things always make news when information is transmitted to other states. It is true for every state. Others' understanding of China depends significantly on their information source. But we don't have our own platform that can offer the source. (c3)

For others, the increasing demand for China-related information was seen as another motive for the media push with the aim of enhancing acceptance through deeper understanding:

The primary role of China's international media is letting the world accept us as who we are. We were not good at telling our stories. Of course, the increase of national strength is essential for the outside interest which is the chance of our media to be a good information source for the Chinese story. When China is becoming stronger, we suddenly find out that the outside world is curious to hear what role China is playing in international affairs, what is exactly happening in China. The topics in our program like social insurance, education, are talking about how bad they are; these are hot topics for the research bodies in top universities in the world. They want to discuss with us. So it is not we who are trying to tell China's story well, the truth is the world is interested in us. (c2)

One main task of our media is to provide explanations for the issues that cause negative judgements. We are not going to debate with others, but we should present China as a country like other countries. We should not be treated differently. (c4)

However, media's functions were seen to have their own boundaries. Media acted more as a projector of what is happening in a state and had its own mechanism. People-to-people interactions played a more significant role.

Media cannot shape the image of a state but it can reflect it. (c12)

Media is the channel to project soft power. But what is important is whether they are capable of telling stories. We have international media outlets. But the audience do not have to listen to you. You must learn to understand media use preference, their [Westerners'] discourse system and their narrative. We still lack the intercultural communication talents. (c2)

Media is only part of international communication. People-to-people interactions are more important. It is unrealistic to expect too much from media. (a12)

In the Chinese context, the expectations of media seemed to be more significant than just as a projector, especially for state-run media outlets like CCTV NEWS. According to a producer, it could be a broker in international affairs that can convey China's stance on world affairs.

We not only telling China's story. CCTV NEWS is acting more and more like a mediator in international affairs. For example, when others accuse China of not sharing responsibility in world affairs, we could tell the world what China has done. When examining issues like Middle East, we could ask 'who has caused the chaos today? Is there anyone who is fighting against terrorists seriously?' No! How to express these opinions on world affairs should be the mission of our international media outlets. (c2)

Australian framing of media

This sub-section reveals the Australian public diplomacy elite's views on media and their media use habit. For Australian participants, there were various information channels for getting China-related knowledge, and most were personal channels and Western media. Catching a glimpse of their media use habit and their views on the role of media can lay the ground for the understanding of the framing differentiation among the Chinese communicators, media and the target audiences in Australia. The findings in this sub-section are from the in-depth interviews with Australian public diplomacy elites.

As mentioned earlier in this chapter, the participants had different degrees of personal interactions with Chinese communities. Beyond that, media still played an important role in their acquisition of China-related information. Here, 'media' refers to not only traditional media like newspapers and television but also social media and other forms of information dissemination like newsletters. Table 4.10 provides details of media use habits of the participants.

Beyond the people-to-people interactions, Australian media were the major information sources with the widest audiences compared with the other channels listed here. The media from other Western countries, although not as prevalent as the Australian ones, enjoyed the highest level of audience loyalty and were characterised as reliable sources whenever they were mentioned by the participants. For the Chinese media, however, the words used by most participants were 'occasionally' or 'very occasionally', and they usually were not sure if they could be reliable sources. A couple of participants mentioned that they knew that the mission of CCTV NEWS was to spread the Chinese

Table 4.10 Channels for China-related information

Participants	Media for China-related information				
	P2P channel	Australian media	Other Western media	Chinese media	New media
A1	Business trip	*The Australian*/ABC	Economists	CCTV NEWS occasionally	Newsletters
A2	Study/Diplomatic exchanges	SCMP/SMH			Newsletters
A3	Friends/Work	ABC/SBS	BBC	Used to watch CCTV NEWS	Facebook
A4	Seminars/Friends	SMH/SBS	CNN		WeChat
A5	Travel	Western press, newspapers, mostly SMH			China-related accounts on Facebook
A6	Study/Teaching diplomatic exchanges	SMH	BBC	CCTV when visiting China	–
A7	Travel business partners	SMH	Economist/CNN	CCTV NEWS very occasionally	–
A8	Travel/Friends/Research/ Language class	SBS, ABC, SMH		Articles from Chinese newspapers/ Watch CCTV NEWS when travelling abroad/Used to watch CCTV in Australia	Internet
A9	Family/Friends	Music TV	BBC	China National Radio	Online TV shows/ Podcasts
A10	Friends/Chinese class teachers	–			–
A11	Travel/Family	SBS	Economist	TVB	Internet

(continued)

Table 4.10 (Cont.)

Participants	Media for China-related information				
	P2P channel	Australian media	Other Western media	Chinese media	New media
A12	Travel/Friends	SMH	–	A little bit of CCTV- NEWS	Youku
A13	Family/Friends	SMH/SBS	–	–	Baidu
A14	Travel/Teaching	ABC/SMH	–	CCTV occasionally	Internet/ WeChat
A15	Personal connection with Australian foreign correspondent in China	SMH	Economist/BBC	CCTV- NEWS when visiting China	–
A16	Friends and Family	ABC/SMH/SBS	CNN/Bloomberg	–	–
A17	Travel	ABC	–	–	Friends on WeChat, *Shanghaiist*
A18	Friends	–	Al Jazeera	–	Weibo
A19	Study	–	–	China Daily	–
A20	Study/Language class	SBS	–	A lot of Chinese movies/Series.	–
A21	Academics/Business people who do business with China.	SMH/*The Australian*	Bloomberg	Very occasionally watch CCTV NEWS	Internet
A22	Business visit/Talking with friends and family	SMH	Documentary	China Daily online occasionally	Internet

perspective. They were aware of the propagandist nature of CCTV NEWS; they accepted that, but what they wanted from it was a faithful rendition of the Chinese perspective.

There were a couple of trends discernible in the Australian participants' understanding of China's international media strategy. First of all, how to deal with China was viewed as a heated topic in Australian discourse. The underlying problem was how to evaluate China – as a friend or as a potential threat? One view advocated strengthening cooperation with China positing that Australia had failed to understand China, and one reason for that was Australian media's failure to present a true picture of China. Bob Carr, former Australian foreign minister, commented thus at a seminar:

> *[From] Australian media's coverage of China, I find out virtually nothing about the Chinese economy development [...] from reading the Australian media and [...] I didn't remember the last article that answer my curiosity about these aspects that are quite important in China.* (Australian Bureau of Statistics 2016)

Others expressed their expectation of viewing English-language news in media run by China in Australia.

> *I do think Chinese English language [news], both television and newspaper, should be more visible here or we should all use it more or interview the correspondents or [be] having them on their programs or to talk about the view from China.* (a20)

The need for some elites was to help Australia access multiple points of view.

> *When I visited China, I watched CCTV NEWS, I don't watch [it] here. I think it's a good thing and China should do it. I think our international media is too much dominated by the US; it's good to have other points of view. So it would be good if China could develop good quality, not just reporting on China but also reporting maybe on central Asia or South East Asia using their overseas correspondences. We will have more sources of information about what's going on in the world. I am sure they will cover China first but they could do more. They could cover, for example, China's projects in Africa, they could report on that. It will be interesting, too.* (a2)

However, demand was one thing, how satisfactory the audience would be with the media products was another. CCTV NEWS's constant improvement in appearance and content received positive feedback from some participants. However, there were also problems in the media content that Australian audiences were not familiar with. For example, participant a20 found that the Chinese media content may not be interesting enough for local audiences because the style was not colloquial. Another issue was getting used to the liberal media environment; the audiences were expecting an adversarial role vis-à-vis the government. Even soft criticism was rare in state media like CCTV NEWS. For example, for participant a8, a good programme format for current affairs was reported as a panel discussion with guests from opposite parties expressing opinions and then letting the audience make their own decisions. But he expressed that in his mind, because of the one-party system, this could not be possible in China's state media. Thus, doubts on state media's credibility arose:

> *CCTV has come a long way and now it's a modern-looking channel, but the issue is, is it believable, can it be trusted? The state media like RT, is called Putin's channel; but if you look BBC, it is never any Prime Minister's channel. It will give government a hard time if there is a problem. So I wonder what way it (CCTV NEWS) will take.* (a7)

To better understand audience views on CCTV NEWS, their general views on media as a whole could offer a triangulation. First, under the liberal system, media's established role was to challenge the authority. This was what the media should do in the eyes of both Australian journalists and audiences.

> *From a journalist's perspective, I don't get paid just to push government views in the West and in Australia; and I think you would know journalists are supposed to question government, question authority, question what's being done, that sort of thing.* (a21)

At the same time, it was revealed in the comments that liberal media in the West were suffering from a low level of trust:

> *Most information is incorrect; they are making news to appeal to audience, what they say is usually wrong.* (a10)

> *But I think Westerners are still quite used to the situation that media run everything down and say everything is terrible. Western media tend to be negative to everything, obsessively negative about everything.* (a14)

> *It is a kind of paradox, broadcasting in the West has the freedom to do whatever it likes within respected or certain lines, but they are biased. The only thing which is slightly balancing is if you've got different channels like CNN, ABC, MSNBC, etc., they are broadcasting a particular point of view and you've got Fox who presents an alternative view. I agree that they only value freedom but they are blind about ideology,*

they want America to project an ideology and they want the Americans to follow that ideology and that's in my opinion contrary to their best interests. (a1)

This chapter presented these findings under the following three parts: (1) the Chinese public diplomacy elites' framing of China; (2) the Australian public diplomacy elites' framing of China; and (3) the understanding by Chinese and Australian public diplomacy elites of the role of media as a tool for soft power promotion. These findings show that both Chinese and Australian public diplomacy elites understood China through their own cultural (in the broad sense) lenses, although a small number of people on each side held different opinions from their own group. The complexity of China was reflected in the views of both groups but with different focuses. For the Chinese side, the acceptance of the current situation and expectation of improvement were at the core of detected frames. Acknowledgement of achievements, acceptance of the current situation, a modicum of suspicion and a measure of angst were embedded in the Australian frames. For the latter, personal engagement was their most reliable source for information related to China, the second being Western media. Most of them had the experience of consuming Chinese media (mostly English-language ones) but were not sure about its reliability.

References

Chitty, Naren. 2007a. "Public Diplomacy: Developing Road Rules." *Submission to the Senate Foreign Affairs, Defence and Trade Committee Inquiry into the nature and conduct of Australia's public diplomacy http://www. aph. gov. au/senate/committee/fadt_ctte/completed_inquiries/2004–07/public_diplomacy/submissions/sub15. pdf2007.*

Chitty, Naren. 2007b. "Toward an inclusive public diplomacy in the world of fast capitalism and diasporas." Foreign Ministries: Adaptation to a Changing World.

Gamson, William A, and Andre Modigliani. 1989. "Media discourse and public opinion on nuclear power: A constructionist approach." *American journal of sociology*:1–37.

Goffman, Erving. 1974. *Frame analysis: an essay on the organization of experience.* Cambridge: Harvard University Press.

Li, Xiufang, and Naren Chitty. 2009. "Reframing national image: A methodological framework." *Conflict and Communication Online* 8 (2):1–11.

Wang, Jianwei. 2000. *Limited Adversaries: Post-Cold War Sino-American Mutual Images.* Oxford: Oxford University Press.

Chapter 5

BELT AND ROAD INITIATIVE IN THE FRAMING PROCESS

The previous chapter presented the findings of the frames by the Chinese and Australian public diplomacy elites and their views on the role of media in soft power strategy. These findings hopefully provide a parameter for understanding the way the Australian target audiences react to the media frames. To investigate the role CCTV NEWS plays in China's soft power strategy, this book uses China's BRI to examine how it is framed by communicators (the Chinese government), the media (CCTV NEWS) and the target audiences in Australia on these three contexts in the information flow.

BRI is known as the Silk Road Economic Belt and 21st Century Maritime Silk Road, China's newest development initiative and framework, which aims, in the official lexicon, to boost connectivity and cooperation among China and Eurasian countries. It was first proposed by China's president Xi Jinping in 2013. In March 2015, the guiding document *Vision and Actions on Jointly Building Silk Road Economic Belt and 21st-Century Maritime Silk Road (Vision and Action)* was co-issued by China's National Development and Reform Commission, the Ministry of Foreign Affairs and the Ministry of Commerce of the People's Republic of China with the authorisation of the State Council. Corresponding to the plan, two financial institutions, the AIIB and Silk Road Fund, were founded to support infrastructure constructions and businesses along the areas. In 2017, the first Belt and Road Forum for International Cooperation (BRFIC) held in Beijing drew 29 foreign heads of state and government and representatives from more than 130 countries and 70 international organisations. The Second BRFIC was held on 25–27 April 2019.

The proposal of BRI with a broad coverage of more than 60 countries in the corresponding areas has drawn great attention and debates on the initiative itself and its impact on responding areas among policy makers and academia around the globe (Wang 2015). The Chinese government has attached exceptional importance to the initiative since the notable pledge of $40 billion to the Silk Road Fund in late 2014 and the setting up in the same year of the Leading Group on the Construction of the Belt and Road[1] in 2015; a team consisting of top leaders serving under a vice premier, to oversee the implementation of the initiative; and the Asian Infrastructure Investment Bank. In addition to the institutional development, multiple means have been employed to promote the initiative. For example, an official website has been set up with data, news and information on policies, cooperation priorities, international cooperation and enterprises relevant to BRI (see Belt and Road Portal 2015). Special versions of major Chinese media outlet websites have been launched, such as at Xinhua News Agency, in multiple languages (see Xinhuanet 2016). With the conceptualisation of the head of the National Development and Reform Commission of China, this commission being where the initiative is centred, and under the co-supervision of the Office of the Leading Group on the Construction of the Belt and Road, the Publicity Department, CPC and the State Council Information Office, PRC, CCTV produced a four-episode documentary on the initiative in multiple languages. Also, seminars and workshops have been convened by government organisations and academics at various levels to interpret the initiative and discuss the achievements and difficulties. Its supporters posit that the initiative will create business opportunities and aids in needy economies. At the same time, criticisms and concerns have been expressed by some. For example, the initiative has been regarded as China's version of the (US) Marshall Plan with the aim of seeking dominance in the neighbouring area and challenge world order, and thus calls for prudence in decisions to embrace it (Tiezzi 2014; Wade 2016). While seeing potential economic potentials, many worry about the geopolitical and geo-security implications in the context of world power transformation (Chitty et al. 2018).

Three factors contribute to the selection of the BRI case:

1. It is a strategic complex, an Incipient Hegemon's Public Diplomacy Plexus (Chitty et al. 2018), which has the potential to increase China's influence through not only its economic approach but also involving economics, politics, cultural aspects and so on, and thus could arouse interest among relevant countries and sectors, which is a base for audience interest.
2. The initiative has drawn a lot of attention over the years and has triggered both positive and negative perceptions among different countries. This provides a perfect up-to-date case of frame formation regarding China-related topics.

---

1 The English title 'Leading Group' has been used in different ways over the years. Leading Group on the Construction of the Belt and Road is officially used on the official website of the initiative, which was set up in 2015. The usage is adopted here.

3. Media coverage on this topic will reflect the effectiveness of CCTV NEWS in spreading the Chinese voice as a state organ. It is first a comprehensive strategy in economic cooperation among the world: how the state media as the mouthpiece of the government frame reflects the mechanism of China's state-run international media in spreading the country's discourse as well as its effectiveness.

In this case study, the focus is on BRI in the communicative process from China's state framing of the initiative, the media framing of it and the target audiences' responsive framing. These three framings were collected from three sources: the government document about the initiative, relevant government interpretation reflected in *Vision and Action*, and media clips consisting of two 30-minute episodes of the weekly feature show *Closer to China with R. L. Kuhn*. The programme 'deals with the substantive, sophisticated and sensitive issues that China faces, primarily domestically but also internationally' with the aim to 'bring the true, complex story of China to the world through candid, intimate discussions with China's thought leaders and decision makers in all sectors'. The host, Robert Kuhn, is a China-based political/economical commentator and has worked with China's leaders and the Chinese government for over twenty years. He is widely known as the author of the biography of former Chinese president Jiang Zemin (CCTV 2014). These programmes were selected because they comprehensively projected BRI and provided a panorama through not only a detailed introduction to the initiative but also a discussion on the disputes and doubts. The videos were divided into 6- to 10-minute clips based on the themes and played to Australian target audiences. Most of the data were collected through in-depth interviews. During the interviews, the participants were shown one video clip ranging from seven to 10 minutes in length and then asked to talk about their impression of the content. The participants who were not available for face-to-face interviews were initially asked to go to a link to fill in some demographic information and their general interest in and impression of China, and then back to the page to choose at least one video and then leave their takeaway frames and their opinion on how well the content was framed.

BRI in State Framing

Vision and Action was released in March 2015, the very first state-level document that comprehensively introduced the background, working principles, framework, priorities, operational mechanisms and China's current engagement on BRI. The master document located the initiative in the context of complex and profound changes in the world: the lingering impact of the international financial crisis, the slow recovery of the world economy and uneven global development, the huge adjustments in the international trade and investment landscapes and rules for multilateral trade and investment, and the major developmental challenges facing many countries. As claimed in the document, BRI aims to promote cooperation among the countries along the BRI routes through policy coordination, facility connectivity, unimpeded trade, financial integration and people-to-people bonds.

Various discussions have been held around the world by academics, media and policymakers with different interpretations. Seeking economic dominance in the region by China is a widely echoed view. Concerns and cautiousness are usually blended with enthusiasm in the discussions. An investigation on the way the initiator and the recipients frame the issue could help in creating a better understanding of the initiative and the appeal it may have to different stakeholders. The framings were uncovered through the analysis of the state document *Vision and Action*. The focus was to identify the main frames, the function of the frames and the devices used.

The main purpose of *Vision and Action* is to explain to potential partners what the initiative is about and how it works. It also calls for action. As presented in Chapter 3, the frames consist of the defining elements, which are composed of themes and positions or functions and presenting elements that include a variety of framing devices. As a call-for-action plan, *Vision and Action* is undoubtedly focusing on the bright side of the initiative. In this regard, its position is obviously positive, so the functions are singled out in this part instead of the position. Five main frames have been identified in the document: the cooperation frame, the development frame, the rule-abiding frame, the open and mutual benefit frame, and the frame of China's role.

Cooperation frame

As indicated in Figure 5.1 below, 'cooperation' is the most frequently used word in the *Vision and Action* document. In the 6,000 or so Word document, the word 'cooperation' has been used 128 times and in almost every section.

The cooperation frame is the main thread through the whole document. It starts with the introduction of the Silk Road Spirit of peace and cooperation, openness and inclusiveness, mutual leaning and mutual benefit in the *Preface* of *Vision and Action*, and explains the necessity of carrying on the Silk Road Spirit at the time of complex international and regional situations. It describes the trend of the world as 'towards a multipolar world, economic globalisation, culture diversity and greater IT application', and, thus, working together on BRI is an ideal solution for the interests of the world community – reflecting the common ideals and pursuit of human societies:

Figure 5.1 The word frequency in *Vision and Action*

[…] encouraging the countries along the Belt and Road to achieve economic policy coordination and carry out broader and more in-depth regional cooperation of higher standards; and jointly creating an open, inclusive and balanced regional economic cooperation architecture that benefits all.

[…] and regional economic cooperation, strengthen exchanges and mutual learning between different civilizations, and promote world peace and development. It is a great undertaking that will benefit people around the world.

The Belt and Road Initiative is a systematic project, which should be jointly built through […]. (National Development and Reform Commission 2015)

Except for the ideal aspect, *Vision and Action* provides concrete details about cooperation in the initiative: the cooperation scope and the mechanism. In the document, the cooperation scope refers to two aspects: the scope of potential partners and the scope of working fields. As for the potential partners, as indicated in the title, they refer first to the countries along the Belt and Road route. However, there are also indications in the document that the targeting partners are not confined to the regions along the BRI:

The Initiative will enable China to further expand and deepen its opening-up, and to strengthen its mutually beneficial cooperation with countries in Asia, Europe and Africa and the rest of the world.

The Initiative is open for cooperation. It covers, but is not limited to, the area of the ancient Silk Road. It is open to all countries, and international and regional organizations for engagement [...].

[...] and the 'biggest common denominator' for cooperation so as to give full play to the wisdom and creativity, strengths and potentials of all parties.

The second aspect relates to fields of cooperation. It is usually viewed that infrastructure investment is a major dimension of the initiative. However, it is articulated in *Vision and Action* that the foci are on five areas: 'policy coordination', 'facility connectivity', 'unimpeded trade', 'financial integration' and 'people-to-people bond'. The whole proposal addresses not only the width but also the depth of the cooperation in each area. For example, in the facility connectivity section, the proposal mentions not only railway and port construction but also information and communication passageway construction:

We should build bilateral cross-border optical cable networks at a quicker pace, plan transcontinental submarine optical cable projects, and improve spatial (satellite) information passageways to expand information exchanges and cooperation.

Trade in the proposal means not only the exchange of goods but also the involvement of labour division and research and development.

We should improve the division of labour and distribution of industrial chains by encouraging the entire industrial chain and related industries to develop in concert; establish R&D, production and marketing systems; and improve industrial supporting capacity and the overall competitiveness of regional industries.

People-to-people bonds are seen as a way of assuring 'public support for the implementing the initiative'. Similarly, the proposal gets into specific details:

[...] carry forward the spirit of friendly cooperation of the Silk Road by promoting extensive cultural and academic exchanges, personnel exchanges and cooperation, media cooperation, youth and women exchanges and volunteer services [...].

Third, cooperation is proposed at multiple levels involving the government, political organs, corporations, students, research organisations and so on:

We should give full play to the bridging role of communication between political parties and parliaments, and promote friendly exchanges between legislative bodies, major political parties and political organisations of [...] We should carry out exchanges and cooperation among cities, [...] focus on promoting practical cooperation, particularly cultural and people-to-people exchanges, [....] We welcome the think tanks in the countries along the Belt and Road to jointly conduct research and hold forums.

We should strengthen cooperation with neighbouring countries on epidemic information sharing, the exchange of prevention and treatment technologies and the training of medical professionals, and improve our capability to jointly address public health emergencies.

We should send more students to each other's countries, and promote cooperation in jointly running schools.

The mechanism of cooperation is based on existing bilateral and multilateral mechanisms as well as kinds of international forums, exhibitions and festivals convened particularly for the initiative:

We should enhance the role of multilateral cooperation mechanisms; make full use of existing mechanisms such as the Shanghai Cooperation Organization (SCO), ASEAN Plus China (10+1), Asia-Pacific Economic Cooperation (APEC), Asia-Europe Meeting (ASEM), Asia Cooperation Dialogue (ACD) [...].

We should continue to encourage the constructive role of the international forums and exhibitions at regional and sub-regional levels hosted by countries along the Belt and Road [...].

We should support the local authorities and general public of countries [...] to explore the historical and cultural heritage of the Belt and Road, jointly hold investment, trade and cultural exchange activities [...].

The mechanism involves cooperation not only at the international level but also at the domestic level. In *Vision and Action*, the regions in each direction in China were allocated corresponding international areas according to their advantages, for example, Xinjiang with Central, South and West Asian countries; and Russia with Heilongjiang, Jilin, and Liaoning provinces.

Devices of exemplars, depictions and appeals to emotion have been used to articulate the theme (see Table 5.1). For example, the mention of the ancient Silk Road and Silk Road Spirit helps to explain the aspiration of the initiative and importance of communication and cooperation. The use of words such as 'jointly' and 'integrate' indicates the emphasis on the expectation for wide participation. With expressions like '[The silk spirit has] passed from generation to generation', 'promoted the progress of human civilisation',

Table 5.1 Cooperation frame

Theme	Function	Devices			
		Exemplars	Metaphors	Depictions	Appeal to emotion
Cooperation frame					
Cooperation is the need of the hour	Appealing	Silk Road Spirit	–	Benefit all/Jointly/Integrate	Progress of human civilisation/Historic and cultural heritage shared by all countries around the world/Common ideals and pursuit of human societies/Community of shared interests, destiny and responsibility
Cooperation scope	Informing	Asian Infrastructure Investment Bank/BRICS New Development Bank/Shanghai Cooperation Organization (SCO) financing institution / The Silk Road Fund / China-ASEAN Interbank Association /SCO Interbank Association	Biggest common denominator	Not limited to/Coordination/Connectivity/Integration	
Cooperation mechanism	Informing	Shanghai Cooperation Organization (SCO)/ASEAN Plus China (10+1)/Asia-Pacific Economic Cooperation (APEC)…	–	Bilateral/Multilateral/Leverage the strengths	–

'contributed greatly to the prosperity and development of the countries along the Silk Road', 'symbolising communication and cooperation between the East and the West', 'the *Silk Road* Spirit is a historic and cultural heritage shared by all countries around the world', 'coexist in peace', 'common prosperity', 'works to build a community of shared interests, destiny and responsibility' and so on, the emotional side of common memories and well-being is likely to be awakened in the target audiences and, in turn, may prompt action.

Development frame

Development is another key frame in the *Vision and Action* document. First, development is portrayed as one of the themes of common human society. The narrative places the initiative in the context of the development of mankind, the whole world and the countries in the region.

> *[…] making greater contributions to the peace and development of mankind.*
>
> *[…] will inject new positive energy into world peace and development.*

In addition to the conceptual connotation of development of mankind, development has been put in a more specific context – the development of specific fields and areas:

> *[…]exploration and development of coal, oil, gas, metal minerals and other conventional energy sources; advance cooperation in hydropower, nuclear power, wind power, solar power and other clean, renewable energy sources; and promote cooperation in the processing and conversion of energy and resources […]*
>
> *We should increase the openness of our service industry to each other to accelerate the development of regional service industries.*

Development of relations among the countries along the Silk Road is another dimension of development:

> *We should strengthen bilateral cooperation, and promote comprehensive development of […].*

Development is also revealed in the document as an approach to implementing BRI, where cooperation occurs and progress is made:

> *The connectivity projects of the Initiative will help align and coordinate the development strategies of the countries along the Belt and Road.*

Table 5.2 Development frame

	Theme	Function	Devices	
			Exemplars	Depictions
The development frame	Development in conception	Appealing	–	Peace and development of mankind
	Development in specific areas	Informing	Development of regional service industries	Comprehensive development of bilateral relations
	Development as an approach of BRI	Informing	Align and coordinate the development strategies	Diversified, independent, balanced and sustainable development

[…] and realise diversified, independent, balanced and sustainable development in these countries.

The conceptualisation theme in the development frame has the potential to appeal to audiences to join the initiative for the well-being of partners. The other two themes with specific information will help others learn about the details. The devices found in this frame include exemplars and depictions, listed with examples in Table 5.2.

Rule-abiding frame

Rules are an important factor in international cooperation. The way rules, norms and regulations are defined would indicate the approach of the initiator implementing the cooperation. The concerns regarding BRI in many countries are partially the suspicion of lawful performance. In *Vision and Action*, China defines the BRI within the framework of rules:

The Initiative follows market operation. It will abide by market rules and international norms […].

The Belt and Road Initiative is in line with the purposes and principles of the UN Charter. It upholds the Five Principles of Peaceful Coexistence […].

Countries along the Belt and Road should work to ensure that the WTO Trade Facilitation Agreement takes effect and is implemented.

Table 5.3 Rule-abiding frame

	Theme	Function	Devices	
			Exemplars	Depictions
Rule-abiding frame	Rules and norms in concept	Assuring	WTO Trade Facilitation Agreement	Abide by/Work to ensure ... is implemented
	Rules and regulations in specific area	Informing/ Appealing	Financial regulation	Comprehensive development of bilateral relations
	Establish rules and agreements during the cooperation	Informing/ Appealing	–	Protect the lawful rights and push forward negotiations

As in the development frame, rules and norms are not just mentioned in the conceptual sense but are also embedded in specific fields:

> *Countries along the Belt and Road should enhance customs cooperation [...] and mutual assistance in law enforcement [...].*
>
> *We should strengthen financial regulation cooperation, encourage the signing of MOUs on cooperation in bilateral financial regulation, and establish an efficient regulation coordination [...].*

The emphasis on rules is also reflected in the establishment of rules and agreements:

> *We should increase cross-border exchange and cooperation between credit investigation regulators, credit investigation institutions and credit-rating institutions.*
>
> *[W]e should speed up investment facilitation, eliminate investment barriers, and push forward negotiations on bilateral investment protection agreements and double taxation avoidance agreements to protect the lawful rights and interests of investors.*

The abstract theme in this frame has the function of assuring potential partners that China will abide by rules in the BRI. For the remaining two themes, on the one hand, the call for rules and agreements inform the audience of China's stance and, on the other hand, call for the action of all parties to work together to sustain a lawful environment in implementing BRI. The framing devices used include exemplars and depictions (See Table 5.3).

Open and mutual benefit frame

BRI is said to have been proposed under the background of China's further opening-up strategy and the open world in the official discourse. 'Open' indicates cooperation with other partners, and mutual benefit might be the most important factor that determines the enthusiasm of the potential partner's participation. *Vision and Action* sets the open and mutual benefit tone for the BRI:

> *The Belt and Road Initiative is a way for win-win cooperation that promotes common development and prosperity [...] by enhancing mutual understanding and trust, and strengthening all-round exchanges.*
>
> *Countries should work in concert and move towards the objectives of mutual benefit and common security.*

According to the document, the potential benefit lies in the creation of a cooperative environment for mutual benefit among neighbours by striving to improve investment and trade facilities, removing barriers in the region and taking advantage of complementary resources and economic.

Mutual benefit is also elaborated on within specific contexts such as investment, information technology, healthcare and so on. It is not simply a trading interaction; it is also the mutual building of certain mechanisms and the mutual recognitions of rules.

> *We should expand mutual investment areas [...].*
>
> *We should promote in-depth cooperation with other countries along the Belt and Road in new-generation information technology [...].*
>
> *Countries along the Belt and Road should enhance customs cooperation such as information exchange [...].*

In *Vision and Action*, mutual benefit is designed between China's domestic regions and the neighbouring countries, for example, the proposed cross-border trade and tourism and culture cooperation between the Tibet Autonomous Region and neighbouring countries like Nepal, and the 'regional interaction and cooperation and industrial concentration' around the inland provinces.

The tone of open and mutual benefit might have the function of appealing to potential partners to join the initiative. The other two frames have the function of informing the audience of China's intentions and thus might also have the effect of appealing. The framing devices are mainly exemplars and depictions, with the examples listed in Table 5.4.

Table 5.4 Open and mutual benefit frame

	Theme	Function	Devices	
			Exemplars	**Depictions**
	The tone of open and mutual benefit	Appealing	–	Win-win/Work in concert
	Open and mutual benefit in specific areas	Informing/ Appealing	Mutual investment areas	Mutual recognition of regulations and mutual assistance in law enforcement
Open and mutual benefit frame	Mutual benefit connecting domestic and international regions	Informing/ Appealing	Border trade and tourism and culture cooperation between Tibet Autonomous Region and the neighbouring countries	Make use of the advantages

Role of China frame

What role China will promise to play is an important question regarding its role and intention in BRI. Most people with concerns think that it is China's ambition to dominate economically in the Silk Road regions. An investigation on how China defines its own role in the master document of *Vision and Action* will help understand its position in the initiative.

Vision and Action repeatedly mentions China's intention of further opening up and promoting cooperation:

> *China's economy is closely connected with the world economy. China will stay committed to the basic policy of opening up [...].*
>
> *China will fully leverage the comparative advantages of its various regions, [...] and comprehensively improve the openness of the Chinese economy.*

Also, as the initiator, efforts have been made to promote the initiative from the highest level of leadership, such as the state visits by the president and premier:

President Xi Jinping and Premier Li Keqiang have visited over 20 countries, attended the Dialogue on Strengthening Connectivity Partnership [...].

In the document, China also positions itself as a cooperator who hopes to work together with other countries along the Silk Road in planning and implementing BRI:

China will join other countries along the Belt and Road to substantiate and improve the content and mode of the Belt and Road cooperation [...].

China will work with countries along the Belt and Road to carry out joint research, [...] so that they will gain a better understanding and recognition of the contents, objectives and tasks of the Belt and Road Initiative.

China will work with countries along the Belt and Road to steadily advance demonstration projects [...].

As always, China continues to define itself as a country that takes responsibilities:

China is committed to shouldering more responsibilities and obligations within its capabilities, and making greater contributions to the peace and development of mankind.

China provides 10,000 government scholarships to countries along the Belt and Road every year.

During the framing, the first theme provides the basic information about China's position as an initiator. The cooperator and responsibility-sharer themes, to a certain extent, provide assurance to potential partners about its role. The framing devices used here include exemplars, depictions and sponsors. The examples are listed in Table 5.5.

Framing BRI in CCTV NEWS

The previous section presented China's framing on BRI. As an official document, *Vision and Action* showcases the bright side of the initiative. In reality, however, there are other perspectives, such as suspicions and concerns. In this section, framing of BRI in two episodes of a news magazine programme in CCTV NEWS's *Closer to China with R. L. Kuhn* will be analysed. Although CCTV NEWS is a state-owned medium, the programmes did provide coverage of a wide range of topics around BRI. Together with *Vision and Action*, these programmes can be viewed as part of Chinese framing of the initiative directed at the world audience.

Table 5.5 Role of China frame

	Theme	Function	Devices		
			Exemplars	**Depictions**	**Sponsors**
	The initiator of opening up and cooperation	Informing	–	Further expand and deepen its opening up	President Xi Jinping and Premier Li Keqiang
Role of China frame	The cooperator	Assurance	Mutual investment areas	Join other countries/Work with countries/ Jointly	–
	The responsibility sharer	Assurance	China provides 10,000 government scholarships	shouldering more responsibilities	–

The two programmes selected here are in-depth discussions with face-to-face interviews as the main format. Different from the state document, television programmes have their own framing techniques. For example, apart from the syntax elements, the ways of introducing the topics, visual devices and structures, and the sponsors representing certain viewpoints are widely used for the purpose of attracting audiences. Differently from the individual framing (in which framing devices are mostly a subconscious happening), the framing devices in television programmes might be used with the intention of presenting certain points of view instead of others. In the analysis of the programmes, except for the identification of the themes and the position/ function, attention will also be paid to the elements mentioned above. Again, in order to get an all-round picture, an inductive approach was be used to identify as many frames as possible.

Professionalism as an index of media culture

As shown in the previous chapter, being familiar with the liberal media, Australian public diplomacy elites are suspicious of CCTV NEWS's reliability as an information source – although they also have concerns about Western media's credibility issues (see the sub-section 'Australian framing of media' in Chapter 4). With the expansion in other countries and the employment of local staff, CCTV NEWS is increasingly becoming a transnational organisation

Table 5.6 Interviewees during observation

Interviewee	Background	Code
Chinese 1	Executive with both Chinese and Western training in journalistic practice	C1
Chinese 2	Executive with Chinese training in journalistic practice	C2
Chinese 3	Programme producer	C3
Chinese 4	Programme coordinator	C4
Chinese5	Official at Publicity Department	C5
Chinese 6	Official at SAPPRFT	C6
Western staffer 1	Western training and journalistic practice	W1
Western staffer 2	Western training and journalistic practice	W2
Western staffer 3	Western training and journalistic practice	W3
Western staffer 4	Western training and journalistic practice	W4
Western staffer 5	Western training outside journalism and non-journalistic practice	W5

that accommodates media workers who exercise mobility across borders and face different professional-value contexts. This sub-section presents findings of the media workers' understanding of their organisation, CCTV NEWS, based on data through observations of their editorial meetings in Beijing from mid-December 2015 to mid-January 2016, in Washington, DC, of CCTV America in March 2016 and interviews with two officials from the watchdogs of CCTV (the Publicity Department of the CPC and the State Administration of Press, Publication, Radio, Film and Television of the People's Republic of China) and four Chinese and five Western staff during the course of observation research. Reporting of interview results is presented below. C refers to Chinese and W to Western staff, and each interviewee is identified with a letter and number (Table 5.6).

Structurally, at the time of research, CCTV NEWS consisted of three parts: the headquarters in Beijing with about five hundred Chinese staff and sixty foreign staff; CCTV America in Washington, DC, with eight Chinese, who are mainly in management positions, and more than 120 local staff who are in charge of the daily operation of news-making for the English-language programmes; and CCTV Africa in Nairobi, with about 150 staff in total and a similar proportion of Chinese and local staff to that of CCTV America. By March 2016 when the field research ended, the Beijing head-quarters provided 10 hours of first-time broadcast programmes, CCTV America five hours (expected increase) and CCTV Africa two hours for the whole day's programme. The research was conducted mainly in Beijing and Washington, DC. In CCTV America, as in CCTV Africa, the operational structures are relatively flat with the director, two editorial managers who are Chinese and the main production teams made up of local staff with, on average, one Chinese staff member in each team. The local staff are the main force behind programme production, and the Chinese make sure that China-related information is accurate and that certain sensitive topics will not hurt China's interest. For example, in early March 2016, before the 'two sessions' conferences in China, when the research was conducted at Washington, DC, the local production editor, during the editorial planning meeting, mentioned leaving a large time slot for the coverage of 'two sessions', but the manager decided it was too early because the conferences would not start until the week after, and that week some warm-up coverage was enough. The mixture of Chinese and foreign staff creates a new sort of media professional culture that may be different from both Chinese and Western cultures in the traditional sense. The understanding of their own perceptions of their values helps us to understand the operational principles which in turn determine the media content. The background factors, the organisational and professional perceptions of the staff will be presented bellow as the clues.

In CCTV NEWS, the hiring of Western staff is a way to open markets in the West, and their expertise in Western journalism is the bargaining chip Western staff members have with which to negotiate their autonomy of practice. There are comments made by CCTV America's Jim Spellman who said in a TV interview with his former employer, CNN, that no one tells staff directly what to do or what not to do. Also, 'censorship' (at least in effect) exists in different forms. In the West, the pressure comes from ratings, while in CCTV NEWS, it may come from the consideration of national interests (C1, C2 and W3). Participants from supervising organisations mentioned censorship as a guide not on a daily basis (C5 and C6). But without any doubt, on certain sensitive issues that may influence national interest or social stability, the watchdogs have the ultimate say over the media organisation. This kind of power has the absolute hegemonic role that prevents the media workers from crossing the line.

Another background factor is that the entry of CCTV NEWS into certain markets, like the United States, was in the context of a slump for Western media with many lay-offs (C1). As one participant said, 'It is just a job' (W5). Their willingness to work with the network comes after considering the existence of certain taboos – that are derived from national interests (C1, C2 and C3).

Regarding journalistic values in China, it should be repeated that one of the missions of media in China is to facilitate governance for a stable environment for development. It is not only the doctrine of a socialist system but also, as one participant commented, the historical tradition. From the earliest form of journalism in ancient times, its function has been to facilitate social governance (C5). This is echoed in the earlier mention that journalists in certain Chinese contexts have the obligation to take on the social responsibilities of traditional intellectuals. Participant W5 observed that Chinese journalists feel a certain sense of privilege for working for the organisation within the system. Of course, it is under the ideal normative context. In reality, the hierarchy within the system may make it very difficult, especially for young people, to secure the position and at the same time find comfort in the context of the collision of professional values and the ever-increasing pressures of everyday life. This makes it hard, even in Beijing, to find enough talent adept at English-language media practice. That is also one of the reasons for the recruitment of foreign staff.

> *In Beijing, we are short of professional staff. Many of our new staff were young graduates in English language, and have no media experience.* (C2)

Shortage of qualified guests is another driving factor behind the employing of local staff, as C3 and C2 mentioned:

> *When the world needs us to tell Chinese stories well, you will find out that we have to rely on the foreigners. In China, almost all the top talents in every field are in Beijing, but in Beijing, there are only 100 people who are qualified to be our guests [in terms of language and performance on TV].* (C3)
>
> *In China, we don't have many experts who can speak good English; the officials don't want to speak to media. It is very hard for us to invite big figures to our studio except for some scholars.* (C2)

Also, the channel is under rapid development. Participant W5 shared a 'reminder' that she received more than a decade ago, which listed 'major hot buttons' associated with the usage of certain terms. For instance, 'the Chinese mainland' must not be referred to as 'Mainland China'. But as participant W1 said, with live broadcasting, correspondents did sometimes lapse into using 'Mainland China' and no one noticed the breach of rules. Furthermore, in relation to the strategy of offering Chinese perspectives to the world, foreign staff mainly focus on affairs in prescribed areas; there is little chance to cross the rhetorical line set to protect Chinese interests.

The combination of management staff from China and the United States and the international expertise at CCTV America make the channel more competitive in the broadcaster market than a purely monocultural one. The internationalisation of broadcasting staff follows the early CNN model. Ma Jing, the director general of CCTV America described its launch as a natural development for CCTV. She attributed the expansion of CCTV into Washington, DC, to the saturation of the domestic market with 42 channels in China in an interview with Public Broadcasting Service (PBS) (PBS 2012).

The senior consultant of CCTV America, Jim Laurie, expressed a view similar to that of the Chinese executives in an interview, indicating that as a big power, China wants to follow suit the international media strategies of BBC and CNN (Folkenflik 2013).

Both Chinese executives and Western employees consent that the motivation behind the foundation of CCTV America is unbalanced news coverage about China – in terms of both volume and agenda, even in the principal media organisations that enjoy a huge professional reputation. Participant W2 thinks that CCTV NEWS provides audiences interested in China and international relations with responsible and credible television programmes. Participant C2 views the move of CCTV NEWS as filling the gap of an unuttered Chinese voice in the international news market.

According to the participants, the pressure of ratings has resulted in a shrinking of international reporting, even among the international channels. But with the growth of China's role in the world, the demand for information and stories is growing accordingly. CCTV NEWS can fill the void in this sense. With the increasing status of China on the world stage, there is an increase in the demand for Chinese stories globally. However, international reporting has been shrinking globally because of financial pressures based on dependence on ratings. CCTV America can offer China focused content in voluminous amounts unlike other media outlets, say *The Wall Street Journal* (participant W3).

However, there is a concern about the lack of audience research in the eyes of some participants: CCTV NEWS operates under the overall CCTV structure and audience research is under a department external to CCTV NEWS. Also, audience research takes place under budget constraints. Participant W2 admitted that although they sense the demand for China-related information, the channel seldom undertakes the kind of comprehensive audience research that many other international broadcasters usually undertake. This is because audience surveys are under the budget control of the overall CCTV structure.

In addition to the quantitative deficit in China-related news in the West, most participants agree that an agenda slant is very obvious in news produced by Western broadcasters. Cases demonstrate that in the coverage of international affairs, national interest and nationalism are at the forefront even in reputed media organisations. For example, participant W2 mentioned in the interview that 'what Western media cover [about China] is partial with the emphasis on human rights, conflicts; it is because the perceptions, of what journalism is, are different'. Participant W4 expressed a similar view.

He observed that in a case like the South China Sea, US media such as the *Washington Post* always cite US sources. But CCTV America will include voices from China as well. This is what participant W3 called stories 'inclusive of the Chinese agenda'.

Another factor that provides a rationale for Western broadcasting practitioners working for CCTV NEWS is the deterioration of professional standards in the Western news industry because of the market pressure (W3 and W4). Participant W4 noted that there is a lot of 'low cal news but very little appetite for important [high cal] news in Western media. CCTV America, unfettered by ratings pressure, is able to cover 'stories with meaning'.

Professional norms and self-perception of the role of a journalist is another factor that may have an impact. As previously mentioned, in spite of the mouthpiece identity of Chinese media, professionalism is a hot topic in media practice and scholarly debates in China. The interview results in this project show that the understanding of professionalism among CCTV NEWS staff has both broad and narrow aspects. For example, participant W1 viewed that professionalism is associated with how a channel looks at, sets and presents a programme.

It could be regarded as one of the contributions of the Western employees with the new look and operational style. The Western employees and display formats become signs of professionalism. 'It's changing very quickly,' former anchor Yin said in an interview. 'I can tell you even from the time that we came on-board here to where we are today, we've changed a lot. We're covering stories from sometimes very controversial angles' (Folkenflik 2013).

Both interviewees, who were Chinese management staff, emphasised the importance of objectivity, balance and fairness in their operational norms although they admitted that no broadcaster applied 100 per cent of the norms. Participant C1 listed objectivity, balance, fairness and diversity as most important elements in their perception of professionalism. Participant C2 stated that in the coverage of issues like Syria they were doing well, in speaking of balance, by presenting the story of both the government and the opposition.

While being aware of the doubts about whether Chinese media adhere to professional values, Western staff working for CCTV NEWS were also aware of the limitations in professional practice in Western media. For example, participant W3 read about shortcuts taken by many Western broadcasters. To participant W5, bias exists in every media; the difference is just a matter of degree.

Another professional value emphasised by CCTV NEWS is inclusivity. It is the journalists' view, the Chinese perspective to offer a unique character to the channel that is different from that of Western broadcasters (participant

W4). In addition to a Chinese perspective, they emphasise solidarity with developing countries.

One participant noted that their perception of a media organisation is determined by people's perception of journalism. In the West, raising doubts, challenging authority and covering conflict are the main responsibilities of journalism. One thing is clear among the participants in this project: they perceive CCTV NEWS and the practitioners themselves as information disseminators aiming to fill the gap of the stories and voices of China and other developing countries which are usually ignored or overlooked in international broadcasting market.

Framing BRI in Closer to China

Closer to China with R. L. Kuhn is a weekly news magazine co-produced by CCTV NEWS and the Kuhn Foundation, an organisation, described, in its own words, as focusing on the dissemination of understanding in science and philosophy, which supports cultural endeavours and promotes good relations between the United States and China. The Kuhn Foundation is the producer of the TV series *Closer to Truth* broadcast on the US PBS. According to the official webpage of the programme, *Closer to China* aims to reveal China-related matters through in-depth discussions with China's decision makers and opinion leaders.

The selected episodes 'Closer to China: "One Belt One Road" I – Economic Development and Cooperation' and 'Closer to China: "One Belt One Road" II – International Affairs and Diplomacy' were broadcast on 22 March and 29 March 2015, respectively. These episodes focused on the detailed explanation of BRI and the challenges facing it. As a news magazine, most of the content is presented through interviews with Chinese officials and experts or stakeholders in relevant areas both from China and other countries.

The analysis of this book focuses mainly on frames of the content with the facilitation of device identification. Figures 5.2 and 5.3 showcase the timeline of the programme and the general topics covered:

This part reveals the frames demonstrated in the programme through the various sponsors. The topics are framed in the two main aspects around BRI: explaining it and deconstructing concerns associated with it.

Defining BRI frame

At the beginning of the programme, the host introduced BRI as a 'strategic initiative' and a 'foreign policy priority', and raised the question of why it was proposed. The first interviewee, a vice-ministerial-level official then in

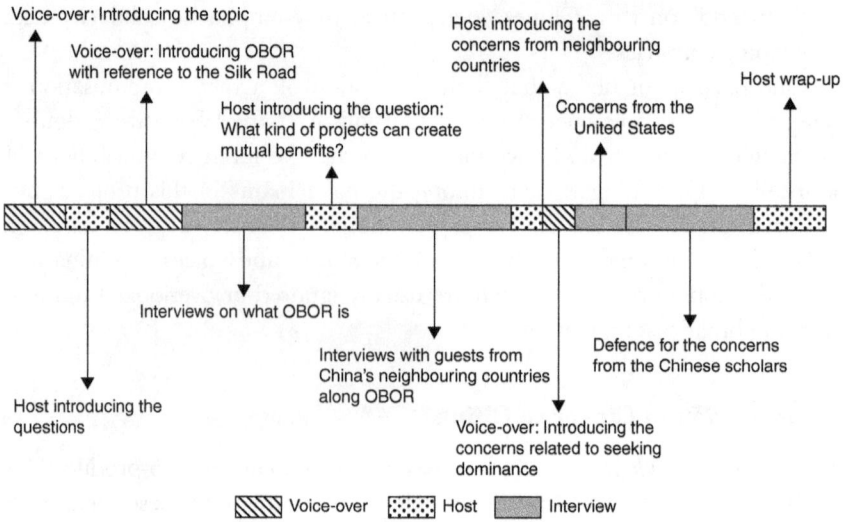

Figure 5.2 Timeline of the programme and the topics in *Closer to China I*

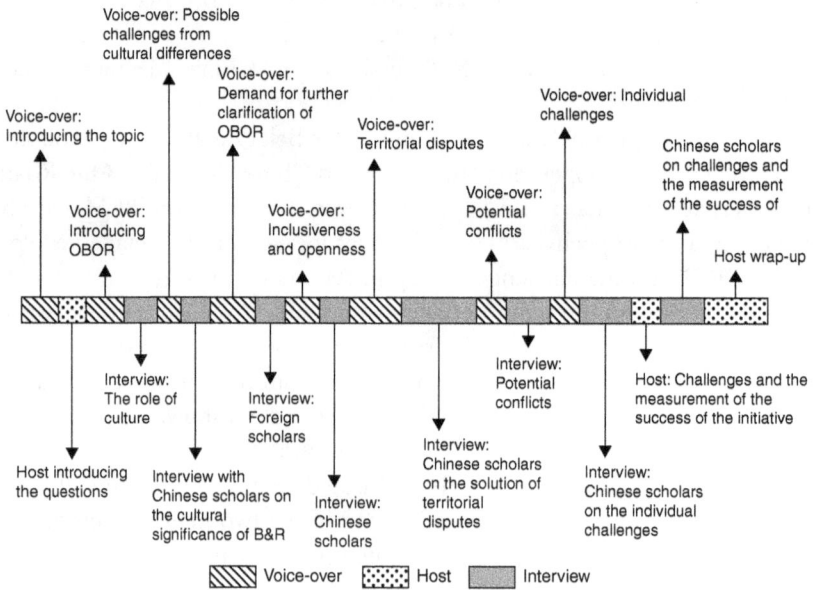

Figure 5.3 Timeline of the programme and the topics in *Closer to China II*

charge of the China International Publishing Group, an organisation with the mission of introducing China to foreign countries through publications and websites, stated that 'the strategic relevance, regional relevance and the overall relevance are extensive'. He believed that the international response to it 'is generally positive, because everybody knows that we are entering into a new era, or rather, the new normal of economic and social development' and to solve the problems by regional cooperation is a widely shared agreement. He said that the proactive posture reflected in BRI is a way to show China's consciousness of responsibilities as an economic power:

> *Now China's economy has grown this high with, enormous economic clout and China has become one of the biggest international traders and is the biggest trading partner for 120 countries. [...] will have to be conscious of its responsibilities as an economic power [...] to meet the global community's expectations.* (Zhou Mingwei, President of China International Publishing Group)

The 'positive response' was presented through three other interviewees, from China's neighbouring countries Kyrgyzstan and Pakistan – from the business, government and media sectors – and a businessman from a Saudi Arabian oil company who thought BRI was a mutual, beneficial, open-minded and cooperative initiative in a new era. One interviewee compared China's investment with the United States and Russia and concluded that China is the most active investor for their country. Also, China's development was seen as an inspiring factor for the developing countries to follow.

> *It is a more positive and beneficial way [of doing business] with China.* (Emil Umetaliev, Businessman, former minister of economy, Kyrgyzstan)
>
> *China's investment is better for Kyrgyzstan. US aid through grants and donor money not investments, Russia is a big investor in energy sectors. The most active investor is China.* (Zhyldyz Satieva, Ministry of Economy)
>
> *BRI is a very open-minded concept [...] and it shows the broad mindedness to share the hard-earned fruits of development of China with the other developing countries of the World. Pakistan, being a developing country looking forward to benefiting from it in a win-win situation.* (*Daily Mail International*, Pakistan: Babar Amin)

But some observers from other relevant countries thought more clarification on the initiative was needed – although it interests other countries – because of the generalness of the concept, its freshness and its non-specific reference to rules.

Even the Chines themselves not really define the concept. It's a quite general concept. (Fraser Mac Taggart Cameron, EU-ASIA CENTER, UK)

I don't know yet [what BRI is] [...] because I think that this can be a very important starting point for new politics but should not be a political mean to exercise power. (Patrizia Catiori, L'Orientale University of Naples, Italy)

[...] Chinese government has not informed what exactly the ABCDs of the Silk Road are. We keep hearing that the 21st century Silk Road will be based on certain rules, we do not know what exactly of those rules except for a few blank statements about win-win cooperation and so on. (Srikanth Kondapalli, Chairman, Centre for East Asian Studies, Jawaharlal Nehru University)

The Chinese interviewees showed a detailed understanding of the initiative highlighting cooperation, openness and cultural connections. Their understanding of the initiative was in line with the state narrative in a strategic outlook – to solve the common challenges of the world, to cooperate towards a win-win result; the topics they covered included historical heritage, cultural rejuvenation, economic and trade cooperation and future innovation.

In *Vision and Action*, people-to-people bonds and mutual benefit are two key themes; in the programme, Chinese experts also interpreted them and their relationship with economic development through the cultural lens. For example, an appeal to history was always a common tactic for the interviewees. The 2000-year history of cultural exchanges and people-to-people connection were always referenced in this regard. From a cultural prism, mutual benefits and development through friendship is based on an understanding of historic traditions, culture and current demand.

Countering concerns frame

Concerns prevail on the international stage about China's motivation and its territorial disputes with other countries, which may pose challenges for the implementation of BRI. The two episodes drew concerns of experts from other countries and explanations from Chinese experts.

One concern is the perception in some states of the initiative's analogy with colonisation. Asked by the host whether China is an exploiter in the cooperation proposed in BRI, a businessman from a Saudi Arabian oil company denied it from a historic and mutual benefit perspective:

This relation is [...] from history. Since the early stage of Silk Road, [...] mutual understanding, mutual benefit is the essence of the entire relation. [Through mutual investment] we have collateral relation, your interest is my interest and your interest is what my interest as well. (Ibrahim Al-Buainain, President, Aramco Asia)

The second concern referenced by the host is that with its growing influence, China will try to dominate all of Asia and conflict may be inevitable, especially with the United States. This view was echoed in the programme by famous American realist international relations scholar John Mearsheimer, who thinks competition in the ocean area is very much a zero-sum game where the United States has deep-seated interests. Thus, maintaining control of the Indian Ocean or the Arabian Sea would be the position of the United States, which might be a conflict point between China and the United States.

The Chinese experts denied the China-centric purpose of BRI by emphasising the openness of BRI, even to the United States.

> *BRI is open to developed countries. Literally the countries are identified. But all these countries have very close economic ties with US and Japan. It is impossible to exclude any countries.*

As presented, the concerns arose not only from the states but also from the individuals. A Chinese scholar who addressed this problem seemed to be well aware of the problem, but he did not propose much of a solution, apart from waiting for mutual understanding on China's behaviour to deepen.

> *The influence, through individual engagement, will cause unexpected results, for example conflicts with locals. After all, we cannot control the behaviour of individuals. And we know that we also have our share of problems, some of us are not very well-behaved.* (Li Peilin, Vice president, Chinese Academy of Social Science)

Territorial disputes were another problem which not only concerned the observers but also influenced the decisions of engagement with BRI by countries like India.

> *[T]he Silk Road possibly passing through some of the disputed territories of Kashmir and that is one concern for India because it is a sovereignty-related issue for India.* (Kondapalli)

The programme also presented a Chinese expert's explanation of the Chinese solution to the disputes of the South China Sea. According to a Chinese expert on South China Sea Studies, BRI or the Maritime Silk Road targets cooperation instead of seeking solutions to territorial disputes. Cooperation is seen as a way to establish mutual political trust. China's proposal for the South China Sea issue is a double-track strategy: negotiating with specific countries over specific disputes and working with countries of the Association of Southeast Asian Nations (ASEAN) to manage and control issues for the purpose of maintaining regional peace and stability. Maritime Silk Road would involve problems at the two levels.

Economic cooperation and development were viewed by some Chinese experts as solutions to territorial disputes, based on observation of other countries' experiences. Cases of confrontation between France and Germany, and Argentina and Brazil were interpreted as examples of mitigating non-economic conflicts through regional economic cooperation. BRI was seen as a channel to build mechanisms to ease disputes.

The basic structure of the programme proceeded in a linear manner: the voice-over with pre-recorded videos to lead into the topic, then the shot with the host's (Kuhn) monologue introducing the questions followed by the discussion between the host and one guest each time. Occasionally, pre-recorded questions from people who are interested in the topic or video clips relevant to the Silk Road were inserted between the questions. Each episode consisted of several segments like this and was followed by a summary by the host, which echoed the official discourse about the initiative.

Host lead-in (Episode One):

Why did President Xi Jinping propose the BRI strategic initiative for China? Why did he call the Silk Road a foreign policy priority? What relevance today of these ancient trade routes connected East and West? How does BRI help achieve China economic objectives and diplomatic goals?

His summary of Episode One reviewed the principles of BRI with an emphasis on economic cooperation in energy, infrastructure and commerce, which was seen as the natural result of China's economic requirements, integrated with the developmental needs of other countries; the necessity of a partnership between government and business because of the huge investment the 'grand vision' requires; and the measurement index of the success of the initiative: by bilateral trade, economic integration, infrastructure development and new growth areas, higher employment enhanced domestic growth and reduced risks. He concluded that it is in China's core interest to secure global peace and stability and to promote global development and prosperity, which are required for China's own continuing development, and BRI articulates well with China's overarching policy and exemplifies China's increasing importance on the global stage.

Host lead-in (Episode Two):

Kuhn: *The BRI strategy – the Silk Road Economic Belt over the land and the 21st century maritime Silk Road over the oceans – is President Xi Jinping's new initiative for multinational development. How does it exemplify his strategic thinking? How will it affect other nations? What are the challenges and obstacles ahead? Let's seek an organising principle to analyse China's BRI strategy in terms of China's overall foreign policy objectives. That will get us closer to China*

We cannot ignore China's maritime border disputes, particularly in the South China Sea, the origin of 21st century maritime Silk Road. How will competing claims of sovereignty affect the overall strategy?

In the wrap-up of Episode Two, the host summarised BRI as an exemplar of China's new proactive foreign policy in a multipolar world involving 50–60 countries. He listed the complex issues, such as economic inequalities, religious tensions and terrorism, which require plans coordinated to foster regional cooperation, joint effort and multi-channel and multi-level exchanges. He concluded with a reference to the principles of the Silk Road Spirit proposed by China's president: mutual learning between civilisations, respecting the choice of developmental path and mutually beneficial cooperation, dialogue and peace.

The framing was mainly facilitated by the sponsors from China and other countries that expressed their interpretations of BRI and their concerns based on their own stances; the programme structure, or the syntactical structure, as Pan and Kosicki (1993, 59) call it, that is, the arrangement of the segments which the question/doubts followed by the responding answers and the highlights of the key points by the host, and the visual devices at the beginning and during the transition between shots which might help viewers understand the topics (see Table 5.7).

The Australian Reception of BRI Frames

Since the proposal of BRI in late 2013, the initiative has drawn massive attention in policymaking circles, academia and media. Most of the Australian participants in this project expressed their knowledge of it, although their knowledge varied. The following two sub-sections present the Australian participants' frames of BRI and their reaction to CCTV NEWS's framing of BRI in *Closer to China*.

Australians' understanding of BRI

The interview results showed that most participants had previous knowledge about BRI, although most of their knowledge focused on only one or two aspects. Most of the participants were aware of the economic and trade aspects (a1, a6, a8, a9 and a14).

Table 5.7 Framing BRI in *Closer to China*

	Theme	Function	Devices		Visual image
			Sponsors	Syntactical structure	
	A proposal responding new era call	Explanation	Chinese officials and people from neighbouring countries	Question-explanation sequence/ Highlights with host's summary	Automation maps/Scene of Xi's speech/Shots with different peoples, architectures with different styles/ Scenes related to Silk Road, e.g camel troops in desert
	A proposal of cooperation	Explanation/ Clarification	Chinese officials and scholars	A proposal of openness	Defence/Clarification
Defining BRI	Chinese officials and scholars	A proposal of mutual benefit	Defence/Clarification	Chinese officials, scholars and Saudi Arabian businessmen	A proposal for cultural connection
	Explanation/ Clarification	Chinese officials and scholars	Countering Concerns	Analogy with colonisation	Defence
Explanation/ Clarification	Saudi Arabian businessmen Chinese scholars	China domination	Clarification/Defence	US scholars (pro) Chinese scholars	Territorial disputes

It a strategy put up probably in the last 3 years also by president Xi, to sort of re-establish economic ties I guess, increase trade along that classic traditional Silk Road, but also have a maritime route. (a21)

Some thought economy is the foundation of the initiative:

[BRI] is a good idea, another form of free trade area, with countries with joint binderies with china; you've got different cultures, different histories, different perspectives and religions, all sorts of differences but they can be united under common economic interest to advance trade. (a1)

There were others who thought that trade was an ultimate end and China would gain an increase in economic influence in the world through the initiative:

[BRI] is a strategic building connection between countries to do trade along this line, connecting them together boost trade. (a9)

China will become more globalised, especially through this BRI, and it's going to spread its economy elsewhere all over. America is withdrawing. (a14)

Another theme reflected in the participants' responses was that it was a strategic move towards power dominance against the United States:

Basically China tries to connect all the countries along Silk Road, recreate the Silk Road, basically to sort of […] countering the US dominance. (a11)

It is interesting that Xi Jinping and the associated government institutions are using history to promote China's future greatness. The museums are filled with people and their children who are hungry for knowledge of the past. (a23)

BRI is a […], by historically, it's a ring next to the Silk Road in terms of its contemporary relevance; it's a turn to the East as a counter balance, to a less extent EU, but definitely to the US. The US Obama administration is promoting its TPP, it excluded China, and so BRI draws a different set of connections across Eurasia. It is really interesting because it's diplomatically interesting, it requires China and Russia to have an agreement, and I think Turkey is in it in an interesting way. I just think it probably stems from a sense the West has done a lot of damage in Middle East and there are new opportunities for the strategic partnerships. (a15)

Only one participant mentioned the soft side of the initiative: the flow of ideas in the initiative:

BRI is sort of 21st century Silk Road, trying to draw people together to improve trade, communication the flow of ideas and products. It is a good thing. I was very disappointed at Britain's decision at Brexit, because I believe the way to forward is to try and improve the flow of ideas, to reduce barriers. (a8)

The participants' attitudes towards BRI were diversified although, as shown above, some thought it was a good concept:

I think it's a big concept which should be good for, particularly for those countries in central Asia which are china's neighbours. It's good for China to develop. (a2)

But most of them thought that it was no more than a political narrative for resource exploitation:

This is another [example] of China's mentality, it takes quite a bit of getting used to make up very implausible stories and think people are going to believe them and this happens all the time. Of course it is not totally bad, colonialism isn't totally bad. It depends on what they are doing in the countries. In Africa for example, there is iron ore, they build railroads and they are happy with that, but the main use of the railway is to transport iron whatever to the port and bring it back to China. So I tend to believe that there is no such thing as a free lunch. Countries just don't give away huge amounts for no reason. (a6)

Participant a1 expressed his disdain of the idea that China was trying to provide a Chinese solution for the world through BRI because of its own domestic problems:

BRI is great, but China itself has got real social and economic problems going forward. I don't believe the policy will solve China's problems let alone anyone else's problems. It is wrong to suppose your own idea can work for all. (a1)

Also, the suspicion of the possible political imperative made some very cautious towards BRI and thus want to learn more about it:

I am very unclear on what the political imperatives; are there any, what they are trying to do politically or is it just economic? [...] but it has been a bit hard to sort of pin down exactly what it is that is the Chinese vision for BRI, is it just try it? (a21)

They may think there are some other intentions. E.g., Australia refused a Chinese telecommunication companies contract because of the suspicion that they may use it to collect information. (a7)

Beyond the suspicions, other participants mentioned further possible challenges facing the initiative, such as the notorious corruption problems in countries along the BRI target region:

BRI means more relations with neighbouring countries, but there are also a lot of problems, like infrastructure, also with corruption, not corruption in China, corruption in countries like Kazakhstan. So it's not easy to overcome those problems, but it's good to have a vision on what you are going to achieve. I think one of the great things about China is to take a long term point of view and plan for the future, our government, especially our present government is not good at it at all. (a2)

I see the greatest problem for China (in pushing BRI) is the overcoming of the corruption associated with gift giving – Guanxi. (a23)

Response to the CCTV NEWS framing of BRI

This following part contains the results of the in-depth interviews on the participants' responses to the *Closer to China* videos. As mentioned earlier, being qualitative research, this project will not make any effort to attribute causality. The foci of the questions in this part were the following: general impressions of the production values, the way BRI was framed, whether or not there was an informing or persuasion intent factor that participants could detect in the videos and their response to that.

A balanced stance by some of the participants who watched the videos was observed, although CCTV NEWS was always accompanied by the label of 'propaganda'. Some participants thought that different views were presented and, in this sense, the format was not that different from programmes in Western media, which they were familiar with.

I think the program on BRI is interesting. I don't think it is propaganda; it is informative. (a15)

It was good because it is quite good for me to hear that China is quite happy for Western companies to be involved. The information seems well balanced to me. The problems with the maritime Silk Road and China's regional neighbours will be solved in the end by negotiation. (a4)

It was good. The belt and road economic trade route seems like history repeating, just like the Silk Road hundreds of years ago. Once again, [it seems to be] another example of China as a large opportunity for trade and investment. The way of the story telling was not that different from what I usually view in Western media. (a7)

It's interesting in terms of that you hear some people from the smaller countries around China talking about BRI and the way they were looking sort of positively towards the potential benefits to them, closer economic relationships. That was interesting. (a23)

I thought they were good and there was coverage about the challenges and what the disputes are; I thought they were good because you've got different views about that. You need to see Chinese officials being challenged, not necessarily in an aggressive way, but it need to be challenged about whether America is excluded from this or is it just a way for China to insert political influence on that new route or are you going to be working and trying to dominate all those countries and is India is included, why is it go through Kashmir and that is going to upset Indians, have you spoken to each country directly and, [...] so just see they are challenged and therefore they provide more balanced view rather than just, 'Oh this is a grand vision by president Xi and we should all get on board.' The rest of us don't have to unless we understand what it's really all about and how can we all benefit. (a21)

However, some still found the promotion of the Chinese perspective to be very obvious in the programme:

I felt that the presenter was trying to push a positive line. (a4)

The program is not hard to understand. It may be a promotion instead of propaganda. Propaganda would say something like we are good people, it is a good project, and you should support us. (a19)

I have no problem with the Chinese perspective; this is what the channel is supposed to do. (a1)

But some participants thought that largely one-sided perspectives were common for the programmes addressing government agendas, even in Western media. According to their experience, Western media did not fare better in presenting diversified opinions:

Yes, it [the program] is largely one-sided, largely positive of the policy, but at least there was one bit in that video I thought interesting, which was where the criticism was raised – isn't it just a new version of colonialism and I thought that was quite interesting at least that idea has been put forward as a kind of counterpoint to the positive side of it. That wasn't developed in any way but at least was put forward. It was good to a certain extent; there was still at least one opposing view point that was part of the mix. You've got to expect something like that to be largely positive and pro the policy, but at least criticism had still been raised. You've got to kind of expect, you really should expect that from the media anywhere, you can understand any media in any country, they are going to be largely positive in terms of the government agenda, but you won't want the media to raise counterpoints. I don't have a very high opinion of Australia media; I think there is some part of Australian media they tend to be smaller, more independent. But the mainstream media, including Fairfax, I just think they don't get many useful or interesting insights into what's going on, I mean the trouble with the media in Australia is it is presented with slower facts, you have people who have opinions on radio and television usually strongly oriented towards one-sided politics. You just don't see too much counterbalance, you see a little bit with the ABC and SBS, but even those organisations, they self-censor to a light degree often, you just don't see too much diversity of opinion and analysis in Australian media. (a22)

Although some participants expressed their confirmation on the informative side of the programme, the intent to persuade was hardly seen:

I can argue some of the measures the Chinese government is taking, the one I would not be recommending. Policy direction will not achieve what the government says [it wants] to achieve. I don't think it's a long term benefit for the ordinary Chinese people. (a1)

[The program is good], but again, I sort of want to know can I trust this report, who is Robert Kuhn, what views is he putting, is he a China government person, or is he a long time former New York Times reporter or [...], you know I didn't know anything about him. (a21)

For me, I don't mind if it is a Chinese point of view, but I would like to hear something about the islands because that's the thing that worries me as a foreigner. Also, it worries some of the little countries. China said they have developed AIIB, they made the point that America could join it if they want to. Australia has joined it, It's a worry because [...] I don't know what's going to happen because history shows when you've got a rising power, you've got a downing power, sadly that often causes trouble. Also there were few debates, no why. They pose the tone that China is exploiting the countries but then they oppose that Chinese investment is better for Tajikistan. There was a big emphasis on win-win cooperation. It felt like the presenter Kuhn was reading something written for him by the government. The Chinese professor sounded like a spokesperson for the government. Good to hear a different view from the American professor. It would have been good to hear from a Japanese or Korean person. (a4)

This chapter presented the research findings of framing around China's BRI at different stages during a communication process: the initiator – Chinese government, the state media CCTV NEWS and TV news magazine programme *Closer to China with R. L. Kuhn* – and the Australian target audiences' response to the coverage. CCTV NEWS's working mechanism and professional values as a professional hybrid organisation with a mix of Chinese staff and foreign staff were also presented. In the state document, BRI was framed as a project with the aim to boost mutual development of the region and a broader human society with regional cooperation and rule-abiding approaches. The programme presented the frames to clarify the outside concerns on the initiative and, in addition, to explain BRI in the cooperation, open, mutual benefit and culture connection perspectives. Through the analysis of interview data based on the clarification of journalistic identity and professional values, it was found that in the view of employees, CCTV NEWS is an information disseminator about China and other countries that are neglected by Western international broadcasters. The rationale of the existence lies in the inadequacy of information being provided in the broadcasting market. Under this self-image, the media workers define their role as disseminators with professional values of objectivity, balance, fairness and, most importantly, inclusivity. With balanced views, the target audiences' responses to the programme demonstrated that the storytelling techniques of the programme are relatively satisfactory. However, because of the broader concerns on China and the state-owned identity of CCTV NEWS, the effect of persuasion is limited.

References

Belt and Road Portal. 2015. "Belt and Road Portal." https://eng.yidaiyilu.gov.cn/ (accessed 16 Janurary, 2017).

CCTV.com. 2014. Introduction of CCTV NEWS program Closer to China with R.L.Kuhn. edited by Zheng Limin.

Chitty, Naren, Dalbir Ahlawat, Mei Li, and D. Gopal. 2018. "The Chinese Belt and Road Initiative and the Indian Ocean Region: Sentiment towards Economic Prosperity and Security implications." *The Indian Journal of Politics* 52 (1–2):1–20.

Wade, Geoff. 2016. China's 'One Belt, One Road' initiative. In *Parliamentary Library Briefing.*http://www.aph.gov.au/About_Parliament/Parliamentary_Departments/Parliamentary_Library/pubs/BriefingBook45p/ChinasRoad (accessed 15 Janurary, 2017)

Wang, Yiwei. 2015. *One Belt One Road: Opportunities and Chanllenges (YIDAI YILU JIYU YU TIAOZHAN)*. Beijing: People's Publishig House.

Xinhuanet. 2016. "BELT AND ROAD INITIATIVE." Xinhua News Agency. http://www.xinhuanet.com/silkroad/english/index.htm. (accessed 16 January, 2017)

Tiezzi, Shannon. 2014. "The New Silk Road: China's Marshall Plan?" *The Diplomat* 6.

Chapter 6

DISCUSSION AND CONCLUSION

Intended, Mediated and Received Frames

This book has investigated the role of China's international broadcasting in the country's overall soft power strategy. With CCTV NEWS and China–Australia relations as a case, the study takes into consideration the two ends and three stages in the process of framing China in the context of a rising China and the imbalance of information flow. It provides a humble attempt to develop a communicative approach to analysing soft power.

Intended frames

First, the book addresses China's intended images in the framing process. China's intended frames to the world have been examined at two levels: at the first level, the Chinese public diplomacy elites' frames of domains of societal activity where society is able to demonstrate virtuosity that can accumulate soft power strength – economy, culture and science and technology, and the controversial domain of the political system – were examined; at the second level, the state perspective was examined through the case study of the framing on BRI in state documents. It was based on the assumption that public diplomacy plays an important role in framing a country's information, image in the context of noopolitik, and will project soft power. As discovered in the interviews with Australian participants, this level of framing did have some congruence with an individual's framing of specific issues.

The findings show that among public diplomacy elites, the framing of China was generally complicated, mirroring the current situation of China which is at the junction of integrating to the world stage while rapidly ascending in status. The complexity in public diplomacy elites' frames was also reflected in their perceptions of the selected fields of economy, culture, political system and science and technology. Judgements on the various themes and diverse attitudes towards their relevance to public diplomacy elites arose from the interviews, but there was no consensual position on any single theme. For each frame, both positive and negative themes were identified. However, underpinning the various attitudes was the fact that all the participants were positioning themselves to consider the projection of China's image based on China's current situation and to try to understand the outward oriented information/image-delivery questions.

Although inquiries were made in the context of public diplomacy with China's image in the eyes of foreigners, the Chinese public diplomacy elites' basic positions on the issues were defensive and reactive, seeking only for better ways of projecting China's image. That is to say, their intended framing was for countering the assumptions such as 'China threat'. Bearing in mind the biased perception from many Western countries, what most participants expected was that an objective image of China should be sent to the outside world on the basis that China is a country that has achieved greatly, focused on development and designs no threat to other countries – although not all the aspects were positive in their own eyes.

The incongruity among the Chinese public diplomacy elites' frames was obvious. Here, framing incongruence will be used to refer to the incongruity among different frames. In this group, the framing incongruence exists in the themes and positions. This incongruence might reflect the current situation in China: there are traditional values and aspects of cultural heritage, thanks to the county's long history, and the socialist values that have dominated the political system since 1949, but the rapid economic development over the last 30 years has endowed the country with a more modern visage and Western values. It seems that settling on some striking and impressive – and quintessential – descriptors for the country is not easy. This is a condition that creates bewilderment among the citizens of a rising China.

In speaking of BRI, the state framing of it was understandably focusing on the promising side of the initiative with the purpose of informing the potential partners of the possible benefits of the initiative and offering assurances of China's responsible status in the progression of BRI. In the master document *Vision and Action*, China was framed as the promoter of world development and cooperation, the rule-abiding participant and the responsibility sharer – a virtuous 'citizen' on the world stage. This positioning complies with its responsible big power discourse in international relations.

Looking at the two levels as a whole, the framing incongruence between the public diplomacy elites and the state framing vary in scope, that is, the state framing on BRI is focused on the 'sunny side' of everything, while the public diplomacy elites do not confine themselves to the positive side of issues about China but instead recognise benign intentions.

Mediated frames

This book has also examined the state media's framing of China's story through the case of BRI. The framing occurred under two main themes: the interpretation of BRI under the state framework and addressing the doubts and disputes raised by international stakeholders. As the product of a state-owned media outlet, the two-episode programme entitled *Closer to China* unsurprisingly did not pose any fundamental challenge to the initiative. The function it played had three goals: describe the initiative, defend China's stance and dispel any doubts of external parties. At variance with the conventional wisdom in the West that CCTV NEWS resorts to positive reporting, the news magazine programme did raise some thorny issues like power dominance, resistance from some countries and disputes around BRI, such as the one about the South China Sea. But the tendency to resort to apologetics – through defence and clarification – was clear and even inevitable considering that expert guests on the show were mostly from the state sector or foreign policy think tanks. Resolution of divergence was not always offered; lead-ins and wrap-ups by the host left some audience members with the impression that he was a mouthpiece of the Chinese government (see Chapter 5).

A comparison of the frames, frame themes and their functions between the state document *Vision and Action* and the CCTV NEWS programme *Closer to China* shows both similarities and differences. In both the state document and the CCTV NEWS programme, the themes of cooperation, development, open and mutual benefit and cultural connections of BRI were highlighted. Both contain information that would help people understand the initiative. However, each piece has its own unique aspects. For example, in *Vision and Action*, the role that China would be playing and its intention to abide by relevant rules during the implementation of the initiative were presented. Clearly, in this state document, the Chinese government was seeking to give assurances to the potential partners to whom it was appealing. But in *Closer to China*, there were no such assurances.

In the state document, there was narration of the benefits of BRI that was viewed as a technique of appealing, while in the TV programme, there were aspirational elements; no apparent direct appeals were detected, however. In the TV programme, doubts and suspicions had been raised and addressed. Defensive remarks and clarification were provided from the perspectives of the Chinese scholars. Principles for resolution were expressed on issues such as territorial disputes where ultimate resolution was considered possible. In the state document, however, disputes and doubts were invisible. The inclusion and exclusion of certain parts in the state document and the CCTV NEWS programme could be interpreted as products of institution-specific professional practice by both: the government as the initiator of the strategy played its role in informing its target audience of potential BRI partners, of what BRI was about, how the plan could be operationalised and what BRI's significance was; the TV programme showed its audience-orientated coverage both the bright side and the controversial side.

The functions CCTV NEWS performed in framing BRI were also evaluated through professional logic and political logic. Professionally, in the context of news practitioners' global mobility, interviews with both Chinese and foreign staff threw light on the role of professional norms in the practice of CCTV NEWS programme production. Through the analysis of interview data based on the clarification of journalistic identity and professional values, it was found that in the view of employees, the channel is an information disseminator about China and other countries that are neglected by Western international broadcasters. The rationale of its existence lies in the inadequacy of information being provided in the broadcasting market. Under its self-determined position, CCTV NEWS staff defined the channel's role as information disseminators with professional values of objectivity, balance, fairness and – most importantly – inclusivity. Under this self-perception, professionally, it played a role in informing the audience of what the BRI initiative was about and how it would be implemented. Facing a suspicious international public opinion, it introduced doubts and negative understanding that counter the typical Chinese media practice of ignoring the doubts in the environment while spelling out strategies and addressing them in detail from the Chinese perspective. The practice conformed to the employees' self-perceptions of the role of a disseminator of the Chinese perspective. The political logic is that CCTV NEWS is a state-funded media organisation with the aim of flipping the international information flow that is perceived to be imbalanced – against China. Its defensive and clarifying stance could find ground from this perspective.

With the strategy of employing foreign staff, CCTV NEWS has embraced Western professional skills and values. The participants' feedback shows that the presentation of CCTV NEWS has little difference from their Western counterparts. This could be interpreted as the result of its foreign employment strategy. The interactions between the channel and the Western staff demonstrate a certain level of hegemonic rule (Onuf 2014) of the management, on the one hand. On the other hand, the Western staff use their expertise to make space for the channel to reflect some of the Western professional values while presenting the news, although there is a modicum of restriction on topics that are deemed to be of a sensitive nature; chief editors are the arbiters.

Findings indicate that expatriate staff at CCTV NEWS, untrammelled by the yoke of ratings, feel free to produce programmes that are more aligned with some of their professional values – not needing to embellish content to attract audiences. Western commercial media face the need to compromise professional values, for example, in content allocation, because of the need to accommodate advertisers. Expatriate staff have individually constructed conditions of homonomy, however uneasy, through making trade-offs between, in some cases, being without work in a libertarian press culture and being gainfully and visibly employed, with some political constraints but with liberation from enslavement by ratings. While there are some incursions into professional preferences, government intervention is not within the parameters of what is acceptable. Indeed, CCTV America's team has won some journalism awards including an Emmy in 2016 for a feature story. From the management's perspective, the expertise from the Western staff at CCTV America generates quality content – a key to attracting Western audiences. The local staff strives for the greatest leeway in making programmes. This aspect too contributes to their constructions of homonomy even if some consider the need to continuously negotiate stances on certain topics to be a nuisance. As one participant said, CCTV America reported the visits of the Pope and the Dalai Lama to the United States in 2012 but not in 2016.

Accordingly, the professional value they adhere to is the presentation of varied voices and stories. As to the crucial questions of the channel's censorship and credibility deficits, they admit their existence without giving these any emphasis. One of the reasons is that in actual journalism practice, structural pressure is everywhere; the differences are in the form and locus of their presence. For the commercial broadcasters, the pressure comes from ratings and advertisers; for public broadcasters of the ilk of BBC, the 'pressure' may be more of a gentle massage. For CCTV NEWS, it comes simultaneously from the investor and the supervisory body. Self-censorship and the 'invisible scissor' phenomenon are also well known across the world in different types of polities.

It is clear through the above analysis that, following the discussion of role identity and professional values, few international staff at CCTV NEWS who were interviewed mentioned any coercive dynamic in their organisations. Homonomic accommodations of different interpretations of professional values may be seen. In a hybrid cultural organisation such as CCTV NEWS, professional norms demonstrate their hegemonic character in the practice of news making. However, the hegemonic effect is not unidirectional; it is interactive, with a negotiation between power granted naturally by the media system and professionalisation. During the process, a unique working culture, a third space, favourable to hosting homonomy for at least some of the Western employees, is fostered among the staff from multiple backgrounds.

Received frames

Through the findings presented in the previous two chapters, clear characteristics of Australian public diplomacy elites' framing of China can be summarised as follows: from the onlookers' perspective, both positive and negative sides were discerned, but onlookers had their own vision angles. As in the Chinese participants' case, multiple themes emerged from each topic. The differences were that the attitudes were more diversified. From economy to science and technology, each topic was accompanied with positive, negative and – more prevalent – suspicious or worrying attitudes. Perceptions were influenced hugely by participants' experiences: their interaction with China and the contexts they were in. For example, most of those who had personal contacts with China had perspectives of China that were closer to that of Chinese organs than those who depended mainly on media.

In addition, being used to their own political system and culture, scepticism clouded the lens of comparison used to observe China. For example, concerns about Communist Party rule and the possible threat presented by a rising China lurked behind almost every aspect of some participants' understanding of China-related issues. This might explain the situation where the Australian media and government show tremendous enthusiasm for special cases such as human rights issues, react sensitively to political donations made by the Chinese diaspora and cautiously assay Chinese investment in Australia.

Also, living in a multicultural environment, Australians view China in the context of many cultures, in which Western culture is the mainstream. This suggests that Chinese culture is usually regarded as something that could be appreciated or researched by a group of people but is not amenable to being profoundly understood by the wider society.

The above comments all accompanied the prospect of China's rise economically and politically on the world stage, with the rhetoric of 'yes, it has been very successful; it may become one of the strongest economies, but there are problems'. This may indicate scepticism about, or lack of confidence in, China's future development, which has resulted from the information they acquired from different channels. Their conclusions varied dramatically when evaluated from different perspectives. For example, in the eyes of most Chinese participants, China's economic achievements were significant; systemic advantage played roles in them and problems resided in the structure that needed continuing reform. In the eyes of most Australian participants, however, it might be that these were systemic coincidences – ones that would end sooner or later.

Through a comparative lens, the above-mentioned characteristics determine the situation that the framing of China happened in two quite different fields: the framing field of the Chinese and that of the Australians. In each field, a variety of frame themes emerge with different attitudes or positions towards certain topics. These themes differ for each individual inside and outside the fields, but similar trends exist. Underpinning the themes and attitudes are core elements that determine the real difference or the degree to which an individual or a group in one field could trust or accept framing from other fields. The core elements may include social norms, ideology, culture, belief and so on. It is easier to achieve integration among individuals within each field because of the similarity in the core elements. But between the different fields, the congruence might be harder to achieve.

The findings in Chapter 5 indicate that the presentation and format of the *Closer to China* programme on BRI were seen as not much different from that in Western media, which they usually watch. The propagandist tone or format was hardly seen, while the informative function was eminently visible. But obviously, the congruence of CCTV NEWS frames with Australian frames, on BRI, was limited, although a certain viewership particularly sought in CCTV NEWS the Chinese perspective. The problem can be analysed in the following manner: First, due to the participants' previous knowledge, their media consumption habits and the core values they held, CCTV NEWS was viewed as one part of most participants' cautiously constructed frame of China, due to its status as a state-owned media and mouthpiece of the ruling party; for the latter reason, its credibility as a reliable information source was challenged by most participants. Second, Australia has a very open media environment. Beyond the domestic media product suppliers, many world-famous media outlets around the world is accessible by Australians. In this case, although the local media may suffer from credibility and quality issues, many alternative choices are still available, such as media outlets like BBC, CNN and Al Jazeera, and news journals like *The Economist*. These are exemplars that CCTV NEWS had been mimicking in its lifetime of less than two decades. Trying to surpass them and becoming the audience's primary medium, even if only for Chinese news perspectives, requires a quantum leap in the storytelling and topic selection virtuosity of CCTV NEWS; the latter may encounter great barriers under China's current media system which always has taboos on some topics. Although one of the editorial management staff claimed during the interview that there is no topic that cannot be reported, she also expressed that the bottom line in editorial guidelines is national interest. In this case, perhaps CCTV NEWS needs to reconsider its strategies professionally and politically, while focusing on the Chinese perspective, to compete with well-established public broadcasters such as BBC and commercial networks like CNN, and how to make sure the Chinese perspective is delivered with the virtuosity of foreign staff. If the questions cannot be answered satisfactorily through the programmes of CCTV NEWS, it cannot overcome the trap of being viewed as a propaganda tool, a problem which can prevent its bringing congruence to its saying and doing.

An Effective Tool of Soft Power?

The above-mentioned frames at the three stages of the communication process provide evidence to discuss the role of CCTV NEWS in China's soft power strategy. Having evaluated its capacity to influence the audience, the role of CCTV NEWS in China's soft power strategy can be reconsidered through the following aspects: through the lenses of framing process, information flow and, finally, soft power strategy.

Through the lens of framing process

Analysing the findings, the framing of China could lead to two outcomes: framing congruence and framing incongruence. Framing congruence refers to the situation that similar understanding is achieved at the two ends of the process. Framing congruence is a positive sign of reaching mutual understanding. Framing incongruence refers to the difference existing in the framing among different individuals or groups. There is a central factor – called the framing core – that determines the most essential part of framing which allows uncovering the nature of framing incongruence. When framing cores are similar, the framing incongruence is at a surface level and is easier to overcome.

Research findings suggest that from the different levels identified, frames of China and China-related issues in the discourse of state, Chinese public diplomacy elites and the media are not strictly congruent in scope and from interpretative angles, but the core values are highly congruent. That is to say, framing incongruence exists internally on the Chinese side. On specific issues, the incongruence is even more diversified among the public diplomacy elites, but the framing incongruence is at the surface level, not at the fundamental level. Under the international lens, the bias against China and China's weakness in influencing international public opinion were clearly seen in a consensual way among both the state and public diplomacy elites, and thus the externally oriented frames are consistent among the state and public diplomacy elites. In this way, although there is internal framing incongruence at the detailed level, the framing core and externally oriented framing are consistent at the Chinese side. But at the Australian side, the situation demonstrates a similar trend: there is internal incongruence among the Australians in details, but the external framing towards China is consistent with the constraint of apprehension of some fundamental aspects like the values and political system.

Framing congruence on China-related topics is hampered at least by two levels of framing incongruences: the internal incongruence among its own public diplomacy elites and the incongruence between internal and external stakeholders. The difference between the internal framing incongruence and the external framing incongruence lies in the framing cores. For the internal framing incongruence, the differences among different individuals in a group will not determine the nature of framing, and such differences are easy to overcome. For the external framing incongruence, the divergence lies in the fundament factor and is hard to overcome. In the case under consideration in this study, the internal framing incongruence lies in different Chinese participants' views of the same topic from different angles. But when viewing Chinese views of external bias vis-à-vis China, there is a congruent trend that is discernible. However, when comparing the Australian participants' framing with that of their Chinese counterparts, hard attitudinal shells are perceived around each group. A striking example in this study is the Australian audiences' concern about China due to differences in political systems and culture. Many issues, such as media and BRI, were influenced by this kind of concern. The cause of the incongruence is the framing core, the cultural factors that determine their belief system and the way they interpret issues. The core could be permeated by people with expertise in both cultures, but this would be more difficult for others. China's media strategy together with other public diplomacy means can be viewed as a modus operandi to tackle the framing cores. But the gestation period would be lengthy.

The framing quality of China's image in CCTV NEWS depends on two factors. First, from the Chinese perspective, shown in the case of BRI, the state frames were clearly reframed in CCTV NEWS with additional defensive perspectives presented. However, the quality should also be investigated from the target audience's perspective. The audience response to CCTV NEWS's framing revealed in this research is that most participants took cognisance of the format but were not impressed by the content. But there are participants who expressed interest in the Chinese perspective delivered by CCTV NEWS. In this sense, the framing of the Chinese perspective in CCTV NEWS is clear enough to suggest that CCTV NEWS has its living space as an organisation specialised in delivering a Chinese perspective. But one must note that the Chinese perspective per se is a double-edged sword: on the one hand, it could be a unique selling point with which to carve out a share of the audience; on the other hand, it might be interpreted as hard proof, for those who believe that CCTV is nothing more than an organ of propaganda, and result in a refusal to accept it as a reliable media source.

Through the lens of information flow

Information flow is one problem to consider when investigating the international media landscape and power dynamics in which China's international media strategy is grounded. Under constructivist international relations, information flow contributes to the construction of social reality, because as Onuf (1989) puts it, the interaction between speaker and hearer is a process of normativisation in international relations.

China's media strategy aims to draw on the noosphere to, first, flip its negative valence as seen in public opinion polls and, second, to strengthen its own discursive capacity in the international public sphere. To achieve these goals, it needs first to diffuse the noosphere with attractive information to international audiences and, secondly to compete with well-established media outlets and establish its own reputation among media consumers. The first layer of actions demands macro efforts such as investment and policy support, while the second layer needs the development of virtuosity in storytelling, in essence, prowess in framing. Research results show that China has made and is making efforts at both levels. At the macro level, financial support from the state facilitates continuous operation and expansion. The establishment of overseas branches, the recruitment of foreign staff and the incorporation of some Western professional values are efforts at the micro level. According to audience feedback in this research, the format change in CCTV NEWS is obvious. In addition, following China's rise in the ranks of the economically powerful with the status in world affairs that accompanies this, the demand to become familiar with the Chinese perspective has grown among some of the public diplomacy elites in Australia. CCTV NEWS's strategic focus on the Chinese perspective invests it with the potential to fill a market void. But research results also suggest that among a large group of audience members, this potential of filling the market gap is hindered by framing incongruences at the core level, which views CCTV NEWS as being trapped in the myth of communist China and thus having questionable credibility. From this sense, the primary challenge for CCTV NEWS is to consider how to compete with dominant media organisations in framing Chinese perspectives in crucial moments and earn the audiences' trust. But judging from the current reality, solutions beyond the system are out of consideration.

In Chapter 3, the proposal was made in a way that information through media was disseminated in two directions to the audience – directly and through domestic networks. According to the soft power model proposed in the theoretical framework, soft power sources take effect only after the information is accepted in a homonomic frame of mind. Research findings show that compared with media as a source, people tend to believe the information they receive through personal interaction. So the mobility channel through networked communication will definitely weigh more in the information flow. Judging from the hybrid structure of CCTV NEWS with both Chinese staff and foreign staff, professional mobility could be facilitated by the self-construction of a measure of homonomy by expatriate staff. In this sense, the organisation itself becomes a node in a civil diplomacy network (Chitty 2017b).

As discussed previously, CCTV NEWS's capacity is limited in impacting Australian viewers effectively. But it may find a certain degree of fulfilment in its domestic market, because from an early stage, CCTV English language broadcasting has attracted many English-language learners in China. This method of information diffusion may be much easier because there are fewer cultural obstacles to understanding the information. CCTV NEWS narratives can to a certain extent turn into the narratives of people in public diplomacy interactions.

Through the lens of soft power

Soft power is a key concept in this research project and is elaborated under a communication lens. Identifying the ambiguity in mechanisms in Nye's (1990; 2004; 2011) model of soft power resources and its relationship with public diplomacy, this research employs Chitty's virtue and virtuosity model (2017a,b) and examines soft power in information flow. The soft power model of information flow, developed herein, is first a model to test the role of media as a channel of soft power source transition. Different from Nye's blunt claim that mass media plays an important role in soft power, Chitty's model distinguishes between passive and active soft power sources to which news and media belong respectively. This study picked CCTV NEWS as its media example and investigated its role in spreading Chinese frames. As frequently mentioned, the motive behind China's media expansion is to tell Chinese stories for mutual understanding and twist the imbalanced information flow. The motivating factor is civic virtue in Chitty's (2017a,b) civic virtue model of soft power, and the purpose is to frame China as a virtuous state in GRC.

Compared with military coercion and economic inducement, a media approach which focuses on the transmission of intangible soft power values, like cooperation, development and mutual benefit, in BRI can be viewed as a soft use of power which conforms to the spirit of GRC, or *He* in a traditional Chinese sense.

In Chapter 3, Chitty's (2017b) positioning of media as a multiplier of resources of soft power was adopted. Under this classification, the intangible soft power sources – knowledge, behaviour and culture in various forms such as art, education, folklore history, language, news and so on – take effect through the channel and multiplier resources like mobility, electronic networked media and cultural industries. Seen from this sense, news is an intangible passive soft power source and media is a channel and active soft power resource.

First, from the state level, CCTV NEWS is under the national strategy for promoting China's discourse and image together with other media organisations and public diplomacy approaches. It is the channel for information delivery for promoting mutual understanding, or a multiplier of virtuosities, to put it in Chitty's terms. The continuing financial support is proof of that. The public diplomacy elites are also aware of the inconformity between China's rising status and its capacity for influencing world discourse. They thus had expectations on media development. In CCTV NEWS, the staff confirmed their role of promoting Chinese discourse and the consideration of national interest in discourse – based on the judgement of unbalanced international information flow and the widely recognised biased framing in world mainstream public discourse. These three levels of expectations on CCTV NEWS could be interpreted as its soft power resources positioning. This is the positive side of it.

In the CCTV NEWS's point of view, delivery of the Chinese perspective has the potential to promote better understanding of China's BRI and to meet a measure of the audience demand for a Chinese perspective. In this sense, beyond having a channel function, by meeting audience demand, media can be seen by CCTV NEWS managers, who would be looking for influence as a measure of success, to have a soft power effect. To discuss the notion of influence of CCTV NEWS's frames on target audiences in Australia, the term 'influence' should be clarified. In media, the potential to influence could be indicated through multiple dimensions. CCTV's report (CCTV Overseas Centre 2013) looks at effectiveness in terms of expanding the organisation's reach into households. CCTV NEWS may be available to every household in Australia that has Foxtel or a networked computer or mobile phone, but this only amounts to potential to influence, not actual influence. There are also the individual ways in which frames are received that were discussed in Chapters 3 and 4: receivers may negotiate readings, constructing their own counter-hegemonic preferred readings (Fisher and Lucas 2011; Hall 1980). The new frame may be adopted and new knowledge may be added to an existing frame modifying it, or the old frame, perhaps a counter-hegemonic one, will be retained. One could speculate that the influence of CCTV NEWS would likely be seen as very limited if quantitative research were to be conducted. For those who found it useful to learn about Chinese perspectives through viewing CCTV NEWS, there might be some new knowledge added to their framing of China. But for those who started with doubts about the credibility of CCTV NEWS, it is unlikely that there would be substantial positive influence.

CCTV NEWS itself plays a dual role in soft power dynamics: on the one hand, it can be viewed as the information diffuser, a soft power multiplier; on the other hand, it is a player in the field of civil diplomacy in which connections are established. But judging from China's overall soft power strength, little evidence in this study has shown its function to wield soft power. As discussed in Chapter 2, the role an initiative can play can be divided into two levels. The first showcases the virtuosity and attractiveness of one country, which contributes to the accumulation of soft power strength. But the ultimate goal of soft power lies in its effectiveness of achieving policy gains, which can be seen as the second level. In this sense, CCTV NEWS has potential at the first level, but it is still far from playing effectively at the second level. Finally, I would like to hark back to John Burton's advice as a diplomat and international relations theorist.[1] Burton (1965) took the position that it is only sensible that states should seek to better understand each other, as through such a learning process conflict could be avoided, especially at the current moment when an increasing number of signs indicate that we are still struggling in the clash of civilisations.

Reference

Burton, John Wear. 1965. *International Relations: A General Theory*. Cambridge: Cambridge University Press.

---

1 Burton was a former Australian foreign secretary and diplomat who was later at Oxford University, University of Maryland and George Mason University, as an international relations and conflict resolution theorist.

BIBLIOGRAPHY

Al-Rodhan, Khalid R. 2007. 'A critique of the China threat theory: A systematic analysis'. *Asian Perspective* 31 (3): 41–66.

Albro, Robert. 2015. 'The disjunction of image and word in US and Chinese soft power projection'. *International Journal of Cultural Policy* 21 (4): 382–99.

Allison, Graham. 2017. *Destined for War: Can America and China Escape Thucydides's Trap?* New York: Houghton Mifflin Harcourt.

Anderson, John Ward. 2006. 'All news all the time, and now in French'. *Washington Post*, 7 December. https://www.washingtonpost.com/archive/lifestyle/2006/12/07/all-news-all-the-time-and-now-in-french/e6ff5dbb-fd4f-477a-9caa-1ca3081b8dbd/.

Angyal, Andras. 1969. 'A logic of systems'. *Systems Thinking* 1: 17–29.

Ardèvol-Abreu, A. 2015. 'Framing theory in communication research: Origins, development and current situation in Spain'. *Revista Latina de Comunicación Social* 70: 423–50.

Arquilla, John, and David Ronfeldt. 1999. *The Emergence of Noopolitik: Toward an American Information Strategy*. Santa Monica, CA: Rand Corporation.

Australian Bureau of Statistics. 2016. 2016 Census QuickStats. Canberra, Australia. Accessed 7 January 2017. https://quickstats.censusdata.abs.gov.au/census_services/getproduct/census/2016/quickstat/036.

Baylis, John, Steve Smith and Patricia Owens. 2013. *The Globalization of World Politics: An Introduction to International Relations*. Oxford: Oxford University Press.

Belt and Road Portal. 2015. 'Belt and Road Portal'. Accessed 16 January 2017. https://eng.yidaiyilu.gov.cn/.

Berger, Peter L., and Thomas Luckmann. 1966. *The Social Construction of Reality: A Treatise in the Sociology of Knowledge*. Garden City, NY: First Anchor.

Borah, Porismita. 2011. 'Conceptual issues in framing theory: A systematic examination of a decade's literature'. *Journal of Communication* 61 (2): 246–63.

Boyd-Barrett, Oliver. 1980. *The International News Agencies*. Thousand Oaks, CA: Sage.

Boyd, Douglas A. 1997. 'International radio broadcasting in Arabic: A survey of broadcasters and audiences'. *International Communication Gazette* 59 (6): 445–72.

Brophy, David. 2018. 'David Brophy reviews "Silent Invasion: China's Influence in Australia" by Clive Hamilton'. *Australian Book Review*, April. https://www.australianbookreview.com.au/abr-online/archive/2018/218-april-2018-no-400/4663-david-brophy-reviews-silent-invasion-china-s-influence-in-australia-by-clive-hamilton.

Browne, Donald R. 1982. *International Radio Broadcasting: The Limits of the Limitless Medium*. Connecticut: Praeger.

———. 1983. 'The international newsroom: A study of practices at the Voice of America, BBC and Deutsche Welle'. *Journal of Broadcasting & Electronic Media* 27 (3): 205–31.

Bulkeley, Jennifer Caroline. 2009. 'Perspectives on power: Chinese strategies to measure and manage China's rise'. PhD dissertation, Harvard University. Accessed 20 March 2016. https://search.proquest.com/docview/304891214?pq-origsite=gscholar.

Burton, John Wear. 1965. *International Relations: A General Theory*. Cambridge: Cambridge University Press.

Calabrese, Andrew. 2005. 'Communication, global justice and the moral economy'. *Global Media and Communication* 1 (3): 301–15.

Campion, Andrew Stephen. 2016. *The Geopolitics of Red Oil: Constructing the China Threat through Energy Security*. London: Routledge.

Cappella, Joseph N., and Kathleen Hall Jamieson. 1997. *Spiral of Cynicism: The Press and the Public Good*. Oxford: Oxford University Press.

Castells, Manuel. 2004. 'Informationalism, networks, and the network society: A theoretical blueprint'. In *The Network Society: A Cross-Cultural Perspective*, edited by Manuel Castells, 3–45. Cheltenham: Edward Elgar.

———. 2007. 'Communication, power and counter-power in the network society'. *International Journal of Communication* 1 (1): 29.

CCTV. 2014. 'Introduction of CCTV NEWS program *Closer to China* with R. L. Kuhn'. *CCTV.com*. Edited by Zheng Limin. Accessed 8 January 2017. http://cctv.cntv.cn/lm/closertochina/video/index.shtml.

CCTV Overseas Centre. 2013. *Evaluation of International Communication*. Beijing: CCTV Overseas Centre.

CGTN. 2017. 'About CGTN'. https://www.cgtn.com/about-us.

Chilton, Stephen. 1988. 'Defining political culture'. *Western Political Quarterly*: 419–45.

Chitty, Naren. 1994. 'Communicating world order'. *Journal of International Communication* 1 (2): 100–119.

———. 2007. 'Toward an inclusive public diplomacy in the world of fast capitalism and diasporas'. In *Foreign Ministries: Adaptation to a Changing World*, 1–22. Bangkok: Ministry of Foreign Affairs of Thailand.

———. 2009. 'Frames for internationalizing media research'. In *Internationalizing Media Studies*, edited by D. Thussu, 61–74. London: Routledge.

———. 2015a. 'Analysing soft power and public diplomacy'. *Jilin University Journal Social Sciences Edition* 55 (3): 20–27.

———. 2015b. 'The notion of soft power relationship'. *China and the World* 1 (1): 1–12.

———. 2017a. 'Conclusion'. In *The Routlege Handbook of Soft Power*, edited by Naren Chitty, Li Ji, Gary Rawnsley and Craig Hayden, 453–63. New York: Routlege.

———. 2017b. 'Soft power, civic virtue and world politics'. In *The Routledge Handbook of Soft Power*, edited by Naren Chitty, Li Ji, Gary Rawnsley and Craig Hayden, 29–56. New York: Routledge.

———. 2019. 'The rise of blunt power in the Strongman Era'. *Georgetown Journal of International Affairs*, 28 February. https://www.georgetownjournalofinternationalaffairs.org/online-edition/2019/2/28/the-rise-of-blunt-power-in-the-strongman-era.

Chitty, Naren, and Sabina Dias. 2018. 'Artificial intelligence, soft power and social transformation'. *Journal of Content, Community and Communication* 7: 1–14.

Chitty, Naren, Dalbir Ahlawat, Mei Li and D. Gopal. 2018. 'The Chinese Belt and Road Initiative and the Indian Ocean Region: Sentiment towards economic prosperity and security implications'. *Indian Journal of Politics* 52 (1–2): 1–20.

Cho, Young Nam, and Jong Ho Jeong. 2008. 'China's soft power: Discussions, resources, and prospects'. *Asian Survey* 48 (3): 453–72.

Chong, Dennis. 1993. 'How people think, reason, and feel about rights and liberties'. *American Journal of Political Science* 37 (3): 867–99.

Chong, Dennis, and James N Druckman. 2007. 'A theory of framing and opinion formation in competitive elite environments'. *Journal of Communication* 57 (1): 99–118.

Cohen, Yoel. 1986. *Media Diplomacy: The Foreign Office in the Mass Communications Age*. Oxon: Psychology Press.

Concerned Scholars of China. 2018. 'An open letter from concerned scholars of China and the Chinese diaspora: Australia's debate on "Chinese influence"'. *Asia and the Pacific Policy Society*. Accessed 5 February 2009. https://www.policyforum.net/an-open-letter-from-concerned-scholars-of-china-and-the-chinese-diaspora/.

Cull, Nicholas J. 2008. 'Public diplomacy: Taxonomies and histories'. *The ANNALS of the American Academy of Political and Social Science* 616 (1): 31–54.

———. 2009. 'Public diplomacy before Gullion: The evolution of a phrase'. In *Routledge Handbook of Public Diplomacy*, edited by Nancy Snow and Philip Taylor, 19–23. New York: Routledge.

D'angelo, Paul. 2002. 'News framing as a multiparadigmatic research program: A response to Entman'. *Journal of Communication* 52 (4): 870–88.

d'Hooghe, Ingrid. 2008. 'Into high gear: China's public diplomacy'. *Hague Journal of Diplomacy* 3 (1): 37–61.

———. 2011. 'The expansion of China's public diplomacy system'. In *Soft Power in China*, edited by Jian Wang, 19-35. New York: Palgrave Macmillan.

———. 2014. *China's Public Diplomacy*. Leiden: Martinus Nijhoff.

Dahl, Robert A. 1957. 'The concept of power'. *Behavioral Science* 2 (3): 201–15.

Dahlgren, Peter. 2010. 'Public spheres, societal shifts and media modulations'. In *Media, Markets and Public Spheres: European Media at the Crossroads*, edited by Jostein Gripsrud and Lennart Weibull, 17–36. Bristol: Intellect.

De Vreese, Claes H. 2005. 'News framing: Theory and typology'. *Information Design Journal + Document Design* 13 (1): 51–62.

Deng, Xiaoping. 1994. *Selected Works of Deng Xiaoping*. Vol. 2. Beijing: Renmin Chubanshe.

Department of Foreign Affairs and Trade. 2018. 'China Country Brief'. Accessed 1 December 2018. https://dfat.gov.au/geo/china/pages/china-country-brief.aspx.

Deuze, Mark. 2005. 'What is journalism? Professional identity and ideology of journalists reconsidered'. *Journalism* 6 (4): 442–64.

Ding, Sheng. 2006. 'Soft power and the rise of China: An assessment of China's soft power in its modernization process'. A dissertation submitted to Graduate School-Newark Rutgers, The State University of New Jersey.

———. 2010. 'Analyzing rising power from the perspective of soft power: A new look at China's rise to the status quo power'. *Journal of Contemporary China* 19 (64): 255–72.

Edwards, Lee. 2001. *Mediapolitik: How the Mass Media Have Transformed World Politics*. Washington, DC: CUA Press.

Entman, Robert M. 1993. 'Framing: Toward clarification of a fractured paradigm'. *Journal of Communication* 43 (4): 51–58.

———. 2003. 'Cascading activation: Contesting the White House's frame after 9/11'. *Political Communication* 20 (4): 415–32.

———. 2004. *Projections of Power: Framing News, Public Opinion, and US Foreign Policy*. Chicago, IL: University of Chicago Press.

———. 2008. 'Theorizing mediated public diplomacy: The US case'. *International Journal of Press/Politics* 13 (2): 87–102.

————. 2010. 'Framing media power'. In *Doing News Framing Analysis: Empirical and Theoretical Perspectives*, edited by Paul D'Angelo and Jim A. Kuypers, 331–55. New York: Routledge.

Fairclough, Norman. 1992. *Discourse and Social Change*. Cambridge: Polity.

Fifield, Mitch, and Scott Morrison. 2018. 'Government provides 5G security Guidance to Australian carriers'. *Minister for Communications, Cyber Safety and the Arts*, 23 August. Accessed 5 February 2019. https://www.minister.communications.gov.au/minister/mitch-fifield/news/government-provides-5g-security-guidance-australian-carriers.

Finnemore, Martha. 1996. *National Interests in International Society*. New York: Cornell University Press.

Fisher, Ali, and Scott Lucas, eds. 2011. *Trials of Engagement: The Future of US Public Diplomacy*. Diplomatic Studies. London: Martinus Nijhoff.

Folkenflik, David. 2013. 'China seeks soft power influence in U.S. through CCTV'. *NPR*, 25 April. Accessed 7 January 2017. https://www.npr.org/2013/04/25/179020185/chinas-cctv-america-walks-the-line-between-2-media-traditions.

Foucault, Michel. 1979. *Discipline and Punish: The Birth of the Prison*. New York: Vintage Books.

Freedman, Des, and Daya Kishan Thussu. 2012. 'Introduction: Dynamics of media and terrorism'. In *Media and Terrorism: Global Perspectives*, edited by Des Freedman and Daya Kishan Thussu, 1–20. Thousand Oaks, CA: Sage.

Gade, Peter J., and Wilson Lowrey. 2011. 'Reshaping the journalistic culture'. *Changing the News: The Forces Shaping Journalism in Uncertain Times*, edited by Peter J. Gade and Wilson Lowrey, 22–42. New York: Routledge.

Gagliardone, Iginio. 2013. 'China as a persuader: CCTV Africa's first steps in the African mediasphere'. *Ecquid Novi: African Journalism Studies* 34 (3): 25–40.

Gagliardone, Iginio, Maria Repnikova, and Nicole Stremlau. 2010. 'China in Africa: A new approach to media development'. Based on a workshop report of Programme in Comparative Media Law and Policy, Oxford University, and the Stanhope Centre for Communication Policy. Supported by the Economic and Social Research Council. Oxford: Centre for Sociological Studies, University of Oxford. Accessed 20 May 2016. http://global.asc.upenn.edu/fileLibrary/PDFs/chinainafrica.pdf.

Gagliardone, Iginio, Nicole Stremlau and Daniel Nkrumah. 2012. 'Partner, prototype or persuader?: China's renewed media engagement with Ghana'. *Politics & Culture* 45 (2): 174–96.

Gamson, William A. 1988. 'Political discourse and collective action'. *International Social Movement Research* 1 (2): 219–44.

Gamson, William A., and Andre Modigliani. 1989. 'Media discourse and public opinion on nuclear power: A constructionist approach'. *American Journal of Sociology* 95 (1): 1–37.

Gamson, William A., David Croteau, William Hoynes and Theodore Sasson. 1992. 'Media images and the social construction of reality'. *Annual Review of Sociology* 18 (1): 373–93.

Gans, Herbert J. 1979. *Deciding What's News: A Study of CBS Evening News, NBC Nightly News, Newsweek, and Time*. Evanston, IL: Northwestern University Press.

Gilboa, Eytan. 1998. 'Media diplomacy conceptual divergence and applications'. *Harvard International Journal of Press/Politics* 3 (3): 56–75.

————. 2002. 'Global communication and foreign policy'. *Journal of Communication* 52 (4): 731–48.

Gillespie, Marie, and Eva Nieto McAvoy. 2017. 'Digital networks and transformations in the international news ecology'. In *The Routledge Handbook of Soft Power*, edited by Naren Chitty, Li Ji, Gary Rawnsley and Craig Hayden, 203–18. London: Routledge.

Glaser, Bonnie S., and Melissa E. Murphy. 2009. 'Soft power with Chinese characteristics: The ongoing debate'. In *Chinese Soft Power and Its Implications for the United States: Competition and Cooperation in the Developing World*, edited by Carola McGiffert, 10–26. Washington, DC: Center for Strategic and International Studies.

Goffman, Erving. 1974. *Frame Analysis: An Essay on the Organization of Experience*. Cambridge: Harvard University Press.

Golan, Guy J. 2013. 'The case for mediated public diplomacy'. *Diplomatic Courier*. Accessed 3 October 2019. https://www.diplomaticourier.com/posts/the-case-for-mediated-public-diplomacy-2.

Goldstein, Avery. 1997. 'Great expectations: Interpreting China's arrival'. *International Security* 22 (3): 36–73.

Goffman, Erving. 1981. 'A reply to Denzin and Keller'. *Contemporary Sociology* 10 (1): 60–68.

Gorfinkel, Lauren, Sandy Joffe, Cobus Van Staden and Yu-Shan Wu. 2014. 'CCTV's global outreach: Examining the audiences of China's "New Voice" on Africa'. *Media International Australia* 151 (1): 81–88.

Gramsci, Antonio. 1971. *Selections from the Prison Notebooks of Antonio Gramsci*, edited and translated by Quintin Hoare and Geoffrey Nowell Smith: International Publishers.

Gribbin, Caitlyn. 2017. 'Malcolm Turnbull declares he will "stand up" for Australia in response to China's criticism'. *ABC News*, 9 December. Accessed 5 February 2019. https://www.abc.net.au/news/2017-12-09/malcolm-turnbull-says-he-will-stand-up-for-australia/9243274.

Guan, Shijie, and Liya Wang. 2015. 'China' s cultural soft power in U.S.: An international communication perspective'. In *China and the World: Theatres of Soft Power*, edited by Naren Chitty and Qing Luo, 9–29. Beijing: Communication University of China Press.

Gunaratne, Shelton A. 2009. 'Buddhist goals of journalism and the news paradigm'. *Javnost-The Public* 16 (2): 61–75.

———. 2013. 'Go East young "man": Seek wisdom from Laozi and Buddha on how to metatheorize mediatization'. *Journal of Multicultural Discourses* 8 (3): 165–81.

Guzzini, Stefano. 2009. *On the Measure of Power and the Power of Measure in International Relations*. Danish Institute for International Studies working paper. Accessed 18 November 2016. http://pure.diis.dk/ws/files/56324/WP2009_28_measure_of_power_international_relations_web.pdf.

Haas, Peter M. 1992. 'Introduction: Epistemic communities and international policy coordination'. *International Organization* 46 (1): 1–35.

Hacker, Kenneth L., and Vanessa R Mendez. 2016. 'Toward a model of strategic influence, international broadcasting, and global engagement'. *Media and Communication* 4 (2): 69–91.

Hall, Stuart. 1980. 'Encoding/decoding'. In *Culture, Media, Language: Working Papers in Cultural Studies, 1972–79*, edited by Stuart Hall, Dorothy Hobson, Andrew Lowe and Paul Willis, 128–38. London: Routledge.

Hallin, Daniel C., and Paolo Mancini. 2011. *Comparing Media Systems Beyond the Western World*. Cambridge: Cambridge University Press.

Hamada, Basyouni Ibrahim. 2016. 'Towards a global journalism ethics model: An Islamic perspective'. *Journal of International Communication* 22 (2): 188–208.

Han, Z. 2011. 'China's public diplomacy in a new era'. In *The People's Republic of China Today: Internal and External Challenges*, edited by Zhiqun Zhu, 291–310. Singapore: World Scientific.

Hanitzsch, Thomas. 2007. 'Deconstructing journalism culture: Toward a universal theory'." *Communication Theory* 17 (4): 367–85.

Hanusch, Folker. 2008. 'Mapping Australian journalism culture: Results from a survey of journalists' role perceptions'. *Australian Journalism Review* 30 (2): 97–109.

Harari, Yuval Noah. 2014. *Sapiens: A Brief History of Humankind*. New York: Random House.

———. 2018. *21 Lessons for the 21st Century*. New York: Random House.

Harris, Stuart. 2001. 'China and the pursuit of state interests in a globalising world'. *Pacifica Review* 13 (1): 15–29. doi: 10.1080/13239100120036018.

Hartig, Falk. 2012. 'Cultural diplomacy with Chinese characteristics: The case of Confucius Institutes in Australia'. *Chinese Journal of Communication* 5 (4): 477–80.

———. 2016. 'How China understands public diplomacy: The importance of national image for national interests'. *International Studies Review* 18 (4): 655–80.

Hassid, Jonathan. 2011. 'Four models of the fourth estate: A typology of contemporary Chinese journalists'. *China Quarterly* 208: 813–32.

Hayden, Craig A. 2003. 'Power in media frames: Thinking about strategic framing and media system dependency and the events of September 11, 2001'. *Global Media Journal* 2 (3): 146–59.

———. 2012. *The Rhetoric of Soft Power: Public Diplomacy in Global Contexts*. Lanham, MD: Lexington Books.

———. 2017. 'Scope, mechanism, and outcome: Arguing soft power in the context of public diplomacy'. *Journal of International Relations and Development* 20 (2): 331–57.

Herman, Edward S., and N. Chomsky. 2002. *Manufacturing Consent: The Political Economy of the Mass Media*. New York: Pantheon Books.

Hills, Thomas, and Elad Segev. 2014. 'The news is American but our memories are … Chinese?' *Journal of the Association for Information Science and Technology* 65 (9): 1810–19.

Hu, Angang, and Honghua Men. 2002. 'The rising of modern China: Comprehensive national power and grand strategy'. *Strategy and Management* 3 (2): 1–36.

Hu, Jintao. 2007. 'Hold high the great banner of socialism with Chinese characteristics and strive for new victories in building a moderately prosperous society in all'. Hu Jintao's Report to the 17th National Congress of the Communist Party of China, 24 October. http://www.gov.cn/english/2007-10/24/content_785505.htm.

———. 2008. 'Speech at the National Confernce on Propaganda and Ideological Work'. *The State Council Information Office of the People's Republic of China*, 23 January. http://www.scio.gov.cn/tp/Document/332639/332639.htm.

Hu, Zhengrong, and Deqiang Ji. 2012. 'Ambiguities in communicating with the world: The "Going-out" policy of China's media and its multilayered contexts'. *Chinese Journal of Communication* 5 (1): 32–37.

Huang, Yanzhong, and Sheng Ding. 2006. 'Dragon's underbelly: An analysis of China's soft power'. *East Asia* 23 (4): 22–44.

Jacob, Jacob Udo-Udo. 2017. 'Cultural approaches to soft power'. In *The Routledge Handbook of Soft Power*, edited by Naren Chitty, Li Ji, Gary Rawnsley and Craig Hayden, 137–45. London: Routledge.

Jefferson, Ronald L., Peter J. Katzenstein and Alexander Wendt. 1996. 'Norms, identity, and culture in national security policy'. In *The Culture of National Security*, edited by Peter J. Katzenstein, 33–75. New York: Columbia University Press.

Jefferson, Thomas. 1819. 'From Thomas Jefferson to John Adams, 10 December 1819'. *Founders Online, National Archives*. https://founders.archives.gov/documents/Jefferson/98-01-02-0953.

Jeffery, Renée. 2009. 'Evaluating the "China threat": Power transition theory, the successor-state image and the dangers of historical analogies'. *Australian Journal of International Affairs* 63 (2): 309–24.

Jiang, Fei, and R. Yan. 2015. 'China high-speed rail: A "new business card" in the age of public diplomacy'. In *Blue Book of Public Diplomacy: Annual Report of China's Public Diplomacy Development 2015*, edited by Qizheng Zhao and Weizhen Lei, 213–36. Beijing: Socsial Sciences Academic Press.

Jiang, Zemin. 1999. 'Speech for stronger publicity power matching the country's status at the National Foreign Publicity Conference'. 27 February. Accessed 1 June 2016. http://www.people.com.cn/item/ldhd/Jiangzm/1999/huiyi/hy0002.html.

Jin, Zheng-kun, and Qing-chao Xu. 2010. 'National image building: The new task for China's diplomacy'. *Journal of Renmin University of China* 24 (2): 119–27.

Jirik, John. 2004. 'China's news media and the case of CCTV-9'. In *International News in the 21st Century*, edited by Chris Patterson and Annabelle Srebemy, 127–46. Eastleigh, UK: John Libbey.

———. 2008. 'Making news in the People's Republic of China: The case of CCTV-9'. PhD, The University of Texas at Austin.

———. 2013. 'The world according to (Thomson) Reuters'. *Sur le journalisme, About Journalism, Sobre jornalismo* 2 (1): 24–41.

———. 2015. 'The CCTV-Reuters relationship'. In *Media at Work in China and India: Discovering and Dissecting*, edited by Robin Jeffery and Ronojoy sen, 201–27. New York: Sage.

———. 2016. 'CCTV News and soft power'. *International Journal of Communication* 10: 3536–53.

Kagan, Robert. 2017. 'Backing into World War III.' *Foreign Policy*, 6 February. https://foreignpolicy.com/2017/02/06/backing-into-world-war-iii-russia-china-trump-obama/.

Kaldor, Mary. 2003. 'The idea of global civil society'. *International Affairs* 79 (3): 583–93.

Keohane, Robert O., and Joseph S. Nye. 1973. 'Power and interdependence'. *Survival* 15 (4): 158–65.

Kepplinger, Hans Mathias, and Renate Köcher. 1990. 'Professionalism in the media world?' *European Journal of Communication* 5 (2): 285–311.

Kim, Kyungmo, and George A. Barnett. 1996. 'The determinants of international news flow a network analysis'. *Communication Research* 23 (3): 323–52.

Kivimäki, Timo. 2014. 'Soft power and global governance with Chinese characteristics'. *Chinese Journal of International Politics* 7 (4): 421–47.

Kovach, Bill, and Tom Rosenstiel. 2007. *The Elements of Journalism: What Newspeople Should Know and the Public Should Expect*. New York: Three Rivers Press.

Kristof, Nicholas D. 1993. 'The rise of China'. *Foreign Affairs* 72 (5): 59–74.

Kurlantzick, Joshua. 2007. *Charm Offensive: How China's Soft Power Is Transforming the World*. New Haven, CT: Yale University Press.

Lasswell, Harold Dwight. 1950. *Politics: Who Gets What, When, How*. New York: P. Smith.

Lazarsfeld, Paul Felix, Bernard Berelson and Hazel Gaudet. 1968. *The Peoples Choice: How the Voter Makes Up His Mind in a Presidential Campaign*. New York: Columbia University Press.

Lee, Chin-Chuan. 2005. 'The conception of Chinese journalists'. In *Making Journalists: Diverse Models, Global Issues*, edited by Hugo de Burgh, 107–27. Oxon: Routledge.

Lee, Chin-Chuan, Zhou He and Yu Huang. 2006. '"Chinese Party Publicity Inc."conglomerated: The case of the Shenzhen press group'. *Media, Culture & Society* 28 (4): 581–602.

Li, Chenyang. 2006. 'The Confucian ideal of harmony'. *Philosophy East and West* 56 (4): 583–603.

Li, Mei, and Naren Chitty. 2017. 'Paradox of professionalism: The professional identity of journalists who work across media cultures'. *Journalism* (November): 1–19. doi: 10.1177/1464884917743175.

———. 2018. 'An overview on China's public diplomacy in Australia'. In *Public Diplomacy Studies*, edited by Debin Liu, 115–28. Beijing: Social Science Academic Press.

Li, Mingjiang. 2008. 'Soft power in Chinese discourse: Popularity and prospect'. Working paper. https://www.rsis.edu.sg/wp-content/uploads/rsis-pubs/WP165.pdf.

———. 2009. 'Soft power: Nurture not nature'. In *Soft Power: China's Emerging Strategy in International Politics*, edited by Mingjiang Li, 1–18. Lanham, MD: Lexington Books.

Li, Shi. 2012. 'Mass communication research on China from 2000 to 2010: A meta-analysis'. *Asian Journal of Communication* 22 (4): 405–27. doi: 10.1080/01292986.2012.681668.

Li, Xiaoping. 1991. 'The Chinese television system and television news'. *China Quarterly* 126: 340–55.

Li, Xiguang, and Kang Liu. 1996. *Behind the Scene of Demonizing China (Yaomohua Zhongguo de Beihou)*. Beijing: Chinese Academy of Social Science Press.

Li, Xin, and Verner Worm. 2011. 'Building China's soft power for a peaceful rise'. *Journal of Chinese Political Science* 16 (1): 69–89.

Li, Xiufang. 2011. *Reading the Contemporary Giant: China's Images in the ABC's Foreign Correspondent Current Affairs Program in the Early Twenty-First Century*. North Ryde: Macquarie University.

Li, Xiufang, and Naren Chitty. 2009. 'Reframing national image: A methodological framework'. *Conflict and Communication Online* 8 (2): 1–11.

Liu, Fucheng. 2007. *China Media System Innovation*. Guang Zhou: Southern Daily Press.

Liu, Qian. 2014. 'Ambivalence in China's quest for "soft power": A case study of CCTV-America's multiple news standpoints'. Master's thesis. Simon Fraser University, Vancouver, Canada. Accessed November 2015. http://summit.sfu.ca/item/14521.

Liu, Qianqian. 2010. 'China's rise and regional strategy: Power, interdependence and identity'. *Journal of Cambridge Studies* 5 (4): 76–92.

Liu, Yang. 2014. 'Discourse and framing: A content analysis based on Chinese news quoted by New York Times'. *International Proceedings of Economics Development and Research* 77 (5): 19–23.

Livingston, Steven. 1997. *Clarifying the CNN Effect: An Examination of Media Effects According to Type of Military Intervention*. The Joan Shorenstein Center on Press, Politics and Public Policy, John F. Kennedy School of Government, Harvard University. http://genocidewatch.info/images/1997ClarifyingtheCNNEffect-Livingston.pdf.

Louw, P. Eric. 2010. *Roots of the Pax Americana: Decolonization, Development, Democratization and Trade*. Manchester: Manchester University Press.

Lowy Institute. 2018. Asia Power Index. Sydney: Lowy Institute. Accessed 18 January 2019. https://power.lowyinstitute.org/.

Lu, Ye, and Zhongdang Pan. 2002. 'Imagining professional fame: Constructing journalistic professionalism in social transformation (Chengming de Xiangxiang: Shehui Zhuanxing Guozhengzhong Xinwen Congyezhe de Zhuanyezhuyi Huayu Jiangou)'. *Journalism Studies (Xinwenxue Yanjiu)* 71 (1): 17–59.

MacBride, Sean. 1980. *Many Voices, One World: Towards a New, More Just, and More Efficient World Information and Communication Order*. Lanham, MD: Rowman & Littlefield.

Madianou, Mirca, and Daniel Miller. 2013. *Migration and New Media: Transnational Families and Polymedia*. London: Routledge.

Marsh, Vivien. 2016. 'Mixed messages, partial pictures? Discourses under construction in CCTV's Africa Live compared with the BBC'. *Chinese Journal of Communication* 9 (1): 56–70.

Matthes, Jörg. 2012. 'Framing politics: An integrative approach'. *American Behavioral Scientist* 56 (3): 247–59. doi: 10.1177/0002764211426324.

Mearsheimer, John J. 2001. *The Tragedy of Great Power Politics.* New York: Norton.

Medcalf, Rory. 2018. 'Silent invasion: the question of race'. *The Interpreter*, 24 March. https://www.lowyinstitute.org/the-interpreter/silent-invasion-question-race.

Melissen, Jan. 2005. 'The new public diplomacy: Between theory and practice'. In *The New Public Diplomacy: Soft Power in International Relations*, edited by Jan Melissen, 3–27. New York: Palgrave Macmillan.

Men, Honghua. 2007.'"Assessment report on China's soft power'. *International Observations (Guoji Guancha)* 2: 15–26.

Meng, Jian. 2012. Research on national image construction and intercultural communication strategy'. National Office of Philosophy and Social Sciences. Accessed 20 November 2015. http://www.npopss-cn.gov.cn/GB/219506/219507/17591993.html.

Monocle. 2015. Soft Power Survey 2015/16. https://monocle.com/film/affairs/soft-power-survey-2015-16/.

Mowlana, Hamid. 1985. *International Flow of Information: A Global Report and Analysis.* New York: UNESCO.

Mowlana, Hamid. 1997. *Global Information and World Communication: New Frontiers in International Relations.* Thousand Oaks, CA: Sage.

Munro, Kelsey. 2017. 'The dragon and the kangaroo: 45 years of Australia-China relations'. *SBS News.* https://www.sbs.com.au/news/the-dragon-and-the-kangaroo-45-years-of-australia-china-relations.

National Development and Reform Commission. 2015. 'Vision and actions on jointly building Silk Road Economic Belt and 21st-Century Maritime Silk Road'. *NDRC*, 28 March. http://en.ndrc.gov.cn/newsrelease/201503/t20150330_669367.html.

Ning, Jing. 2013. 'CCTV-9's coverage of the Iraq War and the evolution of English language television news in China'. PhD dissertation submitted to the Graduate School–New Brunswick, Rutgers, The State University of New Jersey. Accessed 1 November 2015. https://rucore.libraries.rutgers.edu/rutgers-lib/40635/#citation-export.

Nye, Joseph S. 1990. 'Soft power'. *Foreign Policy* 80: 53–171.

———. 2004. *Soft Power: The Means to Success in World Politics.* New York: Public Affairs.

———. 2005. 'The rise of China's soft power'. *Wall Street Journal Asia* 29: 6–8.

———. 2011. *The Future of Power.* New York: Public Affairs.

———. 2013. 'What China and Russia don't get about soft power'. *Foreign Policy*, 29 April. Accessed 23 August 2016. https://foreignpolicy.com/2013/04/29/what-china-and-russia-dont-get-about-soft-power/.

———. 2015. 'The limits of Chinese soft power'. *Project Syndicate*, 10 July. Accessed 23 August 2016. https://www.project-syndicate.org/commentary/china-civil-society-nationalism-soft-power-by-joseph-s--nye-2015-07?barrier=accesspaylog.

Nye, Joseph S., and William A. Owens. 1996. 'America's information edge'. *Foreign Affairs* 75 (2): 20–36.

Onuf, Nicholas. 1989. *World of Our Making.* Columbia: University of South Carolina Press.

———. 1997. 'Hegemony's Hegemony in IPE'. In *Constituting International Political Economy*, edited by Kurt Burch and Robert A. Denemark, 91–110. Boulder, CO: Lynne Rienner.

————. 2004. 'Humanitarian intervention: The early years'. *Florida Journal of International Law* 16 (4) :753.

————. 2013. *Making Sense, Making Worlds: Constructivism in Social Theory and International Relations*. New York: Routledge.

————. 2014. 'Rule and rules in international relations'. Lecture at the Erik Castrén Institute of International Law and Human Rights, University of Helsinki, 24 April. https://www.normativeorders.net/en/events/lecture-series/38-veranstaltungen/ringvorlesungen/2685-rule-and-rules-in-international-relations-eng.

————. 2016. 'The power of metaphor/the metaphor of power'. *Journal of International Communication* 23 (1): 1–14.

Örnebring, Henrik. 2010. 'Reassessing journalism as a profession'. In *The Routledge Companion to News and Journalism*, edited by Stuart Allan, 568–77. London: Routledge.

Osipova, Yelena. 2017. 'Indigenizing soft power in Russia'. In *The Routledge Handbook of Soft Power*, edited by Naren Chitty, Ji Li, Gary Rawnsley and Craig Hayden, 346–57. London: Routledge.

Pan, Zhongdang, and Ye Lu. 2003. 'Localizing professionalism: Discursive practices in China's media reforms'. In *Chinese media, Global Contexts*, edited by Chin-Chuan Lee, 215–36. London: Routledge.

Pan, Zhongdang, and Gerald M. Kosicki. 1993. 'Framing analysis: An approach to news discourse'. *Political Communication* 10 (1): 55–75. doi: 10.1080/10584609.1993.9962963.

Pang, Zhongying. 2005. 'Connotation of China's soft Power'. *Liaowang (Outlook Weekly)* 45: 62–65.

Paterson, Chris. 2011. *The International Television News Agencies*. New York: Peter Lang.

Public Broadcasting Service. 2012. 'China's Programming for U.S. Audiences: Is it News or Propaganda?' *PBS*, 22 March. Accessed 7 January 2017. https://www.pbs.org/newshour/show/world-jan-june12-cctv_03-23.

Pew Global. 2008–14. *Global Indicators Database: Opinion of China*, edited by Pew Global. Accessed 12 January 2017. http://www.pewglobal.org/database/indicator/24/.

Pillsbury, Michael. 2000. *China Debates the Future International Environment*. Washington, DC: National Defense University Press.

Portland. 2016. *The Soft Power 30*. Accessed 20 July 2016. https://softpower30.com/?country_years=2016.

Powers, Shawn, and Eytan Gilboa. 2007. 'The public diplomacy of Al Jazeera'. In *New Media and the New Middle East*, edited by Philip Seib, 53–80. Berlin: Springer.

Pratkanis, Anthony R., and Elliot Aronson. 1991. *Age of Propaganda*. New York: W.H Freeman.

Price, V. 2005. 'Framing public discussion of gay civil unions'. *Public Opinion Quarterly* 69 (2): 179–212. doi: 10.1093/poq/nfi014.

Qian, Gang, and David Bandurski. 2011. 'China's emerging public sphere: The impact of media commercialization, professionalism, and the Internet in an era of transition'. In *Changing Media, Changing China*, edited by Susan Shirk, 38–76. New York: Oxford University Press.

Ramo, Joshua Cooper. 2007. *Brand China*. London: Foreign Policy Centre.

Rawnsley, Gary D. 1996. *Radio Diplomacy and Propaganda: The BBC and VOA in International Politics, 1956–64*. London: Macmillan Press.

————. 2012. 'Approaches to soft power and public diplomacy in China and Taiwan'. *Journal of International Communication* 18 (2): 121–35.

————. 2015. 'To know us is to love us: Public diplomacy and international broadcasting in contemporary Russia and China'. *Politics* 35 (3–4): 273–86.

————. 2016. 'Introduction to "International Broadcasting and Public Diplomacy in the 21st Century"'. *Media and Communication* 4 (2): 42–45.

Reese, Stephen D. 2001. 'Understanding the global journalist: A hierarchy-of-influences approach'. *Journalism Studies* 2 (2):173–87.

Reich, Simon, and Richard Ned Lebow. 2014. *Good-Bye Hegemony!: Power and Influence in the Global System*. Princeton, NJ: Princeton University Press.

Rimmer, Susan Harris. 2015. 'Why Australia took so long to join the AIIB'. *The Interpreter*, 30 March. Accessed 23 January 2017. https://www.lowyinstitute.org/the-interpreter/why-australia-took-so-long-join-aiib.

Rogers, Everett M. 1962. *Diffusion of Innovations*. New York: Free Press of Glencoe.

Said, Edward W. 2008. *Covering Islam: How the Media and the Experts Determine How We See the Rest of the World (Fully Revised Edition)*. London: Random House.

Scheufele, Dietram A. 1999. 'Framing as a theory of media effects'. *Journal of Communication* 49 (1): 103–22.

Schneider, M. 2015. 'US public diplomacy since 9/11: The challenges of integration'. *International Public Relations and Public Diplomacy: Communication and Engagement*, edited by G. J. Golan, S. U. Yang and D. Kinsey, 15–36. New York: Peter Lang.

Segev, Elad, and Menahem Blondheim. 2013. 'America's global standing according to popular news sites from around the world'. *Political Communication* 30 (1): 139–61.

Seib, Philip M. 1997. *Headline Diplomacy: How News Coverage Affects Foreign Policy*. Westport, CT: Greenwood Publishing Group.

————. 2008. *The Al Jazeera Effect: How the New Global Media Are Reshaping World Politics*. Lincoln, NE: Potomac Books.

————. 2010. 'Transnational journalism, public diplomacy, and virtual states'. *Journalism Studies* 11 (5): 734–44.

Shambaugh, David. 2007. 'China's propaganda system: Institutions, processes and efficacy'. *China Journal* 57: 25–58.

————. 2015. 'China's soft-power push'. *Foreign Affairs* 94: 99–107.

Shao, Baohui, and Qingwen Dong. 2016. 'An exploratory study on journalistic professionalism and journalism education in contemporary China'. *Journalism and Mass Communication* 6 (4): 187–200.

Sharp, Paul. 2005. 'Revolutionary states, outlaw regimes and the techniques of public diplomacy'. In *The New Public Diplomacy: Soft Power in International Relation*, edited by Jan Melissen, 106–23. Hampshire: Palgrave Macmillan.

Shi, Anbin. 2013. 'Chinese media development in Africa: From charm offensive to charm defensive'. Forum Medien und Entwicklung, Promoting Alternative Views in a Multipolar World: BRICS and their Role in Developing Media Markets, Berlin, 10 October. https://fome.info/wp-content/uploads/2014/10/FoME-BRICS-2013.pdf.

————. 2015. 'Chinese media should use the internet to reconstruct a new global communication order'. World Internet Conference, Wuzhen Zhejiang, China. http://news.china.com.cn/2015-12/17/content_37340680.htm.

————. 2016. 'China national strategic communication and the reform of the international order'. *Sina.com*, 11 March. http://news.sina.com.cn/w/zx/2016-03-11/doc-ifxqhmve9096861.shtml.

————. 2018. 'Dialysis of the so-called "sharp strength"'. *Qiushi*, 26 March. http://www.qstheory.cn/llwx/2018-03/26/c_1122588503.htm.

Shi, Anbin, and Yaozhong Zhang. 2016. 'Building new global communication order: Interpreting the historical trace and reality consideration of Chinese solution'. *Journalism Lover* 5: 13–20.

Shi, Zhihong. 2009. 'What kind of new China meant to be built'. *Current Affairs Report* 8: 8–27.

Shoemaker, Pamela, and Stephen D. Reese. 1996. *Mediating the Message in the 21st Century: A Media Sociology Perspective*. New York: Longman.

Siebert, Fred Seaton, Theodore Peterson and Wilbur Schramm. 1956. *Four Theories of the Press: The Authoritarian, Libertarian, Social Responsibility, and Soviet Communist Concepts of What the Press Should Be and Do*. Urbana: University of Illinois Press.

Simons, Margaret, David Nolan and Scott Wright. 2016. '"We are not North Korea": Propaganda and professionalism in the People's Republic of China'. *Media, Culture & Society* 39 (2): 219–37. doi: 10.1177/0163443716643154.

Snow, David A., E. Burke Rochford Jr, Steven K. Worden and Robert D. Benford. 1986. 'Frame alignment processes, micromobilization, and movement participation'. *American Sociological Review* 51 (4): 464–81.

Snow, Nancy. 2011. 'Information war 2011'. *CPD Blog*, 24 November. http://uscpublicdiplomacy.org/blog/information-war-2011.

Sorrells, Kathryn. 2015. *Intercultural Communication: Globalization and Social Justice*. Thousand Oaks, CA: Sage.

Sparks, Colin. 2012. 'Beyond political communication: Towards a broader perspective on the Chinese press'. *Chinese Journal of Communication* 5 (1): 61–67.

Straubhaar, Joseph D. 1991. 'Beyond media imperialism: Assymetrical interdependence and cultural proximity'. *Critical Studies in Media Communication* 8 (1): 39–59.

Straubhaar, Joseph D., and Douglas A. Boyd. 2002. 'International broadcasting'. In *Global Communications*, edited by Yahya R. Kamalipour, 133–56. Belmont, CA: Thomson Wadsworth.

Sun, Wanning. 2009. 'Mission impossible? Soft power, communication capacity, and the globalization of Chinese media'. *International Journal of Communication* 4: 19.

Sun, Wanning. 2015. 'Slow boat from China: Public discourses behind the "going global" media policy'. *International Journal of Cultural Policy* 21 (4): 400–418.

Teilhard De Chardin, Pierre Teilhard. 1965. *The Phenomenon of Man*. Translated by Bernard Wall. New York: Harper & Row.

Tewksbury, David, and Dietram A. Scheufele. 2009. 'News framing theory and research'. In *Media effects: Advances in Theory and Research*, edited by Jennings Bryant and Mary B. Oliver, 17–33. London: Routledge.

Thussu, Daya Kishan. 2006. *Media on the Move: Global Flow and Contra-Flow*. London: Routledge.

———. 2010. *International Communication: A Reader*. London: Routledge.

———. 2013. *Communicating India's Soft Power: Buddha to Bollywood*. New York: Palgrave Macmillan.

———. 2014. 'De-Americanizing soft power discourse?' *CPD Perspectives on Public Diplomacy* 2: 5–25.

Tiezzi, Shannon. 2014. 'The New Silk Road: China's Marshall Plan?' *The Diplomat*, 6 November. thediplomat.com/2014/11/the-new-silk-road-chinas-marshall-plan/.

Toffler, Alvin. 1990. *Power Shift: Knowledge, Wealth, and Violence at the Edge of the 21st Century*. London: Bantam.

Tong, Jingrong. 2011. *Investigative Journalism in China: Journalism, Power, and Society*. New York: Continuum.

Tromble, Rebekah, and Michael Meffert. 2016. 'The life and death of frames: Dynamics of media frame duration'. *International Journal of Communication* 10 (23): 5079–101.

Tuchman, Gaye. 1978. *Making News: A Study in the Construction of Reality*. New York: Free Press.

Tylor, Edward Burnett. 1871. *Primitive Culture: Researches into the Development of Mythology, Philosophy, Religion, Art, and Custom*. Vol. 2. London: Bradbury, Evans.

Van Gorp, Baldwin. 2005. 'Where is the frame? Victims and intruders in the Belgian press coverage of the asylum issue'. *European Journal of Communication* 20 (4): 484–507.

———. 2007. 'The constructionist approach to framing: Bringing culture back in'. *Journal of Communication* 57 (1): 60–78.

Vliegenthart, R., and Liesbet van Zoonen. 2011. "Power to the frame: Bringing sociology back to frame analysis." *European Cournal of Communication* 26 (2): 101–15. doi: 10.1177/0267323111404838.

Waisbord, Silvio. 2013. *Reinventing Professionalism: Journalism and News in Global Perspective*. Hoboken, NJ: Wiley.

Wade, Geoff. 2016. 'China's "One Belt, One Road" initiative'. Parliamentary Library Briefing. Accessed 15 January 2017. http://www.aph.gov.au/About_Parliament/Parliamentary_Departments/Parliamentary_Library/pubs/BriefingBook45p/ChinasRoad.

Walker, Christopher, and Jessica Ludwig. 2017. 'The meaning of sharp power: How authoritarian states project influence'. *Foreign Affairs*, 16 November. https://www.foreignaffairs.com/articles/china/2017-11-16/meaning-sharp-power.

Wang, Chen. 2010. Speech at the 2010 National Publicity Work Conference. *The State Council Information Office of China*. http://www.scio.gov.cn/zxbd/nd/2010/Document/511903/511903.htm.

Wang, Hongying. 2003. 'National image building and Chinese foreign policy'. *China (National University of Singapore. East Asian Institute)* 1 (1): 46–72.

———. 2011. 'China's image projection and its impact'. In *Soft Power in China: Public Diplomacy through Communication*, edited by Jian Wang, 37–56. Hampshire: Palgrave Macmillan.

Wang, Huning. 1993. 'Culture as national power: Soft power'. *Journal of Fudan University (Social Science Version)* 3: 91–96.

Wang, Jay. 2014. 'China's First Lady'. *CPD Blog*, 19 March. https://uscpublicdiplomacy.org/blog/china%E2%80%99s-first-lady.

Wang, Jian. 2011. *Soft Power in China: Public Diplomacy through Communication*. Hampshire: Palgrave Macmillan.

Wang, Jianwei. 2000. *Limited Adversaries: Post-Cold War Sino-American Mutual Images*. Oxford: Oxford University Press.

Wang, Longqing. 2011. 'Journalists, media diplomacy and media- broker diplomacy in relations between mainland China and Taiwan from 1987–2009'. Thesis presented for the degree of Doctor of Philosophy, 30 March. Australia: Macquarie University. Accessed 27 May 2015. https://pdfs.semanticscholar.org/e439/ced24831697476081 5a9852a705fb21aafab.pdf.

Wang, Y. 2008. 'Public diplomacy and the rise of Chinese soft power'. *Annals of the American Academy of Political and Social Science* 616 (1): 257–73. doi: 10.1177/0002716207312757.

Wang, Yiwei. 2015. *One Belt One Road: Opportunities and Challenges (Yidai Yilu Jiyu Yu Tiaozhan)*. Beijing: People's Publishing House.

Wasserman, Herman. 2016. 'China's "soft power" and its influence on editorial agendas in South Africa'. *Chinese Journal of Communication* 9 (1): 8–20.

Weaver, David H., Randal A. Beam, Bonnie J. Brownlee, Paul S. Voakes and G. Cleveland Wilhoit. 2009. *The American Journalist in the 21st Century: US News People at the Dawn of a New Millennium*. New York: Routledge.

Wendt, Alexander. 1992. 'Anarchy is what states make of it: The social construction of power politics'. *International Organization* 46 (2): 391–425.

———. 1995. 'Constructing international politics'. *International Security* 20 (1): 71–81.

Williams, Raymond. 1977. *Marxism and Literature*. Vol. 1. Oxford: Oxford University Press.

WMSDOHA. 2016. 'About World Media Summit'. Accessed 2 January 2017. http://www.xinhuanet.com/english/special/worldmedia160320/index.htm.

Wu, Weihong, and Zheng Huang. 2015. 'Brief analysis on the self-producing capacity of CCTV – NEWS: the comparison of News program of CCTV NEWS, BBC and CNN'. *Global Communication* 2: 49–51.

Wuthnow, Joel. 2008. 'The concept of soft power in China's strategic discourse'. *Issues & Studies* 44 (2): 1–28.

Xi, Jinping. 2013. Address at national conference on publicity ideology work. *People's Daily*, 21 August. http://cpc.people.com.cn/n/2013/0821/c64094-22636876.html.

———. 2014. 'Xi Jinping delivers important speech in Germany, stressing China will unswervingly adhere to the path of peaceful development'. *Ministry of Foreign Affairs of the People's Republic of China*, 29 March. https://www.fmprc.gov.cn/mfa_eng/topics_665678/xjpzxcxdsjhaqhfbfwhlfgdgblshlhgjkezzzbomzb_666590/t1143914.shtml.

———. 2015. Speech at the Second World Internet Conference opening cermony. Wuzhen, Zhejiang Province. *China Copyright and Media*, 16 December. https://chinacopyrightandmedia.wordpress.com/2015/12/16/speech-at-the-2nd-world-internet-conference-opening-ceremony.

Xiang, Debao. 2013. 'China's image on international English language social media'. *Journal of International Communication* 19 (2): 252–71. doi: 10.1080/13216597.2013.833535.

Xinhuanet. 2014. 'Xi: China to promote cultural soft power'. Accessed 25 June 2016. https://www.wilsoncenter.org/sites/default/files/xinhua_xi-china_to_promote_cultural_soft_power_article_0.pdf.

———. 2016. 'Belt and Road Initiative'. *Xinhua News Agency*. Accessed 16 January 2017. http://www.xinhuanet.com/silkroad/english/index.htm.

Yan, Xuetong, and Jin Xu. 2008. 'Sino-US comparisons of soft power'. *Contemporary International Relations* 18 (2): 24–29.

Yu, Chang Sen, and Jory Xiong. 2012. 'The dilemma of interdependence: Current features and trends in Sino-Australian relations'. *Australian Journal of International Affairs* 66 (5): 579–91. doi: 10.1080/10357718.2011.570246.

Zaharna, Rhonda S. 2004. 'From propaganda to public diplomacy in the information age'. In *War, Media and Propaganda: A Global Perspective*, edited by Yahya R. Kamalipour and Nancy Snow, 219–26. Lanham, MD: Rowman & Littlefield.

———. 2009. 'Mapping out a spectrum of public diplomacy initiatives: Information and relational communication frameworks'. In *Routledge Handbook of Public Diplomacy*, edited by Nancy Snow and Philip M. Taylor, 106–20. New York: Routledge.

———. 2010. *Battles to Bridges: US Strategic Communication and Public Diplomacy after 9/11*. New York: Palgrave Macmillan.

Zelizer, Barbie. 2005. 'Journalism through the camera's eye'. In *Journalism: Critical Issues*, edited by Stuart Allan, 167–75. Maidenhead: Open University Press.

Zhang, Jian. 2015. 'China's new foreign policy under Xi Jinping: Towards "Peaceful Rise 2.0"?' *Global Change, Peace & Security* 27 (1): 5–19.

Zhang, Li. 2011. *News Media and EU-China Relations*. New York: Palgrave Macmillan.

Zhang, Xiaoling. 2011. 'China's international broadcasting: A case study of CCTV international'. In *Soft Power in China: Soft Power through Communication*, edited by Jian Wang, 57–71. Hampshire: Palgrave Macmillan.

———. 2013. 'How ready is China for a China-style world order? China's state media discourse under construction'. *Ecquid Novi: African Journalism Studies* 34 (3): 79–101.

Zhang, Xiaoling, Herman Wasserman and Winston Mano, eds. 2016. *China's Media and Soft Power in Africa: Promotion and Perceptions*, Palgrave Series in Asia and Pacific Studies. New York: Palgrave Macmillan.

Zhang, Yanqiu, and Matingwina Simon. 2016. 'Constructive journalism: A new journalistic paradigm of Chinese media in Africa'. In *China's Media and Soft Power in Africa: Promotion and Perceptions*, edited by Xiaoling Zhang, Herman Wasserman and Winston Mano, 93–105. New York: Palgrave Macmillan.

Zhao, Qizheng. 2012. *How China Communicates: Public Diplomacy in a Global Age*. Beijing: Foreign Language Press.

Zhao, Yuezhi. 1998. *Media, Market, and Democracy in China: Between the Party Line and the Bottom Line*. Vol. 114. Urbana: University of Illinois Press.

Zhou, Hailin. 2012. 'An interpretation of the influential power of China development'. *Chinese Journal of Population Resources and Environment* 10 (2): 12–23. doi: 10.1080/ 10042857.2012.10685072.

Zhu, Ying. 2012. *Two Billion Eyes: The Story of China Central Television*. New York: New Press.

INDEX